Gims[o]

'Wonderf[ul]

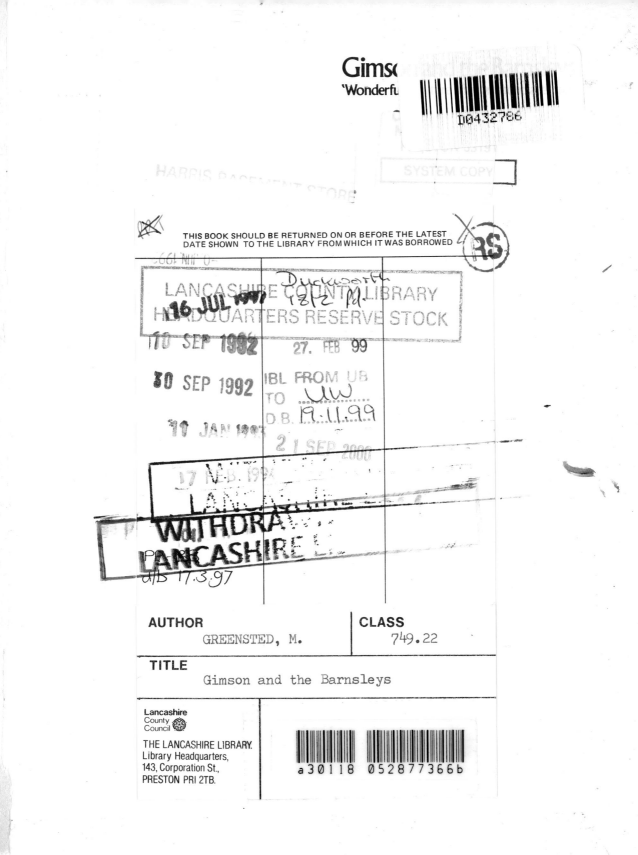

D0432786

SYSTEM COPY

HARRIS BASEMENT STORE

THIS BOOK SHOULD BE RETURNED ON OR BEFORE THE LATEST
DATE SHOWN TO THE LIBRARY FROM WHICH IT WAS BORROWED

RS

Duckworth
18/2 M

LANCASHIRE COUNTY LIBRARY
H[EA]DQUARTERS RESERVE STOCK

16 JUL 1997

10 SEP 1992   27. FEB 99

30 SEP 1992   IBL FROM UB
                TO UW
                D.B. 19.11.99
11 JAN 1993
                2 1 SEP 2000

17 FEB 1994

WITHDRAWN
LANCASHIRE L

d/b 17.3.97

AUTHOR	CLASS
GREENSTED, M.	749.22

TITLE

Gimson and the Barnsleys

Gimson and the Barnsleys
'Wonderful furniture of a commonplace kind'

Mary Greensted

ALAN SUTTON

First published 1980 by Evans Brothers Limited.

First published in this edition in the United Kingdom in 1991
Alan Sutton Publishing Ltd. · Phoenix Mill · Far Thrupp · Stroud · Gloucestershire

First published in this edition in the United States of America in 1991
Alan Sutton Publishing Inc. · Wolfeboro Falls · NH 03896–0848

Copyright © Mary Greensted, 1980

British Library Cataloguing in Publication Data

Greensted, Mary
  Gimson and the Barnsleys: wonderful furniture of a commonplace kind.
  I. Title
  749.22

  ISBN 0–86299–991–X

Library of Congress Cataloging in Publication Data applied for

Cover illustration: Roomset showing furniture by Gimson and the Barnsleys (*Courtesy
Cheltenham Art Gallery & Museums; photograph The Bridgeman Art Library*)

Printed in Great Britain by
The Bath Press, Bath, Avon.

Contents

Fig. 1. Sidney Barnsley's living room at Sapperton, furnished mainly with items from his own and Gimson's workshops. From a contemporary photograph dating from about 1906.

Introduction

Over fifty years have elapsed since Ernest Gimson and the brothers, Ernest and Sidney Barnsley, died, yet it is only recently that their work has been given some of the recognition that is its due. There has been a similar interval between the appearance in 1924 of the only relevant written work, the memorial volume entitled *Ernest Gimson, His Life and Work*,[1] and the publication of this book. In addition, the work of Ernest and Sidney Barnsley and the relationship between all three men throughout their working lives has not been previously tackled at any length. The current revival of interest in the crafts and in handwork suggests that this is a fitting moment to chart the development of their careers and to assess their achievements in the field of handicrafts. Their importance is two-fold; firstly as members of the Arts and Crafts Movement which, after a period of reappraisal, has emerged as the major force in the history of British design during the last hundred years, and secondly, as individuals, for their contribution to the development of twentieth-century furniture design.

The Arts and Crafts Movement emerged as a result of various attempts throughout the nineteenth century to combat the basic conservatism and lack of direction in much Victorian design. The father-figure of the Movement was William Morris, whose writings, lectures and practical work were tremendously influential on the younger generation of architects, decorators and craftsmen between the 1870s and 1890s. It was amongst this wide spectrum of professionals that the ideals of Morris and his precursors, concerning the importance of honesty to function and to materials, and of personal fulfilment through creative work, were put into practice. These tenets of belief were held by men who clung to their individuality with enthusiasm as is indicated by the variety of work encompassed within the framework of the Movement.

After their training in London and their initial efforts in the fields of architecture and furniture design in the eighties and early nineties, Gimson and the Barnsleys made a conscious break by their removal to the Cotswolds in 1893. They settled at Pinbury, Gloucestershire in 1894 and, in 1902, they moved to the village of Sapperton where they spent the remainder of their lives. However, despite their move to a fairly remote part of the country and their absorption in their work, they maintained a close contact with the development of the Arts and Crafts Movement through their many friends and their involvement in a number of important projects. Their continuing relationships with some of the outstanding

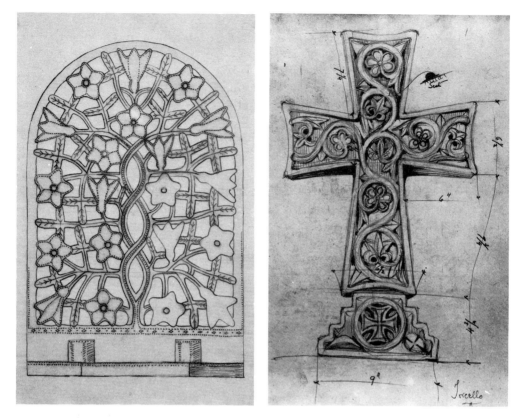

Fig. 2. Design for a candlesconce in brass by Gimson.

Fig. 3. Pencil sketch of a carved stone cross at Torcello, Italy, by Ernest Gimson, 1889.

architects of the period, such as Philip Webb, William Lethaby and Edward Prior, add an extra dimension to their work. In addition, knowledge of their connection with less well-known figures, including the architects, Robert Weir Schultz, Francis Troup, Detmar Blow and Alfred Powell (better known as a decorator of ceramics), adds scope and depth to our conception of the Movement.

Throughout their careers, Gimson and the Barnsleys remained faithful to the principles of the Arts and Crafts Movement. Although many individuals, from A. W. N. Pugin to John Ruskin and William Morris, wrote about the relationship between good design and simplicity, the majority of their work was closely linked to the stereotypes of form and decoration of its period. Gimson and the Barnsleys left very little in the way of written testimonials to their ideals, yet their work often combines the concern for quality, which was so important to the Arts and Crafts Movement, together with a novel approach to design based on clean lines and unadorned surfaces. Particularly significant in the development of the Movement is their early adoption of elements of the Byzantine style in their designs. This characteristic has been described by another twentieth-century woodworker, Eric Sharpe:

It must be noted here how the work drew from other sources of inspiration and research besides the early English woodwork. Gimson had travelled about Europe much, studying and noting information, and Sidney Barnsley measured up a Byzantine monastery in Greece. Nevertheless it is particularly Gimson's work that usually has a Byzantine feeling, and some of his arrangements of pattern definitely derive from that source, particularly the triple loop 'motif' in his sconces [Fig. 2]. But the feeling is a little difficult to describe. I am not referring to the stalls in Bentley's Cathedral or the Khartoum furniture, but to his general domestic work of which these latter are more conspicuous examples. Anyone who has seen the capitals of Torcello, the pierced marble parapets of St Mark's, the shaft of the cross at Bewcastle, or the great church of St Sophia at Constantinople... must have noted the effect of the extreme simplicity of bounding line or form and the intricacy of work contained therein. That is what I mean by the Byzantine feeling. That is what Gimson's furniture in its fullest expression reminds me of; yet it still retained the logical construction of the earliest manner, explicit or implicit.[2]

This Byzantine element is an important aspect of the Arts and Crafts Movement and one which is still to be fully comprehended.

The contribution of Gimson and the Barnsleys to the development of twentieth-century furniture design is also two-fold. Firstly, they showed a fresh and constant appreciation of the materials they used combined with a respect for quality of workmanship and an understanding of construction. The emphasis which they placed on handwork, without being dogmatic, gave rise to a new respect for craftsmanship which has flourished during the present century. The following assessment, although written during their own lifetimes, suggests something of their role in the development of twentieth-century craftsmanship:

The village of Sapperton lies scattered about a winding corner of the Thames and Severn Canal; the canal was busy enough once, but is now stagnant and uncared for, awaiting the time when our villages shall be repopulated and our waterways utilized for the carriage of village-made wares to their 'cheaping-towns'. This is one of Mr Gimson's dreams for the future and meantime his workshops and his smithy employ local labour, and develop the traditional skill in the crafts which is latent in most English villages, though so little called up as to be in danger of dying out altogether.

It is to be hoped that the efforts being made by Ernest Gimson and Ernest and Sydney [sic] Barnsley to save this talent and to utilize it to the best advantage, may be the beginning of a new life for the villages of England. For this reason alone the work from Sapperton presents an important aspect of the Arts and Crafts Movement.[3]

The desire of Gimson and the Barnsleys to revitalise traditional handicrafts and rural communities is echoed in much of the current self-sufficiency philosophy of both craftsmen and environmentalists. More specifically, their work influenced

Fig. 4. Macassar ebony box lined with cherry and inlaid with silver and ivory. Designed by Ernest Gimson and made in his Daneway workshops.

fellow furniture-makers such as A. Romney Green and, through him, his pupils who included Eric Sharpe. A closer link between this tradition and the present day was fostered by Gimson's foreman, Peter van der Waals, who set up his own workshop at Chalford, Glos., after Gimson's death in 1919, and is continued by Edward Barnsley, Sidney Barnsley's son, who has trained an impressive number of contemporary furniture-makers in his workshop near Petersfield, Hampshire, as well as producing furniture made to the highest standards of craftsmanship. The impact which this tradition has had on the teaching of woodwork in the twentieth century can be assessed by even a casual glance at such standard textbooks as *Furniture for Small Houses* by Percy A. Wells and *An Introduction to Decorative Woodwork* by Goodyear and Grimwood.

The principles developed by the three men through their practical work have also influenced the design of furniture for industrial production. The innovatory element in many of their designs enables one to trace features of, for example, the Art Deco style, which dominated the twenties, back to the furniture of Gimson and the Barnsleys in the 1890s and 1900s, [Fig. 65]. In addition, through their impact on contemporaries working on the continent, and on British designers for machine production in the twenties and thirties, they can be said to have made a significant contribution to the simplicity, sense of proportion and fitness for purpose which are fundamental ingredients of the best contemporary design.

Chapter 1
Family background

Ernest Gimson was the fourth of seven children borne to Josiah Gimson by his second wife, Sarah. His father was a self-made man who had begun his career as an iron founder and machinist in Leicester. He established the Vulcan Works, making heavy machinery, in Humberstone Road in the 1850s. The growing success and reputation of this engineering business in the prosperous and expanding city of Leicester brought Josiah Gimson wealth as well as considerable power and influence which he was happy to wield. He became a well-known and respected figure in the community and, in 1877, was elected to the city council as a Liberal. His active and lively mind meant that he took a strong and often unpopular stand on many of the most controversial issues of the day. According to his obituary, printed in the Leicester *Daily Post* on 6 September 1883, 'in theological matters he differed materially from commonly accepted positions', a reference to his position as an active secularist and President of the Leicester Secular Society. At the memorial service held in his honour at the Secular Hall, shortly after his death, Josiah Gimson was described thus by his friend and colleague, Mr G. H. Holyoake:

> He stood for the sanitation of the town, for open parks, for open libraries, for open museums (all forms of sanitation of the mind). He was for bright coffee-taverns for the people, for co-operative devices which tend to establish equality without revolution and equalise fortunes without dynamite.[1]

Ernest William Gimson was born on 21 December 1864 and grew up amidst this enlightened and lively family background. As well as his own brothers and sisters, three of whom survived to maturity, there were five children by Josiah Gimson's first wife. He attended Franklin's School in Stoneygate and, because he was rather a weak child suffering from bouts of ill health, he spent many holidays on a farm in Lincolnshire run by the Morleys, distant cousins of the Gimson family. In 1881, at the age of seventeen, he was articled to Isaac Barradale, a local architect who was responsible for both commercial and domestic building in Leicester in the 1870s and 1880s.

Barradale had set up his practice in 1872, shortly before work was begun on the building of Leicester Town Hall, designed in the Queen Anne style, with additional Dutch elements, by F. J. Hanes.[2] The Town Hall represents an early

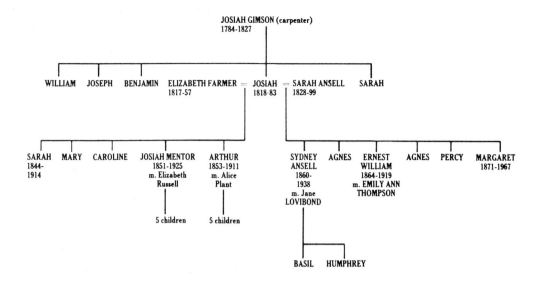

JOSIAH GIMSON (carpenter)
1784-1827

WILLIAM JOSEPH BENJAMIN ELIZABETH FARMER = JOSIAH = SARAH ANSELL SARAH
1817-57   1818-83   1828-99

SARAH MARY CAROLINE JOSIAH MENTOR ARTHUR   SYDNEY AGNES ERNEST   AGNES PERCY MARGARET
1844-   1851-1925   1853-1911   ANSELL   WILLIAM   1871-1967
1914   m. Elizabeth m. Alice   1860-   1864-1919
                       Russell   Plant   1938   m. EMILY ANN
                                                  m. Jane   THOMPSON
                                                  LOVIBOND

                       5 children   5 children

                                                  BASIL   HUMPHREY

and rather isolated use of the new style in the architecture of Leicester, and its innovatory design may have encouraged Barradale to develop his own interpretation based on English vernacular traditions. In 1876, he designed his own offices which were finally built in Greyfriars, Leicester, three years later. This symmetrical brick building is dominated by its regular sash windows, with carefully-proportioned glazing bars, which, on the first floor, run across the entire length of the building. It was in these untraditional offices that Gimson began working for Barradale, easily the most advanced architect of the day in Leicester, at a time when the latter was in receipt of numerous commissions for substantial villas, to be built in the pleasant southern suburbs of the city for its prosperous citizens. One of the most interesting of these houses was designed by Barradale in 1882, during the period of Gimson's apprenticeship, for the principal of the School of Art. The house, in Knighton Park Road was built in English bond brick with a steeply-pitched roof whose stark lines are broken by the introduction of dormer windows. Particularly interesting is Barradale's incorporation of incised plasterwork on the coving between the walls and the roof; this probably provided the young Ernest Gimson with his first close contact with this material in an architectural context.

At the same time, Gimson also enrolled at the Leicester School of Art in Hastings Street. This experience provided an essential part of any architectural training at that time as was explained by a member of the profession, T. G. Jackson, in a paper read to the Architectural Association in 1890:

For although the advantages of pupilage or apprenticeship are so great that they are not likely to be given up, still the student must of necessity supplement the experience gained in his master's office by study and reading of his own; and the office is and should be to him rather the place where he may expect to see put into practice the lessons he has learnt elsewhere rather than the place where he can expect to be taught directly everything he ought to know. He has, therefore, to join classes at Art school and to enter on a course of reading, sketching and independent study of his own.[3]

Ernest Gimson attended classes in advanced building construction at the School of Art and, in 1884, was awarded a silver medal in a national competition for designs and drawings by art students from schools throughout the country. According to *The British Architect*:

> Mr. Gimson's design for a Suburban House (silver medal) though a little crude and harsh in parts, is yet very promising for the future of a designer who is only 18 years of age. We note that the plan has merit – the drawing room and library being nicely placed, though the latter would hardly have the requisite amount of light with the heavy arches veiling its front. . . . In the exterior design the author has been successful in the combination of brickwork and ashlar, the stone band between the floors coming in with good effect.[4]

Only the plan of this design was illustrated in the journal, but the above description indicates Gimson's early appreciation, under the influence of Isaac Barradale, of the use of contrasting colours and textures in his building materials, a recurrent feature of much Arts and Crafts architecture.

In 1885, Gimson completed his studies at the School of Art, obtaining first class results in the examinations. During the same year he once again entered the national competition, winning a third grade prize for a set of drawings of furniture. This was the first indication of his interest in, and flair for, furniture design. Although there is no surviving record of these early drawings, their execution obviously made a significant impression on Gimson for, in 1886, shortly after his arrival in London, he wrote to his mother in Leicestershire asking for them to be sent on to him.

After the death of Josiah Gimson in September 1883, the Gimson family continued to run the business which he had established and to take an active interest in secularism. In January 1884, William Morris visited Leicester to talk on 'Art and Socialism' at the Secular Hall. During this lecture, Morris raised several points which were fundamental to his attitude to art and to creative work, including the importance of every man's having a worthwhile occupation. Sydney Gimson, Ernest's elder brother, has left a vivid description of Morris's lecture and his subsequent visit to the Gimson household in *Random Recollections of the Leicester Secular Society*:

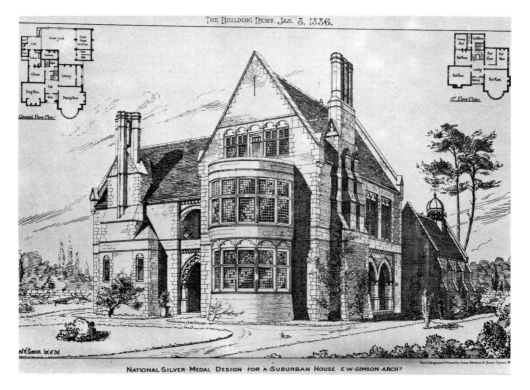

NATIONAL·SILVER·MEDAL·DESIGN·FOR·A·SUBURBAN·HOUSE· E·W·GIMSON·ARCH.T

Fig. 5. A perspective of Gimson's design for a suburban house, executed in 1884 and published in *The Building News* in 1886. It shows a fairly typical High Victorian approach to domestic design with a strong Tudor–Gothic element.

> The bigger event to us was the coming of William Morris. His reputation as a poet and decorative craftsman (the Kelmscott Press had not then been started) was so high that we were definitely very nervous of meeting the great man. Ernest and I went to the station, and, two minutes after his train had come in, we were at home with him and captured by his personality. His was a delightfully breezy, virile personality. In his conversations, if they touched on subjects which he felt deeply, came little bursts of temper which subsided as quickly as they arose and left no bad feeling behind them. He was not a good lecturer. His lectures were always read, and not too well read, but they were wonderful in substance and full of arresting thoughts and apt illustrations. In their phrasing and general form they were beautiful.[5]

William Morris and another guest dined with the Gimsons after the lecture. Towards the end of the evening, they retired to a small smoking room next to Sydney's bedroom to continue their conversation in more relaxed surroundings. Sydney Gimson continued his account thus:

> When Mr Hopps had left, Morris, my sister Sarah, Ernest and I went up there and had a delightful talk which I can never forget. Sarah left us

after about an hour but the other three of us sat talking until nearly 2 o-clock.

I am sure that one reason for this long sitting was that Morris was particularly interested in Ernest, then 19 years old and articled to the Leicester architect, Isaac Barradale, and saw something of the possibilities in him. At any rate when Ernest was anxious to have some experience in a London architect's office, some two years later, he, after much hesitation for fear of intrusion, wrote to ask Morris's advice and perhaps a letter of introduction to a suitable architect. At once Morris sent him three letters of introduction. Delighted and excited, Ernest took the three letters up to London, but he only had to present one, to J. D. Sedding, who at once took him into his office where Ernest stayed for two years.

Whilst in London he joined several Societies and Committees with which Morris was actively associated, and came continuously under his influence, learnt a great deal from him and was imbued with those ideals which governed the rest of his life. Between his first visit to us in 1884 and Ernest's going to London in 1886, Morris paid us several visits and had, no doubt, become sure that Ernest would grow to something worthwhile under the right influence. Ernest went far and was recognised as one of the great craftsmen of his generation. I know that he always felt he owed his great opportunity to the visits of William Morris to Leicester.[6]

A similar family background encouraged Ernest and Sidney Barnsley to embark on architectural careers in much the same way as Ernest Gimson. Their grandfather, John Barnsley, had begun his working life as an apprentice in Matthew Boulton's metal-working factory in the Soho district of Birmingham. In 1826, he set himself up as a builder with premises in Broad Street, Birmingham, but the rapid expansion of the business soon made a move to larger premises in Rylands Street essential. His two sons, Edward and Thomas, were taken into partnership in 1885, by which time the firm of John Barnsley and Sons was one of the leading builders in Birmingham. The entry of Edward and Thomas into the family firm coincided with the development of a close relationship between the builders, John Barnsley and Sons, and J. H. Chamberlain, a young architect working in an original style, who was a founder member and local Secretary of John Ruskin's Guild of St George, and a very vocal and progressive figure in the architectural and cultural life of the City of Birmingham. It may well have been the influence and enthusiasm of the two sons, representing the new ideas of the younger generation, which encouraged this established firm of builders to make a major committment to new developments in the field of architecture under the guidance of a young and relatively inexperienced architect.[7] The partnership was commented on thus in the obituary to Thomas Barnsley printed in the Birmingham *Daily Post* in 1909:

. . . in fact the architect and the builders may be said to have combined to introduce the application of Gothic architecture both in the streets and suburbs of this city.[8]

J. H. Chamberlain also worked on the design of several interiors, where his work was as advanced as it was in the field of architecture. His design for an anteroom at The Grove, Harborne, Birmingham, dating from 1877, features an effective use of panelling in sycamore and oak inlaid with walnut and other woods. This interior has been reconstructed in the Victoria and Albert Museum to provide a period setting for furniture by William Morris's firm, Morris and Co., and his contemporaries.

In the 1870s, the Barnsley family diversified its interests and acquired a partnership in the long-established firm of Meredith and Co. This firm was one of the leading varnish and japan manufacturers in Birmingham, and Edward Barnsley gradually took over responsibility for its management, leaving the control of the building firm to his younger brother, Thomas. Edward Barnsley fathered five children. Of these, Arthur Ernest Barnsley was born on 17 February 1863, the third of four sons, followed by Sidney Howard Barnsley, born two years later, on 25 February 1865. (Arthur Ernest Barnsley was always known as Ernest, whilst, to complicate matters, his elder brother, Ernest William, was known as William.) In common with many other members of the Barnsley family, they lived in Edgbaston, a suburb to the south-west of Birmingham, which was expanding rapidly during the second half of the nineteenth century. The amount and quality of Victorian domestic building in this part of the city indicates its attraction for the wealthy and, in many cases, artistically-inclined middle classes. The Barnsley family was of Wesleyan stock, and Ernest and Sidney regularly attended services at the local chapel. After completing their schooling, they both continued their studies at the Birmingham School of Art. In 1884, Ernest Barnsley won a third grade prize for historic ornament, having attended classes in finished drawing, painting, modelling and design, whilst, in 1885, Sidney Barnsley was awarded a first class certificate in building construction, interestingly an identical qualification to that received by Ernest Gimson in Leicester in the same year.

The backgrounds of Ernest Gimson and the brothers, Ernest and Sidney Barnsley, have certain common features which help to explain both the momentum of their friendship and the similarity between their aspirations throughout their lives. During the nineteenth century, non-conformism in religious matters, which was common to both families, often went together with an enlightened and inquiring attitude to the values of Victorian society. In addition, both families provided a strong technical basis, in the fields of engineering and building, which must have influenced the three men from an early age. Their interests in the more technical aspects of design are illustrated by the existence of drawings by Gimson of machinery from the family firm, and the fact that Sidney Barnsley made a potter's wheel for his friend the ceramic decorator, Alfred Powell, based on a design by Josiah Wedgwood. Both Josiah Gimson and the firm of John Barnsley and Sons were active at a time when the engineering and building industries were expanding rapidly, and were able to exploit these conditions to become prosperous members of the community.

Because of their healthy financial positions, and because Ernest Gimson and Ernest and Sidney Barnsley were younger sons in their respective families, they were not required to enter the family businesses, unlike their elder brothers. In addition, sufficient capital was available in both cases to enable them to train for their chosen careers. Taking these factors into consideration, it is not surprising that all three men chose to train as architects, and enter a profession which required both an artistic and a technical background as well as providing its members with a respected and privileged status in society. In addition, architecture was possibly the most socially-conscious profession involved in the arts in the nineteenth century and consequently attracted many able, public-spirited and individualistic recruits. Because of the scope and historical development of the profession, architects were traditionally involved with all-embracing problems of design and with the role of the arts in society, as well as with the design and construction of buildings.

Ernest Barnsley and his brother, Sidney, went to London to train as architects in 1885. They enrolled with the Royal Academy's architectural school in July and December respectively, through the recommendation of the distinguished architect, Richard Norman Shaw. Amongst their close contemporaries at the Royal Academy were two other architectural students, Robert Weir Schultz and Francis Troup, who soon became close friends of both brothers. Ernest and Sidney Barnsley attended classes at the Royal Academy for two years, during which time they progressed through both the lower and upper schools of architecture. During this period they also began working in the offices of established London-based architects to broaden the scope of their training; it was this that lead to their meeting with Ernest Gimson.

Chapter 2
The Arts and Crafts Movement

From their arrival in London in the 1880s, the careers of Gimson and the two Barnsleys were closely bound up with the Arts and Crafts Movement. It is therefore necessary to discuss the development of this Movement, which had its roots in the early nineteenth century, before one can hope to understand the principles which governed the work of the three designer-craftsmen.

The eighteenth and nineteenth centuries had seen the advance of the process of industrialisation, the effects of which could be seen and felt in the altered character and development of the towns and countryside throughout most of Britain, in the changing nature of people's working lives and in the end-products of mechanised industries. The increasing use of machines in the manufacture of a wide variety of products raised the output of many industries and enabled superficial decoration to be applied cheaply to an ever-increasing range of goods. The concept of industrial design was more or less unknown in the early nineteenth century, and any direction or control in this field came from the manufacturer, who relied on one of the many available pattern books, rather than from the craftsmen developing the decorative features of this work as a direct result of his experience with the raw materials and tools of his trade. As a consequence, stylistic development was stultified and the craftsman no longer had the same enjoyment in and control over his work. It was the combination of a social, humanistic and aesthetic ideology which instilled such moral fervour into the critics of 'the present decay of taste'. The absence of the designer as a recognised professional meant that the role of critic devolved on to the architect, who had managed to maintain his privileged status in society without becoming estranged from everyday life, and had a traditional concern with interior decoration as well as with the building arts.

One of the first individuals in the early nineteenth century to voice this protest was the architect, theatrical designer and Catholic convert, Augustus Welby Pugin. Pugin was responsible for providing the Gothic Revival, whose popularity had previously relied on its supposedly 'English' character, and its appeal to the newly-prosperous middle classes, with strict architectural principles. His written work, as well as his designs, enabled Gothic principles to be taken as seriously as the Italianate and aristocratic classical styles, and paved the way for their widespread adoption in the mid-nineteenth century. Pugin's enthusiasm for the Gothic Revival was increased by its emotional connection, in his mind at

Fig. 6. Carved oak cabinet designed by A. W. N. Pugin for Abney Hall, Cheshire, and made by J. G. Crace Ltd. in about 1841.

least, with the Catholic faith. He was also one of the first promoters of an idealised view of medieval society, and he broached theories of design which were subsequently amplified by John Ruskin and William Morris. In *The True Principles of Christian Architecture*, for example, Pugin stated that

> The two great rules for design are these: first, that there should be no features about a building which are not necessary for convenience, construction or 'propriety'; second, that all ornament should consist of enrichment to the essential construction of the building.[1]

Elsewhere in his writings, Pugin widened the scope of his theories, applying them to the whole field of design rather than to architecture alone. As well as working as an architect on ecclesiastical and private commissions, he was also responsible for the design of furniture and fittings in many of his buildings. He ran his architectural practice from his house in Ramsgate, where he and several assistants also produced stained glass, metalwork, textiles and jewellery. Pugin also designed furniture and, in 1835, he published *Gothic Furniture in the Style of the Fifteenth Century* as part of his attempt to clarify the principles of Gothic design from the muddle of misapplied ornament which he saw around him. His designs for good quality, well-constructed furniture in the Gothic style were executed for his clients by commercial firms.

In the late 1840s, Pugin began working with the firm of cabinet-makers, J. G. Crace Ltd., based in Wigmore Street, London, who produced elaborately carved pieces of furniture to his designs, such as the oak cabinet, made in about 1847, for Abney Hall, Cheshire [Fig. 6]. Although heavily ornamented, these later pieces continued to conform to the basic rectangular structure, consisting of posts and rails, developed by the medieval joiner. They illustrate, above all, a respect for sound construction and the accurate application of ornament. This last aspect of design theory was taken up by several writers in the mid-nineteenth century. In 1856, Owen Jones published *The Grammar of Ornament*, whilst Bruce Talbert's *Gothic Forms Applied to Furniture* appeared in 1867. Talbert's own exercises in furniture design in the Gothic style were very influential, both in his home town of Manchester and in London.

The Gothic Revival architects in the mid-nineteenth century played an important role in the establishment and widespread acceptance of the Gothic style, and of a new approach to furniture design. Particularly where ecclesiastical commissions were concerned, architects such as William Butterfield, G. E. Street and William Burges would often design the interior fittings as well as the building itself. William Burges produced a range of furniture in 1862 which was based on his own researches into thirteenth- and fourteenth-century designs. Burges's furniture was very simple in form but elaborately painted, conforming to his own conception of medieval furniture. Butterfield showed a healthy respect for the marks of workmanship, an attitude echoed in the writings of Ruskin. This quality can be seen in, for example, the library of St Augustine's, Canterbury,

Fig. 7. Oak table designed by the Gothic Revival architect, G. E. Street, for students' bedrooms at the theological college at Cuddesdon, near Oxford, c. 1856.

built by Butterfield in 1845. The interior was panelled with bold, criss-cross timbers, left undecorated apart from some light chamfering on the right angles.

Probably the most important contribution to the development of the Arts and Crafts Movement by the Gothic Revival architects was made by G. E. Street. Like Butterfield, Street preferred to design the interiors of his commissions, and his office in Oxford, and later London, was a valuable training ground for many young architects including William Morris, Philip Webb, Norman Shaw and John Sedding. His influence on Morris and, in particular, on Philip Webb can be clearly recognised when looking at examples of Street's furniture designs. One of the oak tables [Fig. 7] designed by him, and made in about 1856 for students' bedrooms at Cuddesdon College, Oxford, is now in the collections of the Victoria and Albert Museum. Its sound construction is achieved by the simplest of means, using mortise-and-tenon joints pinned with wooden dowels. The only decorative feature is derived from the picturesque use of the club shape to complete both the legs and the mortise-and-tenoned stretchers. Street's approach to furniture design is echoed in Philip Webb's work for William Morris in the 1860s and in some of Sidney Barnsley's early designs at Pinbury in the 1890s. He also designed more elaborate pieces of furniture and was strongly influenced in his choice of inlaid and incised motifs by his involvement with the Gothic Revival.

The furniture designed by the Gothic Revival architects, and by a handful of artists and industrial designers, provided an alternative to commercially-designed furniture for those who could afford to commission its manufacture. 'Art Furniture', taking under its wing a variety of different styles, emerged as a recognisable phenomenon in the second half of the nineteenth century and, at the same time, attempts were made to make it available to a wider public. A spate of periodicals and magazines appeared, all trying to establish a new approach to design amid the indiscriminate abuse of styles and the laboured techniques of decoration found in the conservative products of the furniture 'warehouses'. Perhaps the most influential publication was Charles Eastlake's *Hints on Household Taste*, which appeared in both Britain and the United States in 1869, and popularised the styles and motifs as well as the ideology of the new school of designers.

By the 1870s, 'Art Furniture Manufacturers' were listed separately in the London trade directories, although this was as much an indication of the expanding trade in general as of their recognition by the majority of the furniture-buying public. Other developments in the furniture trade during the nineteenth century, such as the growing popularity of antique furniture, and the consequent manufacture on a large scale of reproduction pieces, had greatly increased the output of the furniture trade. The increased demand for its products was catered for by the invention of woodworking machinery, and the introduction of mechanisation for some of the basic processes, such as sawing, planing and dovetailing, as well as for the decorative techniques of moulding and carving. These inventions, which were intended to carry out processes more quickly and cheaply, were not the sole prerogative of the furniture 'warehouses'. They were rapidly exploited by the manufacturers of 'art' furniture as well as being adapted for use by the growing numbers of amateurs involved in the design of furniture and woodworking. Schools of Wood Carving and classes sponsored by the Home Arts and Industries Association proliferated and, in the 1860s, a small treadle fret-carving machine was marketed for use in the home. William Morris was one of the many individuals who experimented with this machine.

The attempts by architects, industrial designers, writers and public reformers to improve general standards of design were, on the whole, ineffective. Neither the production of expensive furniture nor the publication of exhortatory articles made any great impression on the way of thinking of the great majority of craftsmen, manufacturers, retailers and general public. The Great Exhibition of 1851, in the organisation of which Henry Cole and Prince Albert had attempted to promote greater co-operation between art and industry, and thus to raise the design standards of British manufacturers, was a focal point for discontent. The Exhibition was an outstanding popular and financial success, but it aroused grave concern amongst many commentators, and indeed amongst many of the Exhibition organisers themselves, as to the standard of industrial design in Britain. Owen Jones, who had been concerned with the organisation of the Exhibition and was also a friend of Henry Cole, wrote:

We have no principles, no unity; the architect, the upholsterer, the paper stainer, the weaver, the calico-printer and the potter, run each their independent course; each struggles fruitlessly, each produces in art novelty without beauty or beauty without intelligence.[2]

John Ruskin was one of the most scathing critics of the state of the nation as typified by the exhibits at the Crystal Palace. He concluded that Cole's error had been to tackle the problem on a purely materialistic level, whereas the real solution could only come from fundamental changes of attitude to Nature, to the individual and to the role of work in society. He stressed the importance of work by hand as opposed to mechanical work, for the good of the product and for the well-being of the worker involved in its manufacture. In putting forward these arguments, Ruskin was looking back to a golden age before the Industrial Revolution, much as Pugin had done at an earlier date.

This message was absorbed by William Morris whilst he was still an undergraduate at Oxford. Ruskin's most influential books in the development of the ideas of William Morris and his associates were *The Seven Lamps of Architecture*, published in 1849, and the three volumes of *The Stones of Venice*, published in 1851 and 1853. Of these, the chapter, 'The Nature of Gothic', included in the second volume of *The Stones of Venice*, bore most relevance to Morris's work, and was to become a gospel for the Arts and Crafts Movement in general. In this chapter, Ruskin argued that man-made articles should reveal, rather than seek to disguise, their origins, and that individuality and roughness of workmanship were infinitely preferable to perfection and standardisation, in a free and just society. Ruskin was thus asserting the superiority of the products of the creative craftsman over those of the factory. When the Kelmscott Press reprinted *The Nature of Gothic*, in 1892, Morris wrote in the preface:

To my mind, and I believe to some others, it is one of the most important things written by the author, and in future days will be considered as one of the very few necessary and inevitable utterances of the century. To some of us when we first read it, now many years ago, it seemed to point out a new road on which the world should travel.[3]

Morris's own writings and his lecture tours throughout the country, from 1877 onwards, reached an even wider audience. The strong impression created by Morris's lecture in Leicester on the young Ernest Gimson has already been mentioned, and he also lectured frequently in Birmingham, where his audience may have included Ernest and Sidney Barnsley. In 1880, for example, Morris visited Birmingham twice, lecturing on 'The Beauty of Life' at the Society of Arts and School of Design and on 'Labour and Pleasure versus Labour and Sorrow' at the Town Hall.

However, Morris's greatest influence on his contemporaries was experienced through his practical example rather than his theoretical work. A turning point

Fig. 8. The staircase at the Red House, near Bexleyheath, Kent, designed by Philip Webb for William Morris, c. 1859.

Fig. 9. The oak stairwell at The White House, Leicester, designed by Ernest Gimson in 1897.

in his career came in 1853, when he went to Exeter College, Oxford, intending to take Holy Orders on the completion of his degree. His closest friend at Oxford was Edward Burne-Jones and together they built up a circle of associates, mainly Burne-Jones's friends from Birmingham, who indulged in a similar passion for literature, art (particularly that of the Pre-Raphaelites) and social reform. After his experiences at Oxford, Morris decided that the Church was no longer his chosen career and, instead, articled himself to the architect, G. E. Street, then based in Oxford, in whose office he met Philip Webb, who was to become a life-long friend. Morris left Street's employment in 1858 and, with Burne-Jones, took over premises in Red Lion Square, London, from the Pre-Raphaelite painter, Dante Gabriel Rosetti, to concentrate on painting and on designing furnishings. In 1860, he and his wife, Jane Burden, moved into The Red House, Bexleyheath, built for them by Philip Webb.

In the design of The Red House, and in that of his subsequent architectural commissions, Philip Webb added a new dimension to the role of the architect. According to Goodhart-Rendel:

His ultimate importance in history is likely to derive less from what he built

Fig. 10. Oak table with gouged decoration designed by Philip Webb in about 1870. It is very similar to a round table made by the designer for William Morris in 1858, and now at Kelmscott Manor, Oxfordshire.

himself than from the example which he set to others in his care for minute detail both in design and in processes of workmanship.[4]

Whereas previously, an architect was only superficially involved in the design and execution of the details within his plans, either working from pattern books or relying on the contractor's judgement, Philip Webb's concern was all-embracing. Details such as the pointing of brickwork, the design of staircase rails, window frames and metal window fittings were considered as integral features of the overall scheme by Philip Webb and the generation of young architects influenced by his example. In the same spirit, Webb and Morris, together with many of their friends, designed much of the furniture and furnishings for The Red House.

It was a logical step from this growing absorption with the applied arts purely for personal fulfilment, to the establishment of Morris, Marshall, Faulkner and Co. in 1861, whose members also included Philip Webb, Dante Gabriel Rossetti, Edward Burne-Jones and Ford Madox Brown. The firm set out to produce a wide variety of furnishings and decorative objects including stained glass, wall-paper, textiles and furniture. Unlike their predecessors who had ventured into

Fig. 11. Carved walnut chest designed by George Jack for Morris and Co. in 1892.

this field of design, they made no attempt to reconcile art and industry, but instead based their philosophy on 'truth' in art through individuality, the study of nature and the unity of the arts. The original designers of Morris and Co. furniture were Philip Webb and Ford Madox Brown; Morris himself was not responsible for any furniture designed after 1861. Philip Webb had previously made some furniture for Morris, based on planks and rails fixed by protruding wooden pins, whilst Ford Madox Brown's furniture designs, described in the firm's catalogue as 'of solid construction and joiner made', were also heavy, rectangular and usually without any decoration. The manufacture of the earliest Morris and Co. furniture designs was entrusted to a local Bloomsbury cabinet-maker, but in 1865, when the firm moved to Queen Square, workshops were opened and furniture was produced directly under Morris's supervision. It was not until the 1870s and '80s that Morris and Co. veered away from the production of very simple furniture based on vernacular traditions. In *The Lesser Arts of Life*, published in 1882, Morris wrote:

> Moreover I must needs think of furniture as of two kinds: one part of it being chairs, dining and working tables and the like, the necessary work-a-day furniture in short, which should be of course both well made and well proportioned, but simple to the last degree. . . . But besides this kind of

furniture, there is the other kind of what I should call state furniture, which I think is quite proper even for a citizen: I mean sideboards, cabinets and the like, which we have quite as much for beauty's sake as for use; we need not spare ornament on these, but may make them as elegant and as elaborate as we can with carving, inlaying or painting; these are the blossoms of the art of furniture.[5]

George Jack, who had been a pupil of Philip Webb, became the firm's chief furniture designer in 1890. By then the firm's output was almost entirely in the 'state furniture' category; very well made, elaborately decorated, usually with inlays, and, contrary to Ruskin's teaching, very highly finished. In fact, during the period between 1860 and 1890, Morris and Co. followed the general trend of the furniture trade away from individual craftsmanship, in the sense that even they used machinery quite extensively for carving and shaping wood.

William Morris and Philip Webb were very much the leaders and source of inspiration for the younger generation of architects in the 1870s and 1880s. In 1877, Morris founded the Society for the Protection of Ancient Buildings, which he nicknamed 'Anti-Scrape', and both he and Webb remained active members on its committee throughout their lives. As well as attempting to preserve buildings, and to control restoration work, the Society provided a lively and valuable meeting place for those concerned with the arts and architecture. The architect, W. R. Lethaby, who had been introduced to the S. P. A. B. in 1891 by Gimson, wrote:

> The Society itself was a remarkable teaching body. Dealing as it did with the common facts of traditional building in scores and hundreds of examples, it became under the technical guidance of Philip Webb, the architect, a real school of practical *building* – architecture with all the whims which we usually call 'design' left out. . . . It is a curious fact that this Society, engaged in intense study of antiquity, became a school of rational builders and modern buildings.[6]

Another new organisation was the Art Workers' Guild, founded in 1884 by a group of 25 individuals, all working in the arts, who saw the other professional bodies open to them, such as the Royal Academy or the Institute of British Architects, as too restrictive and isolated. Amongst the founder members of the Guild were John Sedding and W. R. Lethaby. Its main contribution was to provide a meeting place for lectures, discussions and the exchange of ideas, whilst its offshoot, the Arts and Crafts Exhibition Society, gave its members an opportunity to demonstrate their ideology to the public through their creative work. Its foundation, in 1886, provided the original coining of the phrase 'Arts and Crafts'. The Society's first exhibition was held at the New Gallery in Regent Street in October 1888 when the exhibitors included Walter Crane, also the Society's first President, Philip Webb, the potter, William de Morgan and W. R. Lethaby.

A portrait of William Morris, attributed to
C. Fairfax Murray.

Architectural offices:

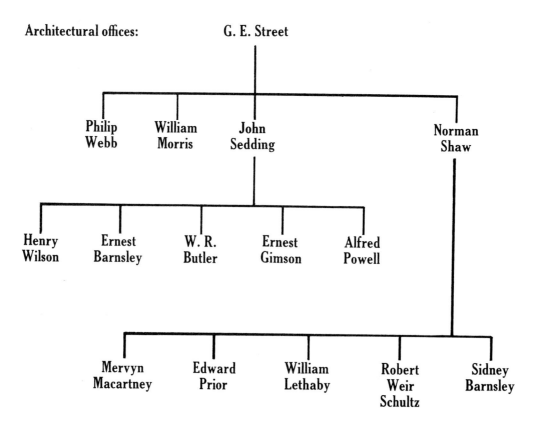

Fig. 12. Turned oak chair designed in
Norman Shaw's office in the 1870s, possibly
by William Lethaby, and retailed by Morris
and Co.

The London-based architects, John Sedding and Norman Shaw were active
participants in these developments and wholeheartedly encouraged the involvement of their assistants and pupils. Norman Shaw, born in 1831, studied architecture under William Burn, and at the Royal Academy Schools. In 1858, after
a period spent travelling on the continent, he entered Street's office as a draughts-
man, taking the place of Philip Webb, in the same year that John Sedding became
one of Street's pupils. In 1862, Norman Shaw set up an architectural practice in
London with W. Eden Nesfield with whom he remained in partnership until
1868. He subsequently built up a large practice of his own, working on public
as well as private commissions, and also designing wallpaper and furniture. His
furniture designs dating from the sixties and seventies show the influence of the
Gothic Revival in their use of elaborate carved and painted decoration. In 1876,
Morris and Co. retailed an oak, rush-seated armchair [Fig. 12], which was
probably designed in Shaw's office. Norman Shaw became known primarily
as a pioneer of the Queen Anne style in his designs for New Scotland Yard, built
in 1888 on the Thames Embankment, and the Bedford Park development in
West London. Under his influence, and with his support, in 1883 a group of
Shaw's assistants and pupils, led by Lethaby, formed a 'Guild of Handicraftsmen
and Designers in the Arts' which was a precursor of the Art Workers' Guild. In
her book on the Arts and Crafts Movement, Gillian Naylor writes:

The conviction that a Socialist Democracy would ensure collaboration rather than competition, and that this collaboration would lead ultimately to the situation in which 'the glorious art of architecture, now for some time slain by commercial greed, would be born again to flourish' led several designers in the 1880s and '90s to embrace the Socialist cause. . . . Norman Shaw's office, while Lethaby was there, gained such a reputation that fathers were loath to allow their sons to associate with the staff.[7]

John Sedding left Street's office in 1865 to join his brother, Edmund, who was working as an architect in Penzance. After Edmund's untimely death in 1868, Sedding moved his practice to Bristol and then, in 1876, settled in London. A year later he met Ruskin and, under his influence, tried to set up a school of masons, carvers and modellers from nature. He disliked the concept of the building as a separate entity from its contents, and therefore designed church furniture, embroideries and gold and silver ornaments for many of his ecclesiastical commissions, following the example of Pugin, of whom he was a great admirer. His inspiration for the design and decoration of his work was almost invariably from nature for, as he wrote, he wanted 'fresh life and reality' in his buildings and designs. In 1890, Sedding completed Holy Trinity Church, Sloane Street, which had been commissioned by Lord Cadogan as his jubilee gift to Queen Victoria. This church is probably Sedding's best-known work; in its design he attempted to unite, in one building, a number of different styles, and the work of different artists. Amongst the many artists concerned in this scheme were Edward Burne-Jones, William Morris, and the sculptor, F. W. Pomeroy. Gimson wrote of this architectural enterprise to W. R. Butler thus:

> The other memorable things of the year are Shaw's Police Offices and Sedding's Chelsea Church – Shaw's is the finest public building since Wren's day and Sedding's is the finest Church since the Gothic Revival.[8]

The interior of Holy Trinity Church was only completed during the decade after Sedding's death in 1891, by his assistant, Henry Wilson, who commissioned some metalwork fittings from Gimson as part of the overall design.

Chapter 3
Architectural students

In 1886, Ernest Gimson entered into articles with the architect, John Dando Sedding. Sedding's office premises in Oxford Street, London, were situated next door to the showrooms of Morris and Co. These showrooms, with their wealth of new designs by William Morris and his associates, must have been a powerful attraction and talking point for the young architects. Amongst Gimson's fellow-students in Sedding's office were Ernest Barnsley, who had come to London a year previously, and Alfred Powell. Through Ernest Barnsley, Gimson came into contact with Sidney Barnsley and the other young architects, including W. R. Lethaby and Robert Weir Schultz, working in the prestigious office of Richard Norman Shaw. The two Barnsley brothers thus strengthened the contacts between the offices of two of the most influential architects working in London at that time. Gimson and Sidney Barnsley, in particular, struck up a close friendship which was to last throughout their lives.

As well as working for Shaw and Sedding, the three men spent the second half of the 1880s undertaking architectural study on their own account. Sidney Barnsley entered a set of measured drawings of St Mary's Cistercian Abbey, Old Cleeve, Somerset, in the competition for the Institute of British Architects Silver Medal in 1886. He was awarded a certificate of merit for his entry and his drawings, which were illustrated in three consecutive issues of the major architectural periodical, *The British Architect*, and were described by that journal as 'amongst the finest of their kind'. The clarity of the drawings, together with the obvious sympathy with their subject matter, were qualities which Sidney Barnsley was to exploit later in his career. In 1889, he entered the Institute's Owen Jones Studentship competition, and was again awarded a medal of merit. One of his drawings, featuring a black and white marble pavement in the Baptistry, Florence, was again illustrated in *The British Architect*.

On the lighter side, they also took part in many of the friendships and activities which London had to offer. Some of Gimson's letters, written from London, have survived, and show a great enthusiasm for their way of life. Although shy, he had a keen sense of fun, and participated in the pranks and entertainments which were an inevitable part of a young student's existence. During this period he was dismissive of anyone choosing to live anywhere other than London, although in his later life he treated a visit to the capital, or indeed to any other big city, as a necessary chore which should be dispatched as quickly as possible.

Gimson joined Morris's 'Anti-Scrape' in 1889, and gave a lively account of its meetings:

> I have joined the Anti-Scrape Society. Morris was good enough to propose me as a member. I attend committee meetings every Thursday afternoon. Morris, Philip Webb and many interesting people are always there. After the meeting we all adjourn to Gatti's for tea and have an hour's talk of which, of course, Morris is the life and soul.[1]

Gimson also attended meetings of the Art Workers' Guild but, unlike Morris and many of his friends and colleagues, he had no strong political convictions. In February 1888, he wrote to Ernest Barnsley thus:

> Schultz and I went to Butler's the other evening. They did their best to make a proselyte of me for 3 or 4 hours. It was interesting but not profitable. On Friday we had the delight of listening to Morris on art at the Art Workers' Guild. Lethaby and Schultz and Butler were in their element applauding his socialism to the echo. 'It's a d——d wicked world'.[2]

Gimson and the Barnsleys paid neither homage nor lip service to the current socialist doctrines, unlike many of their contemporaries working in the arts. Indeed politics of any persuasion seem to have played a negligible role in their lives, a factor which partly explains their wholehearted conviction in the importance of personal fulfilment, throughout their careers.

Despite all the interest and pleasure which London had to offer, the three men did not neglect any opportunities to travel. Gimson and Ernest Barnsley went together to France and Italy in 1887, making copious notes of architectural work and decorative details which were re-worked on their return to England. Sidney Barnsley made a similar trip at the end of that year, whilst Gimson was to return to the continent on his own in the spring of 1889. He sent Ernest Barnsley this lively account of his travels, from Arles in France:

> The loveliest week of my tour was spent at Torcello. Another man, Cross by name, and I stayed in a little cottage there. There was an old couple, their children and grand-children. We sat round a jolly open fireplace with them in the evenings and made tea and played with the youngsters. We lived on Macaroni, Polenta, Salami, Eggs and Wine. The bed was the most unsatisfactory part of the proceedings, as it had a considerable population of its own which violently resented our intrusion. I've the marks on me yet. From Torcello we went back to Venice for two or three days, and then on to Ravenna. Ravenna's the place. Our time there was for me, complete happiness.[3]

A drawing from this period by Ernest Gimson of a statue of St Trophime from the cloisters of the church of the same name at Arles is illustrated here [Fig. 13].

St. Trophimus from the Cloisters of S. Trophimus, Arles.

Ernest W. Gimson

Fig. 13.

Gimson also spent many months travelling through England, visiting sites in Northumberland, County Durham, Yorkshire, Kent, Warwickshire and Gloucestershire. An undated letter to Ernest Barnsley, written during one of these tours, corresponds with one of Gimson's surviving sketch books from this period. He wrote from Berkeley, Gloucestershire:

> I caught my train at Worcester but foolishly indulged in a nap which caused me to miss Tewkesbury and go on to Gloucester. However two or three hours there did not come amiss. I went on to Tewkesbury in the evening and stayed till Wednesday morning when I came on here. I did no work in the Abbey but spent my time seeing things of interest in the neighbourhood. Deerhurst – jolly Saxon Church – Birsmoreton Old Court, such a lovely place, I walked there, 7 miles, through lovely country and then another seven miles on to Ledbury Church among the hills – one of the most interesting Churches I have seen. Berkeley is a fine place. The Church is decorated all over with the most gorgeous old frescoes in wonderful preservation – floral designs – most of them.[4]

Gimson has left a visual as well as a verbal record of this journey in a sketchbook filled with notes of the particular sights which aroused his interest. Another sketchbook from the same period contains a detailed study of Ditcheat Church in Somerset. There are several drawings of the Elizabethan rose motif carved on the transept of the roof, which he later adopted for use in many different media. From a stone carving in Winchester Cathedral, Gimson copied a squirrel, which was subsequently incorporated into designs in plaster, metal and wood. The same sketchbook contains drawings of everyday seventeenth-century furniture, such as cradles and chairs, which had survived in houses and churches visited by Gimson, as well as architectural drawings of vernacular buildings such as tithe barns and cottages.

Most of Gimson's surviving letters from this period were written to Ernest Barnsley, who had completed his training in John Sedding's architectural office by the middle of 1887 and had moved from London back to Birmingham. He married his wife Alice shortly after his return to his home town and, by the end of 1888, he was the proud father of a girl, Mary. His domestic bliss and pre-occupation with family life during this period were commented on by Gimson in this indulgent fashion:

> How is the potter's wheel? The very name brings up visions of hoary patriarchs. When are you going to begin? Mrs Barnsley would approve of it I'm sure – it is such a domesticating occupation. You would work side by side in the dining room – she, at her sewing machine and you at your wheel – and the little family would amuse herself by handing clay to the father and needles to the mother till she was absolutely unrecognizable.[5]

Ernest Barnsley and his family set up home in Stirling Road in the suburb of

Fig. 14. Pencil sketches showing details of
leadwork at Haddon Hall, Derbyshire,
by Ernest Gimson, c. 1890.

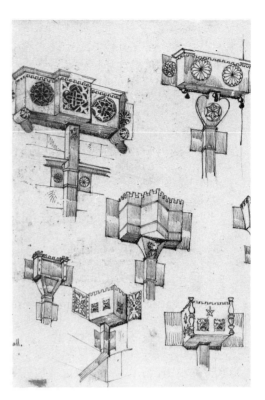

Fig. 15. Detail of a firedog showing a
polished steel roundel in the form of a
squirrel, designed by Ernest Gimson and
made at the Daneway smithy in about 1904.

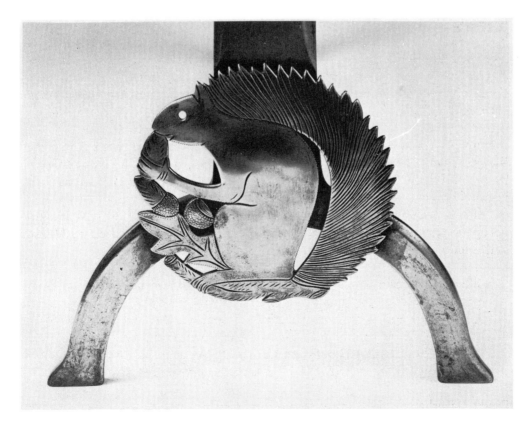

13th Century.

12th Century.

11th Century.

ST·JOHN'S·CH:
CHESTER.

Chancel.   Nave.

Chapel Tower.

Tower.

Porch.

The Black shews plan as at present.

Ernest W. Gimson
Ar.t

1941: 225:59

Edgbaston, and he also established his own architectural practice with offices in Temple Row, in the city centre.

Very few examples of his architectural work in Birmingham have survived, either physically or in contemporary records. His first commission came from his eldest brother, Charles Herbert Barnsley. Ernest Barnsley designed a house for him, which was built at 320 Hagley Road, Edgbaston, by the family firm, John Barnsley and Sons, in 1887. This house [Figs. 17 and 18] remains more or less unaltered, and illustrates the influence of the Queen Anne style, as practised by Norman Shaw, on the young Ernest Barnsley. It was built, characteristically, in red brick, with a darker variety providing a decorative outline for important features such as the chimneys and windows. A typical ingredient of this style of domestic building is the high, steeply-sloping roof, balanced by the tall chimney stacks. The solid regularity of the design is relieved by the asymmetrical siting of a three-sided bay on the ground floor at the front and rear of the house. Ernest Barnsley's design for 320 Hagley Road illustrates the technical competence, appreciation of style and sense of proportion which he was able to bring to bear on his first architectural commission, and this house remains the best-preserved example of his work in Birmingham.

At about the same time, a house was built for William Barnsley, Ernest Barnsley's elder brother, at 324 Hagley Road. It is quite likely that Ernest Barnsley may also have been the architect of this house, but no documentation has survived. The house itself, particularly the frontage, has been extensively altered. In May 1888, he submitted plans, no longer in existence, for a house in Barlows Road, Edgbaston, and, two years later, further plans were submitted, this time for a varnish manufactory and house for the firm of Meredith and Co. with which his father was closely connected. Neither the plans not the buildings themselves, on the proposed site in Western Road, Birmingham, have survived. Perhaps inspired by the shortage of commissions, Ernest Barnsley built a country house for himself, his wife and daughters near the village of Barnt Green in the Lickey Hills, Worcestershire, some time between 1890 and 1892. Their occupation of this new home was cut short by their removal from the area, and neither the exact site nor the house itself, which was called Elmfield, are known today.

Sidney Barnsley and Ernest Gimson left the architectural offices of Norman Shaw and John Sedding respectively in 1888. In the spring of that year, Sidney Barnsley and his fellow-student, Robert Weir Schultz, set off on an architectural tour of Greece, at the instigation of William Lethaby. The two men returned to England briefly in 1889, but were offered a scholarship by the British School at Athens to continue their architectural researches, with a view to publication. The scholarship was funded partly from the School's resources, and partly by individual donations from a variety of individuals, including the Marquess of Bute, Dr E. H. Freshfield and the painter, Edwin Poynter. Sidney Barnsley and

Fig. 16. The interior of St John's Church, Chester, drawn in pencil by Ernest Gimson in about 1890.

Left Fig. 17. 320 Hagley Road, Edgbaston, Birmingham, designed by Ernest Barnsley and built by John Barnsley and Sons in 1887.

Below Fig. 18. The rear of the house. The dormer window frames are not original.

Right Fig. 19. Robert Weir Schultz and Sidney Barnsley (standing), photographed during their travels in Greece, c. 1889.

Schultz returned to Greece in the autumn of 1889, and spent most of the following year making a systematic study of Byzantine churches throughout the mainland. At a later date, they drew up a memorandum to record the scope of their own work, and to suggest areas which warranted further study. The following extract has been taken from this memorandum, illustrating something of the extent of their task and the enthusiasm with which it was undertaken:

> ATHENS: architectural plans of all the Churches with elevations, sections and details. A good set of photographs of ditto also full notes of the Christian work on the Acropolis.
> NOTE: of the church of the monastery beyond the British School we have only got the plan. A complete iconographic study of this with diagrams or coloured drawings showing the disposition of the various subjects and also drawings showing the individual arrangement would be extremely valuable and could be published in the school journal or elsewhere as a set by them-selves. We have also got a good collection of drawings and photographs of the principal Byzantine fragments which were lying about the Acropolis in 1880–90 and which have since been removed to the Central Museum. We should be glad however to have this supplemented and would send rough notes of what we have to anyone who would care to do it.[6]

On the lighter side, Gimson described their travels thus in a letter to W. R. Butler:

Sid Barnsley is in Greece again with Schultz. They went last October and will not return until after next Christmas. They are measuring up the remains of Byzantine Churches for the British School in Athens: and of course are having all their expenses paid. Little B. writes to me occasionally and gives wonderful accounts of the glories of their travels. It *is* travelling too. There are no trails, and it all has to be done on horseback or by coach. And there are no inns. Their lodgings are either at the Monasteries or in some peasant's cottage where all the family sleep in one room – girls as well as fellows!!!![7]

The two men spent a large proportion of their time in Greece producing measured drawings, photographs and decorative studies of the Monastery of St Luke of Stiris in Phocis. This monastery, better known as Osios Loukas, is one of the major surviving Byzantine sites in Greece. At that time, situated as it is in an inaccessible mountainous area north-west of Corinth, this monastery was little known and rarely visited. The remoteness of the site was vouched for by Leonard Woolf who, in the third volume of his autobiography, recounted the hazardous expedition undertaken by himself, his wife, Virginia, and Roger Fry to view this monastery during a journey to Greece in 1932. Today, however, its situation, only a short detour from the main route between Athens and Delphi, has made this site a popular tourist attraction. The study of Osios Loukas by Sidney Barnsley and Schultz was the only section of their work ever published. Even this limited publication was only made possible by the generosity of Dr Freshfield, who made a substantial guarantee towards the costs, enabling the British School at Athens to publish *The Monastery of St Luke of Stiris in Phocis and the dependent Monastery of St Nicholas in the Fields, near Scripou, in Boeotia* in 1901. Their experiences in Greece awoke a lasting interest in Byzantine art in both Sidney Barnsley and Robert Weir Schultz, which was shared by Lethaby and several others connected with the Arts and Crafts Movement, and which was to remain a constant influence on their work.

It was his work in Greece which also won Sidney Barnsley his first architectural commission on his return to England, towards the end of 1890. It came from the above-mentioned Dr Freshfield, a prominent member of the Anglo-Hellenic Society, and Sir Henry Cosmo Orme Bonsor, who commissioned him to design a church for their parish at Lower Kingswood in Surrey. The result, the charming and richly-endowed Church of the Wisdom of God, was dedicated in July 1892. Its plan was derived from that of St Eirene, an ancient Basilican Church in Constantinople, and it was built in a decorative combination of brick and Ham stone. The interior decoration, employing many different types of marble, provides soft and subtle colour gradations. To achieve this effect, Sidney Barnsley adopted a technique first developed by the Romans, and clad the walls with thin slices of marble arranged so that their graining forms a pattern, in much the same way that veneers are applied to furniture. He also painted, by hand, the wooden beams forming the roof of the nave with a colourful pattern of spring flowers. This pattern is echoed in the design of the mosaic above the central apse, executed by a school of artists attached to the glass-making firm of James Powell of

Fig. 20. The Church of the Wisdom of God, Lower Kingswood, Surrey, designed by Sidney Barnsley between 1890 and 1892. Note the variety of textures achieved by the combination of red brick and Ham stone.

Fig. 21. The interior of the church. The dome-topped clergy chairs, rails, reading stands and altar furniture were probably made to Sidney Barnsley's design by Kenton and Co.

Whitefriars. These craftsmen had been specially trained in the art of mosaic-making in order to carry out designs for the newly-built Roman Catholic Cathedral in London. The church furniture, which was designed by Sidney Barnsley, includes two dome-topped clergy chairs, and a pair of delicate and precisely-chamfered reading stands. These pieces were made in brown ebony with a herringbone inlay, probably by the cabinet-makers employed by Kenton and Co., the firm set up by Gimson, Sidney Barnsley and other colleagues, whose history is discussed in a later chapter.

Sidney Barnsley exhibited photographs of the Church of the Wisdom of God at the 1893 Arts and Crafts Exhibition. They were commented on by *The Studio*, the most progressive art magazine of the period, and a vigorous supporter of the Arts and Crafts Movement:

> Here is a new variation on the Byzantine motive, gained I dare swear from the Mosque of St. Sophia at Constantinople but handled with a reticent feeling and sense of proportion beyond praise. From the chancel with its simple slabs of marble, the probable richness of whose hues one perforce misses in the photographs, to the huge ringed chandelier, quaint in its very severity, nothing jars on one's sense of well-ordered harmony. It is emphatically the work of an artist rather than of a professional man.[8]

This last sentence is a rather sad but telling comment on the reputation of the architectural profession during this period.

Unlike the two Barnsleys, Gimson spent the two years following the completion of his architectural training, in 1888, leading what can only be described as a dilettante existence. He was enabled to do this because he, like Ernest and Sidney Barnsley, was of independent means. He travelled abroad and throughout England, alternating his base between London and Leicester, and entered a number of architectural competitions. Early in 1889, he entered the Institute of Architects Pugin Studentship competition and was awarded a Certificate of Honour for his drawings. Two of his entries, featuring such diverse subjects as the railings in Wells Cathedral, and inlaid panelling in the Church of San Pietro, Perugia, were illustrated in *The British Architect* which wrote:

> These and nearly all his drawings were of such a quality as entitled him, in our opinion, to a better position in the competition.[9]

Gimson too considered that he was not successful enough, and, in June 1889, he wrote to Ernest Barnsley in a half-jocular, half-serious vein:

> I am thinking of chucking up Architecture and of taking to money making instead. This sort of thing: E. W. Gimson, ARIBA, FSA, XYZ, ART ARCHITECT AND SURVEYOR. Home made designs in stock. Please rap at the third door down the entry.[10]

He later wrote to W. R. Butler thus:

> In the autumn of 1889 I took lodgings at Chislehurst in a jolly old house with panelled rooms. There I watched the summer go and winter come – took long country walks every day, and in my spare time went in for the Soane Medallion,[11] which I didn't get. In fact it was not awarded as no design was considered worthy of it. 3 'seconds' were given of which I was one. So got something for my trouble. All the papers said my design was 'distinctly ugly'.[12]

Early in 1890, Gimson decided to base himself permanently in London. It was during this period that he began experimenting with chairmaking and plaster-work, having been inspired in his choice of crafts partly by lectures given at the Art Workers' Guild. It was also at the Guild's lectures that his attention was drawn to the rush-seated ladderback chairs used for its meetings. These chairs were acquired for 10s 6d each, by the Guild, in 1888, from Philip Clissett, a traditional chair bodger in the village of Bosbury, Herefordshire, through the offices of one of its members, the architect, James Maclaren. Maclaren's first meeting with Clissett was subsequently described by his companion on that journey, the journalist and painter, D. S. McColl:

> Shortly before the first Arts and Crafts Exhibition, I think, the late James Maclaren, an architect whom many of my readers will remember, had some work to do at Ledbury, and in a walk we took one day we found, in a little Worcestershire [sic] village, a real survival of village industry, an old man who made rush-bottomed chairs with no other apparatus than his cottage oven for bending the wood. Maclaren made him one or two drawings improving a little upon his designs, which he was quite content to do at eight shillings apiece. When the Art Workers' Guild was formed, these chairs, known to some of its members were adopted and passed from that into many houses.[13]

Gimson went to Bosbury sometime in 1890 and spent a few weeks working with Clissett, learning the basic techniques of his craft. Clissett's skill in using the pole lathe was recounted by Gimson to Edward Gardiner, whom he subsequently employed to make chairs at Sapperton. According to Edward Gardiner:

> Mr Gimson told me how quickly Clissett could turn out his work from cleft ash poles on his pole lathe, steam, bend and all the rest. He seems to have made a chair a day for 6/6d and rushed it in his cottage kitchen singing as he worked. According to old Philip Clissett if you were not singing you were not happy.[14]

In much the same way Gimson spent a short time with the London-based firm of plasterworkers, Messrs Whitcombe and Priestley, learning the various methods employed for the moulding and carving of plaster. Plasterwork was

Fig. 22. Portrait of Philip Clissett (1817–1913) of Bosbury, Herefordshire, by Maxwell Balfour. A lithograph originally published in *The Quarto*, 4th series, 1898.

one of the crafts which were practised during the second half of the nineteenth century as part of the general revival of handicrafts, and renewed interest in the arts of the seventeenth and eighteenth centuries. In November 1887, for example, a lecture on 'plasterwork as applied to ceiling decoration' was given to the Art Workers' Guild. Although William Morris never tackled plasterwork himself, his interest in the craft is shown by this passage from his Utopian prose romance, *A Dream of John Ball*:

> The walls were panelled roughly enough with oak boards to about six feet from the floor and about three feet of plaster above that was wrought in a pattern of a rosestem running all round the room, freely and roughly done, but with (as it seemed to my unused eye) wonderful skill and strength. On the hood of the great chimney a huge rose was wrought in the plaster and brightly painted in its true colours.[15]

Edward Burne Jones experimented with designs for painted plaster and gesso, whilst John Sedding executed a number of plasterwork designs for St Agnes House, Bristol, in the 1860s, including a corridor ceiling design based on a serpentine Elizabethan rose motif. In the first Arts and Crafts Exhibition in 1888, Philip Webb and the young architects, Reginald Blomfield and Mervyn Macartney, all exhibited plaster friezes. Joseph Whitcombe, a partner in the firm of Whitcombe and Priestley, was mentioned in the Exhibition catalogue as being involved in the execution of these exhibits. It was therefore natural that Gimson should go to this firm for guidance when his interest in plasterwork was awakened, although his desire which ran contrary to the approach of most of his contemporaries, to master the execution of his designs was something of a mystery to the plasterworkers. W. R. Lethaby wrote:

> Mr. Whitcombe was puzzled by Gimson's 'messing about with plaster, dirty stuff' but finally explained it as 'just his hobby'.[16]

Gimson mastered the techniques of the craft quickly and, in 1890, he was able to write to W. R. Butler thus:

> I have taken to furniture designing and plasterwork. I spend 4 or 5 hours a day working in a little plasterer's shed modelling friezes and ribbed ceilings. I get on capitally and shall soon be able to undertake work on my own account. I shall have one or two things in the next 'Art and Crafts Exhibition' I hope, and some pieces of furniture as well.[17]

Only one of Gimson's notebooks, as opposed to sketchbooks, has survived from this period, and it is devoted to the study of plasterwork. Its contents show the consuming and wide-ranging nature of Gimson's interest in the subject, for they include passages and notes transcribed by him from a variety of sources, including De Piles on *The Art of Painting*, G. E. Street's *The Gothic Art of Spain* and works by Vitruvius and Viollet le Duc, along with sketches and contemporary references to plasterwork taken from articles, newspapers and lectures. Gimson also listed Elizabethan and Jacobean buildings throughout the country which might yield examples of plasterwork, and his enthusiasm for the craft was rekindled by his study of fine sixteenth- and seventeenth-century examples which still survived, in houses such as Speke Hall, near Liverpool, and Haddon and Hardwick Halls in Derbyshire.

As a result of these researches, and his practical experience, Gimson was asked by the National Association for the Advancement of Art[18] to contribute an essay on plasterwork to a book published in 1892 under the title *Plain Handicrafts, being essays by artists setting forth the principles of design and established methods of craftsmanship*. It was edited by A. H. Mackmurdo, founder of the Century Guild, which is described in greater detail in a later chapter, and included essays on design and the study of nature by Selwyn Image, one of Mackmurdo's colleagues; on cabinet-making by W. R. Lethaby, and on embroidery by William Morris's daughter, May Morris. I have quoted extensively from Gimson's essay in this publication as it was the only occasion on which he committed his principles on the design and execution of craftwork to print. The essay begins with the historical background to the art of plasterwork, its revival in Renaissance Italy and its development in Britain in the sixteenth and seventeeth centuries. Gimson wrote:

Fig. 23. Plasterwork ceiling at Daneway House, by Ernest Gimson.

Fig. 24. Contemporary photograph of plasterwork in the process of manufacture in Ernest Gimson's workshop.

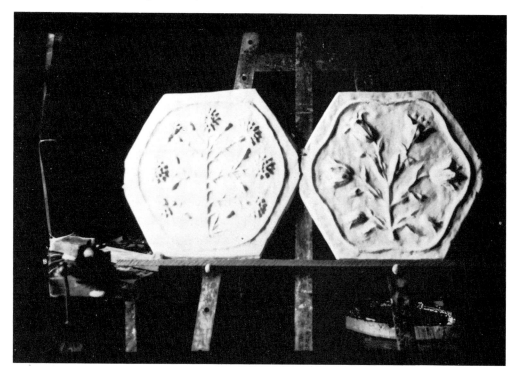

It is interesting to see how the study of nature affected the art when it was first brought into England. Plasterworkers went to nature then, perhaps because their craft was a new one, and possessed no tradition to be followed. But whatever the cause, the effect of it on their art was that though the other architectural crafts were on their decline, and contented themselves with a dead conventionalism, plaster-work was inspired with a life and freedom that sometimes reminds one of Romanesque and Early Gothic Art. A beautiful example of the treatment of nature in old work is to be seen at Knole House in Kent where the lily, the rose, the honeysuckle, the columbine, and many other flowers are all brought within the range of plaster, and worked into the ceilings. The modelling is very simple. There are no sharp lines, no quick curves, no undercuttings, none of those tricks of the modern plaster-worker for making his design 'sparkle'; but instead, dull lines, gentle curves, and little variety of relief. Still it is beautiful, for though it may lack something of realism, it expresses the freshness and healthy growth which is the most vital quality in the natural flower.

Gimson then summarised the materials and techniques available to his contemporaries working in plaster. Lime and ox hair, Keen's cement, Parian cement and selenite cement were all used for internal plasterwork whilst, for external work, Portland cement or the common plaster made of lime, sand and ox hair were recommended. According to Gimson:

The modelling is done with metal tools, and the method of working is much the same for each kind of material. The wall is first coated with coarse plaster. This is scratched before it is dry to give a firm hold to the next coat that is to form the background of the design, and which is of the same material as the modelling. When the background is set the design is drawn on it in chalk, the lines roughly incised, and the solid parts of the design roughened with a tool. It is then dampened with a wet brush and the modelling is applied.

Gimson was critical of much contemporary plasterwork because of the techniques and designs adopted:

In later times plaster-work was confined almost entirely to the one method of casting in plaster of Paris from clay modelling. This, although often producing very beautiful results, is certainly not such a right method as modelling by hand, or even stamping, and the goodness of its effect may be said to be in spite of its means and not in virtue of them. For it has these disadvantages: that it necessitates the frequent repetition of the same idea, that it cannot be worked in position, and that it requires a greater amount of mechanical labour on the part of the workman. . . . The modern plaster-worker, as a rule, robs his work of its right effects because he does not enough consider what are the qualities best obtained in his own material. He is not content to stay within the limits of plaster, but must needs envy the finer qualities and greater range of expression possessed by wood and marble. The custom of teaching modelling in our schools from examples of carving is dangerous for the plaster-worker, in this respect, and tends to lead him into wrong ways of designing, although it may be excellent training, as far as manual skill is concerned.

Finally Gimson discussed his own approach to the design of plasterwork:

> As regards design, the first necessity is that the worker must show in his work something of the pleasure that he takes in natural things. And the second necessity is that he must have knowledge of old work, not that he may reproduce it, but that he may learn from it how to express his ideas, and may learn from it also what the things are that are most worthy and capable of expression in the particular material he has in hand. . . . Of course, with the limited means at his command, it will be impossible for the plaster-worker to get anything more than a suggestion of nature into his work, if he gives any thought to the suitability of the design to the material. But if he is successful in that, and is able to get a certain amount of order and rhythm into his design, his work will be interesting, be the modelling never so lumpy and never so dull. Indeed, something of dulness is always noticeable in good plaster-work, where there is no intention of disguising the material; and it is a quality which, together with the extent of the background, gives it a character of its own, and distinguishes it more than anything else from its sister art of carving. For dulness suggests the softness of the material, and the process of adding and pressing, by which the right relief is obtained, suggests the application of the design to a prepared surface, and the more so when a fair amount of background is maintained.

Many of Gimson's ideas about design and workmanship were thus formulated in relation to plasterwork, particularly the emphasis on the honest use of materials and on the importance of nature and of knowledge of historical work as sources of inspiration. In addition, Gimson's concern for the well-being of the workman through the enjoyment of his work, which was fundamental to his later career, emerged from this essay. Thus, by 1890, Gimson's preoccupation, in common with many of his contemporaries, was taking a very broad approach to the practice of architecture and becoming more concerned with problems of design and the revival of handicrafts.

Chapter 4
Kenton and Company, 1890-92

In the autumn of 1890, the firm of Kenton and Company, 'the business style and title of a company of architects', was set up 'with the object of supplying furniture of good design and good workmanship'.[1] The firm was named, rather prosaically, after Kenton Street, just round the corner from their rented workshop in Bloomsbury in the centre of London. The five active members of Kenton and Co., William Lethaby, Mervyn Macartney, Reginald Blomfield, Ernest Gimson and Sidney Barnsley, were trained architects although, apart from Sidney Barnsley, they are all known to have had some previous experience of designing furniture. The furniture which they designed for Kenton and Co. was made in the firm's workshop by professional cabinet-makers. Though the only experience of woodworking provided by this venture arose from watching these craftsmen in the execution of their designs, the firm gave Gimson and Sidney Barnsley their first opportunity to tackle seriously the problem of furniture design.

The concept of a group of architects combining in a commercial venture in the field of the applied arts was not a new one. The formation of Morris, Marshall, Faulkner and Co. in 1861, with established architects and artists designing a variety of decorative objects and furnishings for commercial production, was an inspiration for subsequent ventures. In 1882, the Century Guild was founded by a group of young architects, designers and artists, led by A. H. Mackmurdo and including Selwyn Image, to 'restore building, decoration, glass painting, pottery, wood carving and metal to their rightful place beside painting and sculpture'.[2] The Century Guild produced some radically simple furniture designed by Mackmurdo and made by a commercial firm. Six years later, in 1888, C. R. Ashbee set up the Guild of Handicraft in the East End of London. He was the only architect involved in this venture, and both he and his assistants were largely self-taught in the production of metalwork, silverwork, pottery and furniture for the Guild. The formation of Kenton and Co. in 1890 was a further development in these attempts to improve standards of design and workmanship. It was, however, one of the few such schemes to concentrate its efforts on a single area, that of furniture design, rather than to attempt to produce a wide range of wares. Because of the Company's self-imposed limitation of its activities to the design and production of furniture, one might have expected its achievements in this area to be all the greater. However, as far as Kenton and Co. was concerned, its importance can in no way be compared to that of these earlier projects, partly because of the absence of any common criteria in the

Fig. 25. William Lethaby (standing) and
Ernest Gimson photographed in about 1890.

design of its products. Moreover the lifespan of the company was very limited,
surviving only for about eighteen months. Its significance exists predominantly
in relation to the subsequent careers of Gimson and Sidney Barnsley and, to a
lesser extent, to that of W. R. Lethaby, for Kenton and Co. provided them with
an opportunity to design furniture and to contemplate a future beyond the
London-based architectural profession.

The events which led up to the formation of Kenton and Co. are complex,
and the poor documentation presents difficulties in pinpointing the exact moment
when the firm came into being. This probably did not occur until the last months
of 1890, after which time Lethaby, Gimson, Sidney Barnsley, Blomfield and
Macartney were all active members of the company. According to Reginald
Blomfield, writing in his autobiography, Lethaby was 'as usual our fount of
inspiration'[3] in the foundation of the company. In April 1890, Gimson wrote to
Ernest Barnsley commenting on his growing friendship with Lethaby and these
two certainly seem to have been the driving-force behind the formation of
Kenton and Co. Two months later, on 22 June 1890, Gimson wrote to W. R.
Butler, a fellow-student in Sedding's office who had recently settled in Melbourne,
Australia, about such a scheme:

> Lethaby, Blow,[4] and I are joining together in a little business. We are going
> to take a shop in Bloomsbury for the sale of furniture of our own design and

make, besides other things such as plaster friezes, leadwork, needlework etc. etc.[5]

All the above mentioned media were featured in Gimson's and Lethaby's contributions to the Arts and Crafts Exhibitions held at the New Gallery in 1889 and 1890. At the 1889 exhibition, the second organised by the Arts and Crafts Exhibition Society, Lethaby's exhibits included designs for chairs and needlework cushions, cast and wrought ironwork and leadwares designed for the firm of Wentham & Waters. In 1890 Lethaby exhibited cast iron designs for the Coalbrookdale Company, and furniture designed for the Leeds firm of Marsh, Jones and Cribb, which Gimson described as 'wonderful furniture of a commonplace kind'.[6] Gimson exhibited work for the first time that year, including a sampler executed by his sister-in-law Phyllis Lovibond, a plaster frieze and furniture.

The enterprise envisaged in June 1890 was more communal and all-embracing than the final arrangement. According to Gimson they were 'to have bedrooms and offices in the same building and share expenses'.[7] This coincides with Gimson's search for a country cottage for himself and his friends, which he mentioned in letters to Ernest Barnsley. In June or July 1890, Gimson wrote to Sidney Barnsley, who was then in Greece with Schultz, asking him to join in this scheme. Sidney Barnsley seems to have taken to the idea with enthusiasm, but it was not until 1 October 1890 that Gimson was able to write to Ernest Barnsley thus:

> I heard from Sidney on Monday. The last letter from me evidently did not reach him. It was full of rejoicings that he was going to make one of the quartet.[8]

From this it appears that the three original participants of the venture, Lethaby, Detmar Blow and Gimson himself, were still the only ones involved.

The last two individuals to become involved in the formation of Kenton and Co. were Mervyn Macartney and Reginald Blomfield. Despite their late participation in the scheme, it seems likely that they played an important part in its organisation, as they were somewhat older and consequently more experienced than the other members. Both men were practising architects in the 1880s. Macartney entered the architectural profession straight from university by joining Norman Shaw's office in the same year as Lethaby. Blomfield attended the Royal Academy Schools and entered the architectural office of his uncle, A. W. Blomfield. His uncle was very much part of the architectural establishment, being President of the Architectural Association in 1861 and Vice President of the Institute of Architects in 1886. He was responsible for restoration work at the cathedrals of Salisbury, Lincoln, Chichester and Canterbury, as well as the execution of many ecclesiastical commissions. Despite his uncle's position in the architectural hierarchy, Blomfield, together with Macartney, was involved in such organisations as the Art Workers' Guild, and in promoting the cause of architectural reform. In 1884, at the start of his professional career, Blomfield took rooms in the same house in Southampton Street as another young architect, E. S. Prior. Through the latter, Blomfield made the acquaintance of 'Shaw's men', including Lethaby and Macartney, and became accepted into their circle. In 1889, Blomfield and Macartney were delegated to select furniture for the Arts and Crafts Exhibition Society, a task which gave rise to the following incident, related in Blomfield's autobiography:

> In collecting exhibits for the shows of the Arts and Crafts Society members of the Committee were deputed to visit the principal London shops and see what they could get. The results were most disappointing. The furniture was bad, the tradesmen would give us no information, and in one large shop in Regent Street the manager was extremely rude and, had he dared to do so, would have ejected Macartney and me then and there.[9]

This attempt made by the Society to broaden the scope of the 1889 Exhibition and to encourage the participation of the furniture trade was not a success, and the experience may have spurred both men to tackle furniture design seriously under the auspices of Kenton and Co. In his autobiography, Blomfield also mentions Stephen Webb as a short-lived member of the company although there is no other evidence of his involvement. Webb was already reasonably experienced as a furniture designer by 1890, specialising in intarsia work, and designing elaborately inlaid pieces for a number of established firms including Collinson and Locke.

The confusion as to the exact date of Kenton and Co.'s formation has arisen because furniture which could be considered as part of the Company's output was exhibited by both Gimson and Blomfield at the third Arts and Crafts Exhibition [Fig. 26], which opened on 6 October 1890. Gimson exhibited a mahogany writing desk with cabinet-work by A. H. Mason and C. Smith and marquetry work by J. Beaner. A. H. Mason, who became foreman cabinet-maker for Kenton and Co., was a trade cabinet-maker connected with the Arts and Crafts Movement. In the 1889 exhibition, Lethaby showed a panel, painted in gesso gilt, for an altar table at Trinity Church, Bothenhampton, Devon by E. S. Prior. The cabinet-work for this piece is credited to A. H. Mason. Gimson would undoubtedly have known of Mason, and could have approached him to execute an individual design. Therefore, although this writing desk is similar in design to later examples of Gimson's work for Kenton and Co., it must be regarded as separate from the firm's output. Mason was probably employed by Kenton and Co. some months after the completion of this piece, possibly on Gimson's and Lethaby's recommendation. Similarly, in October 1890, Blomfield exhibited a mahogany corner cabinet, inlaid with snakewood and ebony, which was later included in the exhibition of furniture by Kenton and Co. in 1891. One can only assume that an informal attitude to the firm's output was taken by the participants, especially by Blomfield himself, enabling a cabinet which predates the formation of Kenton and Co. to be included. This is borne out by the fact that, at the 1893 Arts and Crafts Exhibition, Blomfield, Macartney and

Fig. 26. Furniture at the Arts and Crafts Exhibition, 1890. From left to right: chest of drawers by Ford Madox Brown; table by W. R. Lethaby; corner cupboard by Reginald Blomfield; fall-front cabinet by Ernest Gimson; cupboard by W. R. Lethaby.

Fig. 27. Altarpiece from Bothenhampton Church, Devon, in oak with a decorative gesso panel designed by W. R. Lethaby, cabinet-work by A. H. Mason.

Lethaby exhibited furniture, previously seen at the Kenton and Co. exhibition, in their own names.

More or less at the same time as Kenton and Co. came into being, its participants found themselves in profound disagreement with their professional body, the Institute of British Architects. Blomfield, Lethaby and Macartney were deeply committed to the campaign against the Institute's scheme of registration for architects by examination. According to Blomfield, 'the attempt to make architecture a closed profession . . . is opposed to the interests of Architecture as a fine art'.[10] The three men were amongst the group who resigned their membership of the Institute in protest against its scheme. Their subsequent involvement with Kenton and Co. may have been symptomatic of their disillusionment with the architectural profession although it gave rise to rather caustic comments in *The Builder*:

> We observe that the architects concerned in the firm belong to the party who are opposed to the policy and procedure of the Institute of Architects, and refuse to belong to that body; and (without for a moment suggesting this as the motive of their opposition) we cannot help remembering that if they were members of the Institute they would be debarred from carrying on this company, by the regulation which debars architects from having a pecuniary interest in anything connected with the materials about which they have to advise their clients as to their outlay. . . . It is perfectly evident that if the architects who are members of Kenton and Co. wished to recommend a client to go to them for artistic furniture in keeping with the style and sound construction of his house, they would expose themselves to the reflection (not an agreeable one even when groundless) that in doing so they were acting in their own interests and looking to the increase of their own dividends.[11]

According to Lethaby, writing about Gimson's London days in the *Life and Work* memorial volume,[12] a meeting was held in Blomfield's rooms on the evening of 24 October 1890 to discuss 'the furniture shop scheme'. It is reasonable to assume that Kenton and Co. came into being shortly after this date. Each of the five participants contributed £100 to provide capital for the company, whilst a sixth 'sleeping' partner, Colonel Mallett, a retired colonel of cavalry and an influential friend of Macartney, who was very interested in furniture, contributed £200. According to H. J. L. J. Massé, assistant secretary of the Art Workers' Guild since 1889, he was offered the post of manager to Kenton and Co. by Macartney. Massé rejected this offer because 'it would have been interesting enough, but it had not the necessary element of security: at least such was the advice that was given to me by two experts'.[13] About five professional cabinet-makers were employed, including Augustus H. Mason, as foreman, and stocks of material were bought. Blomfield wrote:

> We used to meet in each other's rooms and undertake designs of our own

Fig. 28. Exhibition of furniture by Kenton and Co., held at Barnard's Inn in 1891. Revolving bookcase, desk and walnut chair by Macartney; inlaid cabinet by Blomfield; gate-legged table by Sidney Barnsley with hexagonal workbox by Lethaby.

> choice and invention more or less in turn, except the Colonel, who held, as it were, a watching brief on the whole proceedings. Each man was responsible solely for his design and its execution, and it was delightful to go to the shop and see one's designs growing into shape in the hands of skilful cabinet-makers. We made no attempt to interfere with each other's idiosyncracies.[14]

Most pieces of funiture were stamped with the initials of the designer and cabinet-maker and the name of the firm. The recognition given in this way by Kenton and Co. to the workmen, as well as to the designers, was applauded by contemporaries and put into practice the theories of Ruskin and William Morris.

As Blomfield suggested, there was no attempt to achieve a common style in the products of Kenton and Co. A wide variety of furniture was designed by the five architects, reflecting the interests and experience of each individual. Most of the furniture followed stylistic trends which had already been established in the design of 'artistic' and trade furniture in the second half of the nineteenth century. However, certain pieces do stand out for their startlingly novel and advanced approach to design and have ensured the survival of Kenton and Co.'s reputation.

Fig. 29. Another contemporary photograph of the 1891 Kenton and Co. Exhibition. From left to right: cabinet by W. R. Lethaby; circular table and cane-seated settee by Reginald Blomfield; two cabinets on stands by Ernest Gimson; the 'ship' chest by W. R. Lethaby.

Mervyn Macartney was said by Blomfield to follow 'the elegant motives of the eighteenth century'[15] and the accuracy of this comment is illustrated by the surviving examples of his work from this period. After many years of neglect, a new appreciation of eighteenth-century furniture had developed in the second half of the nineteenth century. This can be traced back to the revival of the Queen Anne style in the architectural work of Philip Webb, W. E. Nesfield and Norman Shaw. Similarly, D. G. Rossetti and his friends were great admirers of the arts of the early eighteenth century, and Warrington Taylor, who became manager of Morris and Co. in 1865, wrote 'Is not Queen Anne furniture more suited to our wants, constructional but light . . . strongly built but with middling thin appearance?'[16] Subsequently, in the late 1890s, Macartney became involved in designing furniture for Morris and Co., together with George Jack and W. A. Benson. Both this and his earlier work for Kenton and Co. are characterised by the use of slim uprights and a simple but elegantly curving outline. His writing desk in walnut, exhibited at Barnards Inn in 1891, was commented on most favourably by *The Builder*, as having 'elegance of line and solid workmanship'.[17] The same could be said for the revolving bookcase [Fig. 28], exhibited on the same occasion, which relies on the simple mouldings and curving legs to enliven its straightforward construction.

Fig. 30. Two mirror frames inlaid with mother-of-pearl designed by Sidney Barnsley. These pieces were either made by Kenton and Co. or closely resemble Sidney Barnsley's designs for this firm.

Some of the same appreciation of the lightness and elegant proportions of the eighteenth century can be seen in the furniture designs of Reginald Blomfield. His inspiration however came from a later period, the designs of Chippendale and Sheraton. Chippendale furniture was very much in demand during this period, and a great deal of reproduction furniture was produced in this style. Blomfield worked mainly in mahogany and rosewood, and had a fondness for using exotic veneers and inlays to achieve a bold decorative effect. In 1891 he exhibited a large settee in solid rosewood [Fig. 29] with a cane seat and back, made to his design by J. Urand. According to Blomfield, he had to model the curves of the arms in clay, as this was the only way he could illustrate their intricacy to the cabinet-maker. This piece was priced at £50.0.0, allowing only 15% profit. Although *The Builder* described the settee as 'of noble proportions and fine in its sweeping curves',[18] it was critical of the price charged by Kenton and Co. for this, as well as for several other pieces of furniture. This settee was also exhibited in the 1893 Arts and Crafts Exhibition, together with three other examples of Blomfield's Kenton and Co. furniture, which illustrate admirably his use of marquetry and inlay in woods of contrasting figure and colour to create bold, geometric patterns. *The Studio* magazine was most appreciative of his designs, writing:

Mr Blomfield's inlaid sideboard pleases by its very reticence, and by the skill wherewith he has turned to advantage the too academic suggestions of E. Sheraton and Chippendale. Thoroughly honest it is, and yet in this case as in some others nearby, honesty has not been read as synonymous with brutality. So too with his inlaid cabinet, though here as when in front of his sideboard one is tempted to ask whether the art of the inlayer should not concern itself, as its very genius might lead one to suppose, with lines rather than with masses.[19]

Very few examples of Sidney Barnsley's furniture designs for Kenton and Co. are documented, and even fewer have survived either as actual pieces of furniture or in photographs. Blomfield mentioned 'a mirror frame, rather Persian in design, inlaid with mother of pearl designed by Sidney Barnsley and much admired by Leighton'[20] (that is Frederick, Lord Leighton, the painter). This is one of the pieces for which there is no surviving visual record, but Sidney Barnsley made other richly inlaid mirror frames later in his career [Fig. 30], which may bear some resemblance to this early example, and which show the influence of his Byzantine studies in the lavish combination of shapes, colours and textures. The use of inlaid mother-of-pearl to achieve a boldly-contrasting, mosaic-like effect in these designs became a feature of many of the more decorative pieces of furniture, particularly those intended for an ecclesiastical setting, designed by Sidney Barnsley and his colleagues in the Cotswolds. The rich and exotic impact of this type of inlaid decoration would have appealed strongly to Lord Leighton, whose love of the oriental is demonstrated by his own paintings, and the design of his own house in Holland Park Road, with its Arab Hall decorated with sixteenth-century Turkish Isnik tiles, as well as contemporary examples in the same style by William de Morgan.

The large Kenton and Co. wardrobe veneered in Indian walnut and priced at £15.0.0 was probably designed by Sidney Barnsley, although it is only known today through a contemporary photograph reproduced here [Fig. 31]. The use of large, flat surfaces, taking their only decoration from the pattern of the wood grain created by the geometric arrangement of the veneers, shows an almost brutal approach to design, and in many ways this piece of furniture, dating from 1891, bears more relation to the furniture designs of the 1930s than to its contemporaries. The only other piece of Kenton and Co. furniture which can be ascribed to Sidney Barnsley is an oak gate-legged table with an oval top and inlaid herringbone stringing which is included in a contemporary photograph of the 1891 exhibition [Fig. 28]. It illustrates Sidney Barnsley's first attempt at designing a basic type of country furniture, which was to become a feature of both his and Gimson's later work.

According once again to Blomfield, 'Lethaby's and Gimson's inventions ran to simple designs of admirable form in oak'.[21] This is true of a proportion of their work for Kenton and Co., but it rather underestimates their contribution. Lethaby designed a series of plain oak furniture with subject inlay, including a

Fig. 31. Wardrobe in Indian walnut designed by Sidney Barnsley for Kenton and Co. and exhibited at Barnard's Inn in 1891.

Fig. 32. Dresser in stained oak designed by W. R. Lethaby for Kenton and Co. and exhibited at Barnard's Inn in 1891.

Fig. 33. Chest in oak with inlay in the form of sheep designed by Lethaby and made by Kenton and Co. in 1891.

Fig. 34. Chamfered dresser in unpolished oak designed by Gimson for Kenton and Co. in about 1891.

large oak chair, inlaid with sheep in different woods, and two oak chests, inlaid with sheep and ships respectively, which feature an early use of cogged dovetails. All three pieces follow simple, more or less traditional shapes and are soundly constructed. In much the same vein, Blomfield designed an oak cabinet with subject inlay of rabbits eating lettuce, which bears little relation to the rest of his work for Kenton and Co. Lethaby also designed some more sophisticated and unusual pieces of furniture, including a hexagonal workbox in walnut [Fig. 28], with ebony insets which join the six sides, as well as providing the only ornamentation of this piece. Another attractive item designed by Lethaby was a small cabinet in walnut, inlaid with naturalistic and abstract designs in contrasting woods.

Both Gimson and Lethaby designed variations on the traditional English dresser. Lethaby's version was in oak, stained black, with clean cedar inside, and is very typical of much Arts and Crafts furniture, particularly in its use of gently curving details within a severe rectangular outline. In this case, the curves are provided by the inner sides of the legs, and by the vertical and horizontal divisions within the cabinet. Gimson's dresser in oak [Fig. 34], obviously created an impression by its use of chamfered decoration on the plate rack. This seems to have been one of the first occasions when chamfering was used as a decorative technique, even though Bruce Talbert, writing in 1867, mentioned it as an important feature of Gothic design. In commenting on a piece of furniture,

Fig. 35. Late seventeeth- and early eighteenth-century furniture from the South Kensington Museum, from a photograph in Ernest Gimson's personal collection.

designed by Ambrose Heal, at the sixth Arts and Crafts Exhibition in 1899, *The Studio* magazine wrote:

> For ornament a restricted use is made of waggon-chamfering, the traditional decoration of drays, vans and costermongers' barrows and such, that was first applied to furniture, if we mistake not by Messrs. Kenton and Co. some eight years ago.[22]

Both Gimson and the Barnsleys continued to use chamfering as a decorative technique throughout their careers.

A number of cabinets designed by Gimson for Kenton and Co. also foreshadow later developments in the Cotswolds. The mahogany writing cabinet on a stand [Fig. 29], now in the Victoria and Albert Museum, shows an early use of the light and dark inlaid stringing, which became such a characteristic feature of their work. In this case, the inlay is diagonal, flush with the surface and almost half an inch wide. This decorative technique was derived from seventeenth- and eighteenth-century furniture, particularly English and Dutch chests of that period, with which Gimson and his friends would have been familiar through

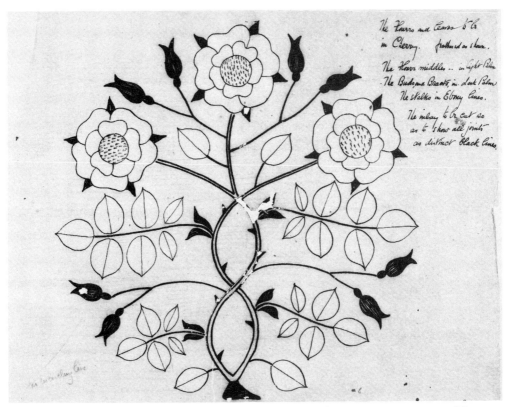

Fig. 36. Drawing in ink on tracing paper by Ernest Gimson for an inlaid design on a fall-front cabinet (see Fig. 29), 1891.
Fig. 37. Drawing in coloured crayons by Ernest Gimson of fourteenth-century frescoes in the nave of Berkeley Church, Gloucestershire.

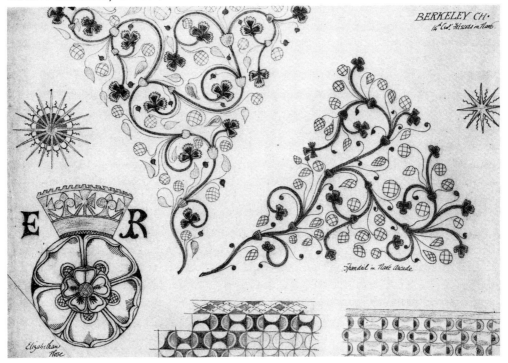

their visits to the South Kensington, now the Victoria and Albert, Museum. Gimson's personal collection of photographs, now held by Cheltenham Museum, included examples of furniture from this period, supplied by the South Kensington Museum. The circular inlaid design in cherry, ebony and palm on this cabinet is a somewhat stilted version of Gimson's later naturalistic designs and features a stylised Elizabethan rose, which became a favourite motif used on woodwork, metalwork, embroidery and plasterwork. The drawing for this design, together with Gimson's detailed instructions as to its execution, is the only one to have survived from the Kenton and Co. period and is reproduced here [Fig. 36]. Gimson's Kenton and Co. cabinet with a bold marquetry surface in cherry, ebony and palm [Fig. 29], was probably the most favourably received piece at the 1891 exhibition, echoing as it does the marquetry designs which were so popular during the Victorian period. Gimson's inspiration for the marquetry design came from the fourteenth-century frescoes at Berkeley Church, Gloucestershire, which he had drawn during a visit made at some time between 1889 and '90 [Fig. 37]. *The Builder* described the cabinet thus:

> The latter is a really fine thing, full of character, and well-constructed and designed in every portion and if it were an ancient work in the furniture gallery of South Kensington it would be one of the most interesting items of the collection and would be sketched over and over again.[23]

Despite its contemporary popularity, this piece was, at first, ascribed to Gimson's mature work, when it reappeared on the art market some twenty years ago. To most experts it appeared to be an innovatory design of the 1910s, having more similarity to the feel and approach of the 1920s than the 1890s. It is fortunate that the Kenton and Co. practice of stamping its furniture, as well as the surviving photographic evidence, has enabled this cabinet to be confidently included amongst the company's output.

An interesting Kenton and Co. piece is a mirror [Fig. 38] designed as well as made by Augustus H. Mason, foreman of the Company, of which there are at least two examples in existence. The design is simple, relying on the diagonal dark and light inlaid stringing, and the double curve on the top of the frame for its decorative effect. The latter feature was adopted by Gimson in his later work and was used extensively on chair backs, plate-racks and rails.

The exhibition at Barnards Inn by Kenton and Co. in December 1891 was a financial, as well as a critical, success, with sales totalling £700. However, the firm's resources could not support the venture much longer without a new injection of capital, and their patron, Colonel Mallett, was losing his initial enthusiasm. They could have raised more capital to finance the firm either amongst themselves, as they were all of independent means, or from outside their circle, but, as Blomfield wrote, 'the time has come to make a definite choice between the practice of architecture and the practice of designing and making furniture'.[24] It must be remembered that most of the participants had been

Fig. 38. A wall mirror in Cuban mahogany designed and made by Augustus H. Mason, the foreman/cabinet-maker for Kenton and Co. The use of inlaid holly and ebony herringbone stringing was quite a common feature of Kenton and Co. designs, but the double curve of the top frame is the first known use of this device, which was subsequently adopted by both Ernest Gimson and Sidney Barnsley for use particularly in the backs of chairs and plate racks.

involved in architectural ventures during the period of Kenton and Co.'s existence. In 1891, for example, Lethaby had been commissioned to design a country house, Avon Tyrell, near Christchurch, Hampshire, for Lord Manners. During this period Gimson was building himself a house, Inglewood, in Leicester, whilst Sidney Barnsley had been commissioned to design the Church of the Wisdom of God, at Lower Kingswood, Surrey. It was therefore decided, some time in 1892, to disband the company. The stocks of material were sold, although according to Blomfield no money was ever received for them, and the unsold furniture was divided out amongst the participants. Lethaby wrote:

> To my share fell what we still call 'the Gimson Cabinet' of walnut, 'left clean' and unpolished, but now mellow and glossy from use; another cabinet which we call 'Blomfield', 'Barnsley's table', 'my Oak Chair' and a little revolving bookcase designed by Macartney. After all, these five pieces with all the fun and some experience gained were not a bad return for £100 down.[25]

As far as the two elder men, Blomfield and Macartney, were concerned, their future lay with architecture and a commitment to their chosen profession had to be made at this stage in their careers. The battle against the Institute's introduction of examinations and formal architectural training having been lost and forgotten, Blomfield built up a successful practice and became President of the Royal Institute of British Architects in 1912, whilst Macartney, as has already been mentioned, became involved with Morris and Co. and, in 1905, took over the editorship of *The Architectural Review*. The year after Kenton and Co.'s disbandment, Lethaby left for an architectural tour of Constantinople and the Near East in between work on a number of architectural commissions. In 1896 he was appointed one of the two principals of the London County Council Central School of Arts and Crafts. In this position, and through his writings and his involvement with the Design and Industries Association from 1915 onwards, Lethaby continued at the forefront of the campaign for good design and craftsmanship.

Blomfield, Macartney and Lethaby exhibited furniture designs at the 1893 Arts and Crafts Exhibition as well as at subsequent shows. It is interesting to note that, unlike their erstwhile colleagues, Gimson and Sidney Barnsley did not submit any furniture to the 1893 exhibition, but instead illustrated their current architectural projects. Their attitude at this stage was captured by Eric Sharpe when, writing in 1945, he stated that they felt 'a desire to make a closer contact with the actual processes of building and with Nature than they felt was possible over the drawing board in a City office, and they held the belief that the revival of architecture lay in the revival of the crafts'.[26] Kenton and Co. was not a framework within which these desires could be fulfilled, and, in 1892, Gimson and Sidney Barnsley were ready to find a more congenial way of life.

Chapter 5
The impact of the Cotswolds

The decision, in 1892, to disband Kenton and Co. encouraged Ernest Gimson and Sidney Barnsley to give serious consideration to their growing aspirations to live and work in the country in surroundings whose natural beauty gave them physical satisfaction. This was to be a crucial development in the course of their careers and that of Ernest Barnsley, partly because their relative isolation in the Cotswolds enabled them to concentrate all their energies on the furtherance of their own ideas, and partly because of the inspiration and encouragement which all three men were to derive from the countryside and from rural pursuits, affecting almost every facet of their working life and leisure activities. It was some time, however, before the final commitment to such a move was made. Gimson must have considered returning to Leicester for, between 1891 and 1892, he bought a plot of land in the southern suburbs of the city on which to build himself a house. This house [Fig. 39], named Inglewood, is situated at 32 Ratcliffe Road, and is similar in its design to Ernest Barnsley's contemporary domestic buildings in Birmingham, showing clearly the influence of Philip Webb's and Norman Shaw's pioneering examples in the use of high chimneys, steep gables and decorative brickwork. It was built in Leicester sand-stock bricks, and roofed with Swaithland slates quarried in the Charnwood Forest. Although Gimson never took up residence in this house, he did decorate its interior with William Morris wallpapers, combined with plasterwork ceilings designed and modelled by himself.

It was towards the end of 1892 that Ernest Gimson and Sidney Barnsley decided to move permanently to the countryside in order to derive more satisfaction from the pursuit of architecture and handicrafts. Their reasoning was probably similar to that of Norman Jewson who followed the same course some fifteen years later. Jewson wrote thus of his own motives for leaving London to become Gimson's assistant at Sapperton:

> Up to this time my life as a young man training to be an architect had followed fairly normal lines. My three years' apprenticeship being now ended, the usual course would have been to have gained further experience in the office of some well-known London architect for another three or four years, first as an 'improver', or unpaid assistant, afterwards for a small salary, in my spare time working at drawings for competitions and attending advanced classes. But such a prospect had no attractions for me. The

Fig. 39. Inglewood, Ratcliffe Road, Leicester. The house was built by Gimson for himself in 1892. The simple yet asymmetrical design and well-proportioned sash windows are reminiscent of the style of his first employer, Isaac Barradale.

professional side of architecture had never appealed to me. I was aware that it was generally considered to be impossible to become a successful architect without living in a town, spending much of one's time making social contacts whilst most of the actual work was done by one's office staff, but for me it was architecture I was interested in, not making a large income as an architect. My own buildings I wanted to have the best qualities of the best old houses of their locality, built in the local traditional way in the local materials, but not copying the details which properly belonged to the period in which they were built. By working on these lines I hoped that my buildings would at least have good manners and be able to take their natural place in their surroundings without offence.[1]

Gimson and Sidney Barnsley may well have been encouraged in their decision to leave London by William Morris; they would certainly have approached both him and Philip Webb for advice. The latter's concern and respect for the two young men is amply illustrated in his correspondence with Sidney Barnsley following their departure from London.

They may also have been spurred on to leave London by their personal inclinations, as they were both retiring and unworldly individuals who were slightly at a disadvantage in their fiercely competitive profession, in which social skills were of paramount importance. Consequently the advantages of living and working in a rural setting must have been an attractive proposition which their independent means made perfectly possible to undertake. Their different personalities may also have made them hesitate to undertake such a major upheaval on their own. In any event, they contacted Ernest Barnsley in Birmingham and persuaded him, apparently against his wife's wishes, to join them in their search for a country setting where they could, all three, practise the arts of building and handicrafts.

Ernest Barnsley had been rather disappointed by the course of his architectural career in Birmingham, and was therefore persuaded by his friend's and his brother's enthusiasm to abandon his practice, sell his newly-built house at Barnt Green and join them in their search for a suitable area in which to settle. As a temporary measure he took rooms for himself, his wife and two daughters in Gray's Inn in London. Ernest Barnsley was a totally different character to Gimson and Sidney Barnsley. He was outgoing, expansive and a good, if rather too easy-going, businessman, who lacked the fierce sense of purpose and dedication of both his younger brother and his friend. It was he, however, who took charge of all the negotiations and business arrangements in connection with the move out of London, and he continued in this managerial role after they had settled in the Cotswolds. Norman Jewson, who later married Ernest Barnsley's eldest daughter, Mary, described him thus:

> There was nothing of the ascetic about Ernest Barnsley. A big, handsome, jolly type of man, fond of good company, good food and good cheer of every sort, he was built on a larger scale altogether.[2]

It is reasonable to assume that, although the move out of London was undertaken initially for their personal satisfaction, the three men were also motivated by other, more wide-ranging aspirations. The first intimations of Gimson's desire to establish a craft community came as early as 1889, in his letters to Ernest Barnsley describing his search for a country cottage for himself and his friends. The move of Gimson and the Barnsleys out of London was their first step in the establishment of an ideal community, which was mentioned by Sidney Barnsley in a letter written to Philip Webb in 1901. According to Sidney Barnsley, their intention was 'to get hold of a few capable and trustworthy craftsmen and eventually have workshops in the country where we should all join together and form a nucleus around which in time others would attach themselves'.[3] Although it was never fully realised, this idea continued to play a part in their philosophy throughout their working lives. It remained of particular importance to Ernest Gimson who, in about 1913, bought some land about two miles from the village of Sapperton, in Gloucestershire, and provided it with a water supply, with the intention of setting up a craft community based on the principle of healthy and useful employment. The outbreak of the First World War was a serious setback

Fig. 40. Sidney Barnsley and his dog, Panda, in Sapperton Valley, from an original photograph taken in about 1905. It was from this spot, on a similar walk, that he first saw Pinbury Park, which is up the valley to the right of the photograph.

to this development but, in 1918, Gimson brought up the idea once more in a letter to his friend, Sydney Cockerell. He asked Cockerell to suggest a suitable partner who would assist him in the execution of this scheme, and would ensure its continuation after his death. Gimson was obviously aware of his failing health at this point, and, sadly, he died before anything could come of his plans.

According to Alfred Powell, the three men scoured the country 'from Yorkshire to the South Downs', before they chose the Cotswolds for their new home. One can only speculate on the reasons for their choice, although the area was certainly familiar to all three. Gimson and Sidney Barnsley had visited parts of the Cotswolds on various architectural study trips, whilst the two Barnsley brothers may well have visited them during their childhood in Birmingham. Their relative proximity and accessibility to Birmingham and London must have been a considerable advantage, while the Fosse Way provided Gimson with a direct route to his home town of Leicester. Their choice of the Cotswolds may also have been suggested by William Morris who knew and loved the area, having acquired the lease to Kelmscott Manor, near Lechlade, Oxfordshire, in 1871. Obviously the beauty and relatively unspoilt nature of the countryside and the rural communities must have been a powerful lure for Gimson and the

Barnsleys, as it was later to be for C. R. Ashbee and many other artists and craftsmen at the turn of the century. Norman Jewson, writing of his first visit to the area in 1907, stated that 'in Gloucestershire, as I found afterwards, many old customs and ways of life lingered on and were to do so for nearly another decade'.[4]

In 1893, Ernest Gimson, Sidney Barnsley and Ernest Barnsley and his family moved to Ewen, a hamlet about three miles south-west of the market town of Cirencester, in Gloucestershire, whilst they continued their search for more permanent accomodation. This was eventually found at Pinbury Park, an Elizabethan house in a beautiful setting, which had been the seat of the Atkyns family before being converted into a farm and allowed to fall into disrepair. Ernest Barnsley negotiated the lease of the house from Lord Bathurst, on whose land it stood, at a very reasonable rent of £75 per annum. He also supervised the necessary repairs and alterations to the house and gardens before moving in with his wife and family. Gimson and Sidney Barnsley, who were still bachelors, moved into adjoining cottages converted from the farm outbuildings. Alfred Powell described Pinbury thus:

> Pinbury was a hill forming the head of one of the little Cotswold valleys. It had been nobly dealt with of old time by one Sir Robert Atkyns, and the Elizabethan House, now flanked symmetrically by enormous grouped sycamores and elms, planted there by him, stood towards the valley — gleaming white gables against the mass of foliage behind. Beneath the house the ground fell away to the valley — well covered with fruit trees in an orchard of thirteen acres, productive of many a pipe of cider, and along the crest of the hill ran the famous Nun's Walk, an avenue of ancient yews from sixty to seventy feet high. At midsummer the sun set in the centre of the vista, while at the eastern end a descent of stone steps led through a darkened stone gate-way into the lower garden, square-walled and grass-pathed between its regular beds. A wall of twenty feet on the north of this garden was, as it were, the foundations of the old house whose gables showed atop of it. Here, round the house used and beautifully kept by Ernest Barnsley, was the front garden with the main entrance, a flagged path leading to the porch.[5]

It must be remembered that although the old traditions still governed the life and work of the majority of the inhabitants of the Cotswold villages, Gimson and the Barnsleys did not walk into a living tradition as far as furniture-making was concerned. The position of the independent cabinet-makers in small towns and villages throughout Britain had begun to decline during the eighteenth century. The growing demand for mahogany furniture was a fashion which the independent cabinet-maker could not supply, and consequently he lost his wealthy patrons to the large furniture-making centres. Similarly, by the late nineteenth century, the carpenter no longer made much furniture for his fellow-villagers, who were more likely to supply their needs from the retailer selling mass-produced wares at the nearest market town. The likelihood of this furniture

Above left Fig. 41. Portrait of Ernest Barnsley by Sir William Rothenstein, 1913. *Above right* Fig. 42. Portrait of Ernest Gimson. *Below* Fig. 43. Sidney Barnsley, his wife and two children, from a photograph taken in 1901.

being 'of shoddy manufacture and poor taste' is borne out by Philip Webb's experience with local workers in Sussex, related in a letter to Alfred Powell:

> Most of the Estate workmen are decent fellows but rough in their work; and inclined to say 'O, that will do' – when it should not: but they agree with me when thought has been put into it, that 'it makes a good job'. They are careless to an injurious degree in using spent lime, with too much of it, inferior sand, and the proportions of both haphazard. When they look at the work as finished, they say, 'that will stand for years' as if endurance was a kind of vice.[6]

This careless way of thinking was echoed through many aspects of working people's lives, making them particularly susceptible to the superficial attraction of the over-ornamented but poorly made artefacts of mass-production.

However, there were still at least two cabinet-makers working in Cirencester when Gimson and the Barnsleys came to the Cotswolds in the 1890s, and most villages in the area still had blacksmiths, carpenters and wheelwrights working within old traditions. Sapperton, which was the nearest village to Pinbury, was particularly well-served in its wheelwright, Richard Harrison, who was to work in close co-operation with Gimson and the Barnsleys. In Kelly's Directory of Gloucestershire for 1894 he was described as a carpenter, provision dealer and beer retailer and, according to Norman Jewson:

> After the Rector and the farmer (not including Gimson and the Barnsleys, who were comparative newcomers), the most important man in the village was Richard Harrison, the wheelwright, whose workshops and yards backed on to Ernest Barnsley's garden. He was a short little man, with a face reddened by exposure, small, humorous blue eyes and a tight mouth holding entirely toothless jaws. . . . If ever a man loved his work, old Richard did. He seemed to live for nothing else, starting work at 6 in the morning and often working as long as it was light in the evening, or at any rate pottering about the shops, seeing all was in order for the next day. When I knew him he only had four men working for him: not many years before he had had up to a dozen, including his younger brother John, who was said to have been the best wheelwright of them all, but he died suddenly three years before. Richard watched his men's work – they were all sons, nephews and cousins that were left – most closely, never letting any slipshod work or faulty material pass. To anyone who really appreciated his craft he enjoyed explaining the reason for using oak for the spokes and elm for the hub and felloes of a wheel, why ash was better for shafts and that the stop-chamfering that added so much to the appearance of a wagon was only, or at any rate mostly, to reduce the weight where that could be done without reducing the strength.[7]

Gimson and the Barnsleys were the first designer-craftsmen to come to the

Cotswolds to practise their crafts. Although Morris and Rossetti had jointly leased Kelmscott Manor in 1871, they were never able to spend long enough away from their London commitments to make any significant impact on the area or to take full advantage of its benefits. Despite the fact that many artists and designers were to settle in the Cotswolds, particularly in the area around the villages of Chipping Campden and Broadway, in the first decades of the twentieth century, Gimson and the Barnsleys' arrival from London in 1893 must have aroused no little interest and comment amongst the local people and was subsequently responsible for a renewed appreciation of traditional handicrafts in the area.

Once settled at Pinbury, the three men were able to indulge in their love for the countryside and in their desire for a rural life to the full. The comfort and cleanliness of this way of life had always appealed to them, even though they were none of them country-born. Gimson and Sidney Barnsley had attempted to bring some of its joys to their shared rooms in Raymond Buildings, Gray's Inn, London in the early 1890s. Their efforts were appreciated by their friends including Alfred Powell who wrote:

> It was wonderful in old smoky London to find yourself in those fresh clean rooms, furnished with good oak furniture and a trestle table that at seasonable hours surrendered its drawing-boards to a good English meal, in which figured, if I remember right, at least on guest nights, a great stone jar of the best ale.[8]

All three men's love of nature is well-documented, and a great deal of their time, particularly whilst at Pinbury, must have been spent on long walks, closely observing the plant and animal life of the Gloucestershire landscape. Alfred Powell testified to Gimson's involvement with the countryside, and to the importance of the impact of particular local characteristics on his work:

> It is to be remembered that throughout this time he was quite alive to the entire necessity to himself and his work of the country and of this Gloucestershire country in particular. Without it he could not have had half the power. He watched and he wondered – absorbing everything around him. If you showed him any notable flower or tree, or bird, or beast, he knew it well, and it opened his mouth to speak what was in him. So with books also. Wordsworth, for whom he was always ready, brought a brightness into his eyes, and opened the way for him to say things about nature and humanity – things he had spent his life considering. Wordsworth spoke to the child in him, and, as a friend who knew him long says, 'he always came out wonderfully to children'. He had a long bed of 'wild' daffodils beside the nut-walk at Pinbury which was one of the real delights of every spring. These things – the seasons, the flowers, and all that grew and changed in the earth – were intensely real to him. I never knew him to speak of them without a touch of music in his voice: he could not take them as a matter of course, and so it

Fig. 44. Small box with faceted sides inlaid with naturalistic motifs in mother-of-pearl, designed by Ernest Gimson and made in the Daneway workshops.

seemed that his flowers, his trees, his grass, were richer in association and more memorable than other people's.[9]

Sidney Barnsley's letters to Philip Webb from Pinbury are full of allusions to the pleasures and beauties of the countryside and country life. A letter dated 30 June 1901 contains the following description of his life at Pinbury:

The gardens are looking most beautiful now after the rains, with roses in masses, hanging over grey stone walls and climbing up in the cottages, but fruit we have none, save gooseberries and currants. Still we have the comforting feeling of 1000 gallons of cider in the cellar to tide us over this barren year but we shall miss the apples for pies during the winter months.

Talking of using the axe and saw, don't you find the wood vanishes quickly. My winter store is just being hauled and when it is all piled up it looks sufficient for a lifetime. 16 tons a year I find I burn – and that means a good deal of sawing and carrying – still, as Thoreau says, it is economical in that one gets warmed twice – once in sawing it, and then in burning it, and the pleasure of splitting a big log and thinking of the future pleasure of watching it burn is worth a good deal. Just now however the sun is rivalling the poor fires and we are really enjoying summer.[10]

Ernest Barnsley and his family also took to country life with great enthusiasm,

Fig. 45. Group photograph dating from about 1895 taken outside Gimson's cottage at Pinbury. From left to right: Sidney Barnsley, Miss Lucy Morley, Ernest Gimson, Mrs Ernest Barnsley, and Ernest Barnsley with his two daughters, Mary and Ethel.

and it allowed him to indulge in his passion for good food and good company to the full. Norman Jewson left this description of Ernest Barnsley's household:

> A real 'bon viveur', he enjoyed not only eating a good dinner but buying the ingredients and cooking it himself, with his wife's and his daughters' assistance. Wherever he went he collected recipes for good dishes or the addresses from whence he could obtain special delicacies. His York hams and Wensleydale cheeses came from farms in Yorkshire direct, Welsh mutton from Brecon and pork pies from Melton Mowbray. Cirencester, being a market town and agricultural centre, had good grocers', fishmongers' and poulterers' shops and one good wine merchant. So, once or twice a week, he would cycle into the town, returning with his bicycle laden with parcels hanging from every possible part of it, riding very slowly, often reading a book on his handlebars. His sloe gin he made himself and loved to regale his many visitors on it.[11]

When the three men first settled in the Cotswolds they did so with the intention of living like country gentlemen; keeping horses, goats, dogs and chickens, growing some of their own food and making some of the staple necessities of life, such as bread and cider. The cooking was done in a large brick oven, a feature which was still found in most cottages in the village, and Sidney Barnsley sent Philip Webb instructions as to this oven's uses, when the latter moved from

London to Crawley in Sussex in 1901. However, Gimson and the Barnsleys' inexperience of country life must have presented them with practical problems in the early days, and, at Gimson's suggestion, one of the Misses Morley, his cousins in Lincolnshire, on whose farm he had spent several holidays during his youth, was asked to join the settlement at Pinbury and give them the benefit of her country upbringing. Miss Lucy Morley, a very capable lady, who seems to have overcome the handicap of her deafness by her strength of character and warm personality, joined them at Pinbury in 1894 or 1895, and shortly after that she and Sidney Barnsley were married. A photograph taken in about 1895 shows them all outside Gimson's cottage at Pinbury. According to Sidney Barnsley's son, Edward, 'it shows Gimson in an unusually solemn mood, but Ernest Barnsley is as I shall always remember him – confident, often smiling, and with an expansive ease of manner'.[12]

The early years at Pinbury must have been amongst the happiest in the lives of all three men. They were visited by many of their London friends and former colleagues who grew to share their love for the area. Both Detmar Blow and Alfred Powell were frequent visitors, either staying at Pinbury or renting accommodation at Sapperton and the other nearby villages. Ernest and Sidney Barnsley's two elder brothers and their families also spent many happy holidays at Pinbury. Such was their affection for the place that William Barnsley named his house at 324 Hagley Road, Birmingham, possibly designed by Ernest Barnsley himself, Pinbury, in about 1899, in memory of happy days spent in the Cotswolds. Philip Webb also had a great affection for the place, for the community established there and for the work they were doing.

> I liked the countryside part of that community with its natural setting, and did not like the thought of dissolution, and possible dispersion; for, had I not met much honest hospitality there and gracious helpfulness in fitting simplicity of manner?[13]

Gimson married Emily Ann Thompson, daughter of the vicar of Skipsea in Yorkshire, in 1900. The couple had originally met during one of Gimson's architectural study trips to that part of the country in the 1880s. She was a keen observer of nature, as is shown by her sketchbooks, and a valuable support for Gimson in his work. Both husband and wife shared a love of traditional English music and did much to encourage its appreciation throughout their lives. Gimson was not the only member of the Arts and Crafts Movement to associate a revival of the crafts with a revival of folk music and entertainments. In 1892, for example, the Century Guild organised three concerts of sixteenth- and seventeenth-century music, performed on the viol, lute and harpsichord, which were held in the home of Mackmurdo and Horne at 20 Fitzroy Street. Both Mackmurdo and Gimson shared the friendship of Arnold Dolmetsch, who reintroduced the use of the recorder, and did much to revive an appreciation of early English music. Dolmetsch was a frequent visitor to Pinbury, whilst Cecil Sharp, the enthusiastic collector of traditional folk music, was to visit the Gimson household at Sapperton.

According to Norman Jewson:

> [Gimson] loved all simple fun, good music and country dancing. . . . He had a good baritone voice and enjoyed singing such songs as 'Turmut Hoeing', 'The Leather Bottel' and a curious old local song called 'Tom Ridler's Oven', as well as many from Gilbert and Sullivan operas. The old folk songs and country dances with their delightful airs, then only just rediscovered, especially delighted him and every Saturday evening he joined the class of boys and girls at the village hall, learning old dances, while Mrs Gimson played the piano. It pleased him when he found that several of the dances had been popular in the neighbourhood within living memory, the postman remembering dancing some of them at Harvest Homes in his boyhood. This postman also knew the old mummer's play and brought the mummers round every Christmas. In various villages not many miles away, as at Bampton and Headington in Oxfordshire, Morris and sword dances as well as country dances still survived, encouraging him to feel that it was not too late to revive this healthy and enjoyable form of relaxation in Sapperton.[14]

One particular event, organised by Gimson and the Barnsleys, was described by the chair-maker, Edward Gardiner, and must have aroused great astonishment and amusement amongst the village audience. He wrote:

> Once Mr Gimson and the Mr Barnsleys got up the play *Mrs Jarley's Waxworks*. The waxwork models were made up of Daneway workmen, my brother and myself, Mr Ernest Barnsley was Mrs Jarley and he wanted to borrow a woman's skirt so he asked a very stout woman named Mrs Arkle to lend him one of hers. She did and remarked she was 'afraid it would be too small for him'. The 'models' were draped and each stood on a chair in a line across the back of a raised platform with only a curtain behind us. I don't remember what the 'models' represented but I know we were supposed to stand stiffly and erect, keep a straight face and not move, while Mr Barnsley and Gimson dragged us and our chair along to the front of the platform and explained the work to a school full of villagers, replace it, and bring out the next 'model'. When they were replacing Harry Davoll, they pushed him and his chair too far back so that he fell through the curtain and off the platform. Messrs. Barnsley and Gimson very cleverly covered up by pretending it was part of the play and few of the audience knew better. Mr Gimson sang those two songs he was always pleased to render, 'Birds of a Feather' and 'The Crocodile'.[15]

The active part which Gimson and Ernest Barnsley in particular took in village life won them the affection and respect of the community. The familiar figure of Gimson in the village is vividly described by Norman Jewson on the occasion of their first meeting in 1907:

> He was a tall, well-built man with a slight stoop, a large rather heavy face,

Fig. 46. Small chair, its splats carved with Cotswold characters, designed and made by Norman Jewson, c. 1914.

except when he smiled, a brown moustache and wide-open contemplative eyes. His expression was that of a man entirely at peace with himself and all the world. His tweed suit hung loosely on him over a soft shirt and collar, with a silk tie threaded through a ring. Being summer he wore a panama hat instead of his usual cloth cap, but in all seasons he wore heavy hobnailed boots made for him by a cobbler in Chalford.[16]

According to F. L. M. Griggs, Gimson and his wife 'taught Sapperton to "enjoy itself"'.[17]

The arrival in the Cotswolds of Gimson and the Barnsleys brought a new awareness to the area and was responsible for the revival of many traditional crafts and of a way of life which had been dying out. Although many other craftsmen, both individually and in groups, followed in their footsteps to settle in the Cotswolds, it was probably Gimson and the Barnsleys who both profited and contributed the most as a result of their move. The largest incursion was that of C. R. Ashbee and the Guild of Handicraft, comprising about fifty craftsmen, and their families, who moved from the East End of London to settle in Chipping Campden in 1902. Obviously the impact caused by the arrival of the Guild, involving nearly 150 people, was much greater on the existing community than that of Gimson and the Barnsleys some nine years previously, and it was inevitable that such a large influx of town dwellers would cause some hostility as well as severe problems of adjustment. Today, the tradition inspired by the Guild of Handicraft has become inseparable from the Cotswolds and, in particular, from Chipping Campden, but, at the time, it was more or less impossible for the craftsmen to become integrated into the community, and to develop local characteristics in their work, because of the large numbers involved. In addition, the craftsmen's work at Chipping Campden had already been developed stylistically in London. The other activities promoted by the Guild, under Ashbee's guidance, such as lectures, gardening, physical drill, domestic science and drama were partly for the craftsmen's benefit, although Ashbee also tried to involve the local inhabitants. The Guild of Handicraft suffered from continual financial problems and finally went into liquidation in 1907, though many of the original craftsmen, such as the silver-worker, George Hart, continued to practise their crafts successfully in Chipping Campden.

As well as their involvement with their own work, Gimson and the Barnsleys continued as active members of the Society for the Protection of Ancient Buildings after their move to the Cotswolds. They provided valuable local information to the London-based committee and were frequently consulted when buildings in their locality were brought to the Society's attention. In May 1900, Philip Webb, the moving force behind the S. P. A. B., wrote to Sidney Barnsley:

> I took your notes, drawings etc. of Matton Church to last Thursday's S. P. A. B. Comm/ee, with the memorandum letter you afterwards sent me; and the members were very thankful for your clear explanation of the circumstances of the case – even as I explained them – and the Committee decided to write to the Parson and advise that, until the *cause* of the mischief to the steeple had been remedied, it would be hopeless to attempt lasting repairs. That is, that the action on the tower and spire of the bell-ringing, had evidently been the cause of the dislocation. The Committee also agreed with me, that it would be necessary to carry down the vibration of the bell cage to the stage below the cage – we all wished the Committee had 20 such reporters on the condition of old buildings as you and your companions.[18]

Fig. 47. 'Gloucestershire Waggon and Team', a chestnut panel carved in relief by William Simmonds and exhibited at the Royal Academy in 1937.

Chapter 6
The Pinbury workshop, 1894-1901

By the summer of 1894, Gimson and the Barnsleys were able to transfer their work, as well as their living accomodation, from Ewen to Pinbury, where one of the outbuildings had been converted into a workshop. Sidney Barnsley's son, Edward, has said that 'at Pinbury it must have been for a long time a very happy set-up indeed, with all three men working together in the workshop and sharing ideas'. This inter-change of ideas and constant discussion of problems of design and technique at the bench was an important element in the development of the work of the three men. A photograph of the joint workshop [Fig. 48], dating from 1896, gives a clear impression of the range of work carried out on the premises. It shows examples of Gimson's plasterwork friezes, together with turned ladderback chairs in the process of manufacture, the construction of which he had mastered since his short sojourn in Philip Clissett's workshop. It was these two aspects of handicrafts which were occupying the greatest part of Gimson's energies during this period.

In the left foreground of the photograph of the Pinbury workshop is a music-cabinet and workbox, combined in a single convex-topped chest, made by Ernest Barnsley and exhibited at the 1896 Arts and Crafts Exhibition. According to the trade magazine, *The Cabinet Maker and Art Furnisher*, in the review of this exhibition:

> One would hardly imagine . . . that it is a 'music-chest and workbox' and yet it proves to be. The lower doors open and reveal shelves of the proper music size, and the top throws back and discovers the usual holes and corners, lined with pencil cedar, for the materials of the needlewoman. Here again, lively marquetry 'stringing' relieves the oak, and the dovetails show that they are not ashamed of their class. That someone will have to kneel to get at the music, or lift a considerable superstructure to find a needle and thread, are not serious penalties to pay for the sight, in the home, of a comely box of tricks like unto this. Mr A. Ernest Barnsley deserves credit for religiously avoiding any relationship with the flimsy and wobbly structures which are usually made for music and workbox purposes, and giving us an article which if not – to all – a thing of beauty, is likely to be a joy and a comfort for at least two or three centuries.[1]

This ingeniously designed chest was also quite a skilful piece of cabinet-work,

Fig. 48. The joint workshop at Pinbury, c. 1895. Left foreground: music-chest and workbox by Ernest Barnsley. Centre foreground: the two ends of an oak chest (see Fig. 50) by Sidney Barnsley. Right foreground: turned ladderback chair in the process of construction by Ernest Gimson. Left background: plasterwork friezes by Ernest Gimson.

with its curved top, sunken panels and herringbone dark and light inlaid stringing, as well as the undisguised dovetails upon which the reviewer commented. Its very skilfulness raises the question of whether Ernest Barnsley had had any previous experience of woodwork and cabinet-making whilst in Birmingham, comparable to that obtained by Gimson and Sidney Barnsley through their involvement with Kenton and Co.

About the same time Ernest Barnsley also made an oak chest, with subject inlay in fruitwood and stained oak, featuring hens, chickens and sprays of flowers, probably inspired by the series of inlaid furniture designed by Lethaby for Kenton and Co. This rather fanciful piece of work was intended for his own household and still remains in the possession of his daughter, Ethel. The basic rectangular structure, joined with exposed dovetails, is reinforced by the heavy bolts and hinges of wrought iron, and slots into two free-standing oak plinths which form the feet. A delicate touch, characteristic of Ernest Barnsley's work, is provided by the row of small gouges cut into the base of the chest and along the sides of the feet. An oak gate-legged kitchen table with a well scrubbed surface, also made for the Barnsley household at Pinbury, illustrates a similar use of this decorative technique which may have been derived from the oak table designed by Philip Webb in about 1870 [Fig. 10].

82

The two ends of an oak chest designed and made by Sidney Barnsley, and now at Rodmarton Manor, can be seen in the centre of the photograph of the Pinbury workshop. This piece illustrates some features of the general approach to furniture making at Pinbury in the 1890s. At this stage in their careers, Gimson and the Barnsleys relied almost entirely on locally obtainable woods; oak, ash, elm, deal and various fruitwoods, and soon developed a close working relationship with Richard Harrison, the village wheelwright at Sapperton, who supplied much of their timber. The solidity and good construction of their furniture was a feature which was almost universally noted, if not always favourably. From the outset, their belief that honesty of construction went hand in hand with the deliberate use of open joinery was fundamental to their designs, so that the wooden pins, mortice-and-tenon joints and dovetails on which their sound and solid structures were based were visible, and were even exploited for their decorative effect, as, for example, the protruding dovetails on the Rodmarton chest. The other major factor dominating their designs was their enthusiasm at this period for making simple and useful domestic furniture. Every item proudly proclaimed its intended use, however mundane. In addition, the almost complete absence of any superficial ornamentation on their designs is quite startling for the 1890s, even amongst Arts and Crafts furniture. Sidney Barnsley made no attempt to add any surface decoration to his oak chest apart from some chamfering down the corners and along the ribs. This piece was exhibited in the 1896 exhibition where, according to the *Studio* magazine, it was 'selected by good judges as the best piece of simple joinery in the exhibition'. It was also commented upon by the *Cabinet Maker and Art Furnisher* thus:

> There is no pretence about this article. Mr Sidney H. Barnsley, the exhibitor, is so determined to secure attention to his excellent dovetails that if you happen to sit on them you feel them. It is a capital and clever piece of work, but I venture to think that the lines of the old Italian chests offer more kindly and pleasing models for such an article than the lines of the coachbuilder. If this were put on wheels it would make a perfect covered truck, and in saying this I am not depreciating the excellence of the idea of the workmanship. Indeed it is one of the best pieces of construction in the Gallery.[2]

It must be remembered that all three men's practical experience of woodworking was very limited. During the short time spent with Philip Clissett at Bosbury, Gimson had acquired some basic skills which he developed through his own practical experiments in chairmaking. Both he and Sidney Barnsley must have acquired some expertise through observing the Kenton and Co. cabinet-makers at work. However, this more or less covers the extent of their knowledge of woodwork and cabinet-making on their arrival in the Cotswolds in 1893. It was Sidney Barnsley, in particular, who extended this knowledge through his dedicated experimentation in the field of furniture design at Pinbury, laying the foundations, both technically and stylistically, for the later work of all three men. Sidney Barnsley's contribution at this stage of their careers, and also within the broader framework of the Arts and Crafts Movement, was a

Fig. 49. 'Chick' chest in oak with wood inlays, designed and made by Ernest Barnsley, c. 1896.

Fig. 50. Oak chest with a coffered lid, protruding dovetails and chamfered decoration, designed and made by Sidney Barnsley, c. 1895.

Fig. 51. Oak gate-legged table designed and made by Sidney Barnsley and exhibited at the Arts and Crafts Exhibition of 1896.

unique one, commented upon by Paul Thompson in his book on William Morris:

> The ultimate logic of Arts and Crafts theory that craftsmen should work on their own designs was scarcely recognised before the 1890s, partly because all the leaders of the movement were architects. Even then, Sidney Barnsley was the only important furniture designer who executed all his own work.[3]

At the 1896 Arts and Crafts Exhibition, Sidney Barnsley also showed a rectangular gate-legged table in oak. The design of this piece has similarities with the oval table designed by him for Kenton and Co. in 1891, although the prominent dovetails and chamfered decoration on the stretchers were new features. The dark and light inlaid stringing which decorates the Kenton and Co. table is absent from the later design. In fact, although Gimson and Sidney Barnsley both used this decorative technique on furniture designed for Kenton and Co., it does not appear on any known example of Sidney Barnsley's work at Pinbury. According to the *Cabinet Maker and Art Furnisher* in its review of the 1896 Exhibition:

> The designer is evidently proud of its primitive character. The prominent and well-cut dovetails, the hand-holes for lifting, and the compact appearance when closed, are all good points. Of course, it is our old friend the 'Sutherland Table' over again, but revived in light oak with a touch of Gothic in its toes and construction. All these elements are salutary, and the table deserves its position of honour.[4]

The two ends of the table are decorated with a row of shallow gouges, a technique already noted in relation to Ernest Barnsley's designs, whilst the gate-legs, when closed, fit snugly into semi-circular bays formed by the stretchers. This table was purchased from the exhibition in London by C. H. St John Hornby, a patron of the Arts and Crafts Movement, and a craftsman in his own right, providing Sidney Barnsley with his first professional sale.

Shortly after 1896, Sidney Barnsley attempted, for the first time, to tackle the design and construction of a large and complex piece of furniture. The bow-fronted oak dresser, dating from about 1897 or 1898, was a major advance from the box and plank structures of chests and tables which had formed the extent of his output up until then. According to Edward Barnsley, the immediate inspiration for the design of this piece came from William Morris. In a lecture entitled 'The Lesser Arts of Life', first given to the Society for the Protection of Ancient Buildings in 1882, Morris laid down the following principles for the design of furniture:

> As to matters of construction, it should not have to depend on the special skill of a very picked workman, or the super-excellence of his glue, but be made on the proper principles of the art of joinery: also I think that, except for very moveable things like chairs, it should not be so very light as to be nearly imponderable; it should be made of timber rather than walking sticks.[5]

It was the last phrase in this paragraph which struck an immediate chord in Sidney Barnsley's imagination. William Morris may well have repeated this lecture at a later date, nearer in time to the design of this dresser, or, equally possibly, he may have expressed the same sentiment in a private conversation.

Sidney Barnsley's dresser was exhibited at the 1899 Arts and Crafts Exhibition where it was not received altogether sympathetically, judging from this comment in *The Builder*:

> In the reaction which is taking place against display and over-lavish ornamentation the new school of designers appear to be losing the sense of style,

Fig. 52. The interior of Sidney Barnsley's cottage at Pinbury, showing the oak bow-fronted dresser which he designed and made in about 1898.

and of dignity of design which accompanies it, altogether. The object now seems to be to make a thing as square, as plain, as devoid of any beauty of line, as is possible, and call this art. Look at the oak dresser, for instance . . . the semi-circular plan is effective, but the details are absolutely clumsy; the turn buttons to the small top cupboards look like the work of a savage; the wooden handles to the lower doors, with the panels hollowed out just beneath them for the fingers, are actually nailed on at one end, the rough nail-head showing at the top. This is not only not artistic work, it is not even good craftsmanship.[6]

However, in reading this review, it must be remembered that *The Builder* was one of the most conservative periodicals commenting on furniture during this period. In fact, all the constructional features which the reviewer singled out for criticism, such as the use of nails, were orthodox methods used in the construction of Gothic furniture, and had the approval of such authorities as Bruce Talbert. Sidney Barnsley first developed the double-dovetail as a constructional feature, in this piece of furniture, to join two pieces of wood in the same plane. He was under the impression that he had invented this technique, in which a piece of wood, dovetailed both horizontally and vertically, formed a key joint reinforced by thin wedges. However, towards the end of his career, he saw the same technique used on a Japanese chest some three hundred years old in the British Museum. Both Sidney Barnsley and Ernest Gimson used the double dovetail joint regularly on table tops.

The most influential feature in the design of this dresser was the emphatic treatment of the vertical plane. The sheer expanse of unornamented oak, which follows the construction of some sixteenth- and seventeenth-century chests by descending vertically to form the two feet, makes a powerful impact which is only slightly relieved by the semi-circular bow-front. The cupboard doors on the bow-front were planed at different angles to create the necessary curve and, as a bonus, each plane catches a varying amount of light. The lattice-work grid treatment of the plate-rack was a recurrent feature of Sidney Barnsley's designs during this period, and bears some relationship to the spatial approach recognisable in the furniture of his contemporaries, the architects and designers, E. W. Godwin and C. R. Mackintosh [Fig. 52]. This plate-rack was originally bisected by a vertical shaped and chamfered support designed by Gimson. This type of curved structure was a feature which Gimson particularly enjoyed designing, and its use on Sidney Barnsley's dresser illustrates the co-operation which must have existed between them in the Pinbury workshop. This co-operation enabled Sidney Barnsley to execute a design by Gimson, an oak box inlaid with mother-of-pearl, which was included in the 1899 Arts and Crafts Exhibition. Unfortunately no visual record of this piece has survived.

Ernest Barnsley was obviously influenced by his brother's dresser in his design of an oak kitchen cupboard dating from about 1899. The two vertical lengths of oak are separated by a shallow bow-fronted construction which provides the main cupboard area. As in the oak dresser, the two uprights flanking the bow-front provide additional cupboard space which is entered into from the sides. Ernest Barnsley gave free range to his enjoyment of chip-carving in the decoration of this piece, and a variety of abstract motifs, reminiscent of Egyptian hieroglyphics, run vertically and horizontally along the ribs of the bow-front. This basic form was reworked and revived many times by all three men, providing dressers, sideboards and cupboards of different sizes and in different woods for their clients.

Gimson's contribution to the development of furniture design and construction at Pinbury was very limited, particularly until about 1900. As well as some plasterwork friezes, and a white linen embroidery executed by his sister, Margaret, he exhibited two turned ash chairs at the 1896 Arts and Crafts Exhibition, one of which was illustrated in the *Cabinet Maker and Art Furnisher*. The drawing shows a rush-seated armchair, typical in its design of the ladderback chairs made by Gimson at Pinbury. However, instead of the curved slats continuing down to the seat, as they do on Gimson's standard design, the back is broken up by two rows of vertical, bobbin-turned supports. The fact that a somewhat similar design had been Gimson's only contribution in terms of furniture to the previous Arts and Crafts Exhibition in 1893 is indicative of the minimal extent of his involvement with furniture design during this period.

Plasterwork was probably the first craft which Gimson took up seriously, and his involvement with it continued throughout his working life, possibly because

Fig. 53. The interior of Stoneywell Cottage, Leicestershire, photographed in the early twentieth century. On the right is the oak kitchen cupboard by Ernest Barnsley.

he enjoyed the challenge of designing within the limitations of the material. He was one of several architects and designers who used plasterwork decoration extensively from the last quarter of the nineteenth century onwards. Others included George Jack, Henry Wilson, R. S. Lorimer, T. Stallybrass and G. P. Bankart. However, Gimson was one of a very limited number, together with Bankart and Henry Wilson's assistant, John Paul Cooper, who actually executed their own plasterwork designs. These men tried to return to a simpler, more appropriate approach to plasterwork which took into account the soft, fibrous nature of the material, and renounced the use of popular techniques such as undercutting and elaborate moulding, which were more suited to wood or stone carving than to decorative plasterwork. At the beginning of his career, Gimson set down his principles for the design and execution of plasterwork decoration in an essay, discussed in an earlier chapter, for the handbook *Plain Handicrafts*, and these principles remained the guidelines for all his work in this field.

Gimson's first major commission came in 1892 for work at Avon Tyrell, the house near Christchurch, Hampshire, which Lethaby had designed for Lord Manners. Gimson spent the summer of 1892 lodging nearby, in company with Lethaby, and carried out plasterwork decoration in most of the main rooms. The dining room is decorated with a simple, repeating, naturalistic pattern which runs along the friezes and beams, setting off the austere fireplace and plain white walls designed by Lethaby. The plasterwork decoration in the drawing room

Fig. 54. The White House, Clarendon Park, Leicester, designed by Gimson in 1897, with exterior plasterwork panels designed by the architect and modelled by G. P. Bankart.

Fig. 55. Drawing by Ernest Gimson of a plaster panel on the exterior of a house in Canterbury.

makes a more powerful impact, consisting, as it does, of a pattern of flowing and intersecting ribs ending in moulded pendentives over the entire area of the ceiling, dividing it into squares, each of which contains a naturalistic design modelled *in situ*. One of Gimson's working drawings for this project has survived in the collections of Cheltenham Museum, and shows designs for overmantel plaster panels. His notes show that most of these designs were made by 'the contrast of a raised rough surface against a smooth sunk surface', a technique which admirably suited the gradual building-up of layers of plaster and the granular surface of the material itself. The work at Avon Tyrell was only the first of several commissions for plasterwork in which Gimson co-operated with Lethaby. A year later, for example, Gimson designed and executed decorative plasterwork at The Hurst, another house built by Lethaby at Four Oaks, near Sutton Coldfield. Although this house has since been demolished, it was featured in the influential volume, *Das Englische Haus*, produced by Hermann Muthesius in 1904.

Gimson used plasterwork friezes to decorate the interior of Inglewood, the house which he built for himself in Leicester in 1892. The White House, in Clarendon Road, Leicester, built by Gimson for his half-brother, Arthur, in 1897, also included decorative plasterwork by Gimson and G. P. Bankart, a friend who devoted his life to the revival of plasterwork through his practical and

Fig. 56. A contemporary photograph of the carved stone fireplace at Pinbury Park.

written work. The White House was built of wire-cut bricks, giving the exterior an uneven texture, and lime-washed. Two bays were given a rough-cast plaster finish and were covered with panels modelled in Keene's cement with a design based on the oak tree. The illustration of these panels in *Plastering, Plain and Decorative* by W. Millar, edited by G. P. Bankart in 1926, credits the design to Gimson and the execution to Bankart himself. This use of external decorative plasterwork was a popular technique up until the eighteenth century. Amongst Gimson's notes on plasterwork is this paragraph which he had copied from an issue of the *Building News* of 1871:

Fig. 57. Gimson's design for a fireplace, panelling and plasterwork in the extension at Pinbury Park built by Ernest Barnsley. Ink and wash drawing on tracing paper, signed and dated 10 June 1903.

Fig. 58. Coloured sketch design for a plaster ceiling to the bay window at Borden Wood by Ernest Gimson, dated 8 June 1903.

> We recently saw, say the 'Guardian', a cottage in Kent of possibly the Elizabethan period in which a gable abutting on the village street was covered with plaster moulded not to imitate stonework, but with a pleasing geometric diaper pattern, sunk slightly into the face of the work.[7]

Gimson's appreciation of this technique is also illustrated by a drawing, dating from about 1890, of plasterwork decoration on the exterior of a house in Canterbury. However the only occasion when he himself employed this technique was in the decoration of The White House.

Plasterwork was the only craft in which Gimson continued to work as well as to design throughout his career. According to Norman Jewson, Gimson would execute his plasterwork designs in the open shed below his drawing office at

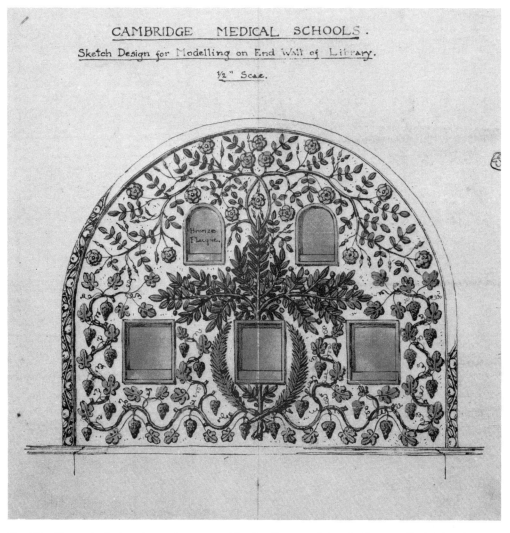

Fig. 59. Gimson's design for a plaster panel in the library of Cambridge Medical School. Ink and coloured wash drawing on paper, dated January 1915.

Sapperton, with the occasional help of Mrs Gimson and Jewson himself, and would enjoy the variety it provided from a normal afternoon spent at the drawing board. Some of his most effective designs in this medium were produced for Pinbury Park, in 1903, for Lord Bathurst, after the latter's family had moved into the house. Gimson first used a squirrel and oak leaf design for a fireplace at Pinbury. This design became one of his most popular motifs and was used in a variety of commissions for plasterwork, including the interior of Borden Wood, a house near Liphook, Hampshire, also undertaken in 1903. His working drawings for this project, some of which are illustrated here, show an effective and lively use of painted plasterwork, another technique revived by Arts and Crafts practitioners of the craft in the latter half of the nineteenth century. The library at Borden Wood was decorated with a frieze of painted plasterwork, consisting of overlapping, concave-sided squares and floral sprays modelled *in situ*, broken up at intervals by round or square modelled panels with moulded frames. The raised areas were painted in tempera with a certain amount of detail wiped or scratched through the surface to show the white plaster below. The use of tempera on plaster produced dull rather than bright tones which complement the character of the material, whilst the actual range of Gimson's palette was limited to greens, yellows and reds. The round and square panels have a solid coloured background enabling them to stand out in the frieze. This slow and laborious process produced a luminous but unobtrusive decorative effect. Gimson's use of coloured plasterwork is also illustrated in his design for the library of the Cambridge Medical School dating from 1915 [Fig. 59].

Gimson was fortunate in having a permanent source of inspiration for his plasterwork designs at Daneway House, near the village of Sapperton, leased by Gimson from Lord Bathurst for use as showrooms from 1902 onwards. The main rooms of the house contain some very early and attractive examples of sixteenth century plasterwork friezes and ceiling decorations. He received a fairly constant stream of commissions for decorative plasterwork until the outbreak of the First World War during which the demand for this type of work inevitably decreased. His major works include designs for Wilsford House, Lincolnshire in 1905, which demonstrate clearly the influence of the sixteenth-century plasterwork at Daneway, for the Council Chamber at Bradford in 1907, for Purton Manor House, Wiltshire, in 1909, and for Sheffield Park, Sussex in 1911. His friendship with the architect, Halsey Ricardo, provided Gimson with a succession of commissions for plasterwork. In 1905, he executed plasterwork designs in the drawing room of Woodside, Graffham, Sussex, built by Halsey Ricardo. The low-relief, flowing vine leaf pattern used by Gimson on the ceiling beams of this room contrasts in both colour and texture with the bright, swirling designs of William de Morgan's 'Islamic' tiles which decorate the fireplace. Gimson's most important commission came from Sir Ernest Debenham, in whose house in Addison Road, Kensington, built by Halsey Ricardo in 1907, many fine examples of Gimson's decorative plasterwork survive intact. In the same year he was asked by Debenham to design plasterwork friezes and ceiling decorations for the interior of the luxurious new department store, Debenham and Freebody's, in Wigmore Street, London. The store is still in operation today (as Hamleys Sport and Leisure Shop, part of the Debenham Group), and, although most of these designs have since been concealed by false ceilings, it is still possible to view one section of Gimson's work in the toy department on the second floor.

He also combined plasterwork with several of his furniture designs using gesso, a material traditionally used with wood to provide a smooth ground for the application of gilt or painted decoration. However Gimson used gesso in its unpainted state to provide panels of relief decoration on furniture. The possibilities inherent in the use of gesso are discussed in *Plastering, Plain and Decorative*:

The best character of the work is direct and simple. It might perhaps at first

Fig. 60. Small oak box decorated by Gimson with a pattern of Elizabethan roses in unpainted gesso.

Fig. 61. Oak coffer designed by Gimson with unfinished floral decoration in unpainted gesso.

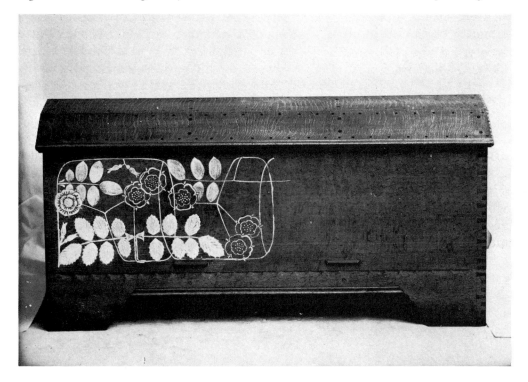

Fig. 62. A piece of plasterwork in the process of manufacture in Gimson's workshop.

sight be thought that a material such as gesso has no particular restrictions or limitations of use essential to character or style. On the contrary, it has most delightful and charming characteristics peculiar to and arising directly from the nature of the medium itself and from the tool or tools, which an artist may tend to emphasise and develop rather than to hide. In the flowing on and building up of a design, brush and medium will combine in favouring particular forms such as dots, blobs and spots, arrangements of lines and of stringy forms, branch, leaf and scroll work, and forms such as naturally arise from a brush full of thick, treacly paste.[8]

There is a very attractive oak box in the collections of Leicester Museum which is decorated in gesso built up into panels containing Elizabethan rose motifs [Fig. 60]. The oak chest in Cheltenham Museum, on which Gimson was reputedly working at the time of his death, has an unfinished floral design, also executed in gesso, which illustrates admirably his free and attractive exploitation of this medium.

Chapter 7
Furniture-making at Sapperton

Ernest Gimson's major involvement with furniture design dates from about 1901, by which time he had reached his mid thirties without having seriously applied himself to any of his undertakings. It was Alfred Powell, Gimson's friend from their student days in John Sedding's architectural office, and a frequent visitor to Pinbury, who urged Gimson to tackle this problem purposefully. Taking his advice to heart, Gimson began to concentrate all his energies on designing and making furniture. He soon found it necessary to employ professional cabinet-makers to execute his designs, partly because he was not physically strong enough for sustained work at the bench, and partly because he considered that the discipline of actually making all his own furniture did not justify the limits, in terms of time and effort, which it put on the interpretation of his ideas. In June 1901, Sidney Barnsley wrote to Philip Webb thus:

> And as to our work, furniture is still being made and sold and things look quite cheerful, the difficulty now being to complete the orders we get, and so we are launching out as business men.[1]

The three men established a second workshop, situated in the yard of the Fleece Hotel in Market Square, Cirencester, where several craftsmen, including Harry Davoll, were employed to make furniture to their designs.

One of the earliest of Gimson's surviving working drawings is a pen-and-wash design, dated January 1901, for a glazed china cabinet and bookcase in solid dark mahogany. The upper part of this piece is divided into small sections by numerous glazing bars inlaid with dark and light stringing. They also incorporate an occasional double curve, derived from the Kenton and Co. mirror designed by A. H. Mason. In contrast to the rather elaborate upper part, the design of the lower half of this cabinet is very simple, deriving its only ornamentation from the contrasting run of the wood grain on the quartered panelling of the cupboard doors. This design was loosely interpreted in the execution of a cabinet, exhibited at the 1903 Arts and Crafts Exhibition and included in a contemporary photograph of the Daneway showrooms [Fig. 64]. Its powerful stand, constructed as a single entity detachable from the main carcass, was a feature of a number of Gimson's designs from this period. A more elaborate version was used in the execution of the store cabinet, veneered in English walnut and dated 1902, now in the collections of the Victoria and Albert Museum. This cabinet [Fig. 65] sits on a two-tier

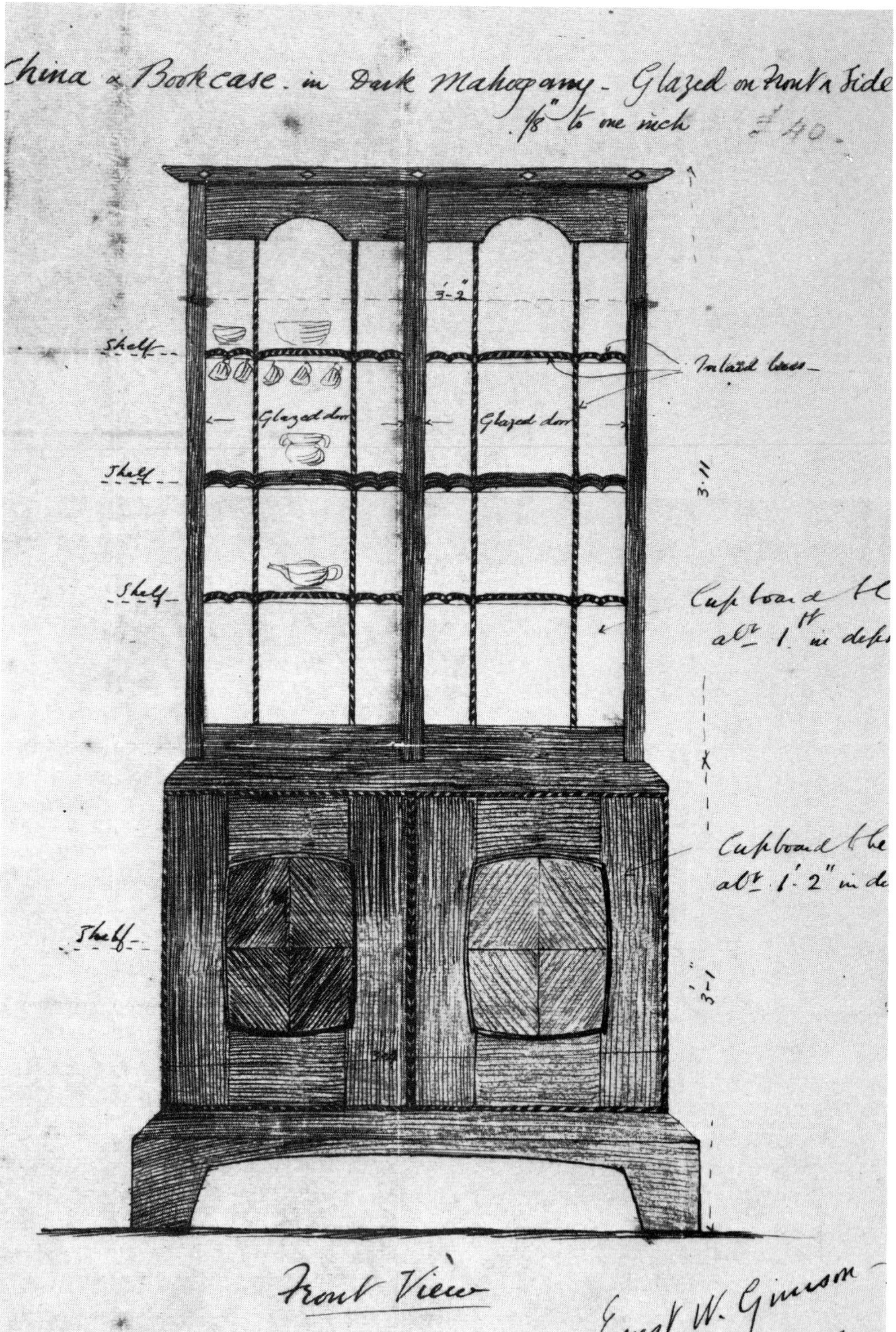

China & Bookcase in Dark Mahogany — Glazed on front & side
1/8" to one inch   £40.

Shelf

Shelf

Shelf

Shelf

Glazed door   Glazed door

Inlaid brass

3'-2"

3'-11"

Cupboard th
abt. 1'. 1" in dep

Cupboard the
abt. 1'. 2" in de

3'-1

Front View

Ernest W. Gimson
Jan. 1901

98

Fig. 63. Design for a china- and book-case in dark mahogany with glazed front and sides by Ernest Gimson, dated June 1901.

Fig. 64. A room at Daneway House, near Sapperton, with a sixteenth-century plasterwork ceiling. This was one of the main rooms used as showrooms for the products of the Daneway workshops from 1902 onwards. Included in the room setting, which dates from between about 1903 and 1905, are the mahogany cabinet and oak corner cupboard mentioned in the text.

plinth in brown ebony, the design of which is reminiscent of Lethaby's dresser [Fig. 32], made by Kenton and Co. in 1891. The use of veneering on this piece shows the continued interest which both Gimson and Sidney Barnsley had in this technique, since their involvement with that firm. The veneered surface of Sidney Barnsley's Kenton and Co. wardrobe [Fig. 31], as well as that on Gimson's store cabinet, show how they were able to achieve a decorative effect purely through the geometric arrangement of the grain on the sections of veneer. Another interesting feature of the store cabinet is the use of panels of floral decoration executed in gesso. This piece was the first of a series of pieces designed by Gimson which relied on a chequered veneered surface for their decoration.

In his initial efforts in the field of furniture-making, Gimson was, to a significant extent, reliant on both the Barnsleys, particularly Sidney Barnsley, because of their greater experience as designers and woodworkers since their removal to the Cotswolds in the 1890s. Many of Gimson's earliest designs, made whilst they were still at Pinbury, were annotated by Sidney Barnsley, and must therefore have been executed in an atmosphere of close collaboration between

100

the two men. The oak corner cupboard, now displayed at Lotherton Hall, Yorkshire, was one result of this collaboration, even though it was made in the Daneway workshops in about 1903. The design for this cabinet first appears, in a slightly modified form, in a drawing made by Sidney Barnsley at Pinbury dating from about 1901. There are several versions of this design which are drawn and annotated by both men, and predate the execution of the corner cabinet. The finished piece can be seen in a contemporary photograph of the interior of Daneway House [Fig. 64]. Although not the best-proportioned piece of furniture, in the relationship between the solid base and the glazed upper part, this does incorporate one significant feature, a heavy central upright with a curved profile, reminiscent of Sidney Barnsley's oak bow-fronted dresser [Fig. 52].

The commitment to furniture-making made by Gimson and the Barnsleys at this stage in their careers, and the growing demand for their work, led to a need for enlarged premises which was recognised by all three men. This need coincided with the decision of their landlord, Lord Bathurst, then serving abroad with the army, to establish a permanent country residence for his family on his estate. Negotiations with Lord Bathurst and his estate manager for the solution to both these problems were left in the capable hands of Ernest Barnsley who, in a letter dated March 1901, wrote:

> When your letter arrived we had under discussion the future development of our crafts, and at the present time, many things promise to make an extension of our influence successful. To ensure this we need more accomodation in our workshops than we have at present, and Cirencester seems the only available centre for this but we should much prefer the workshops nearer to our homes on account of the supervision. I make the following suggestion, merely supposing, from a point to start at, that you would care to make a country residence at Pinbury – which has many attractions not to be found anywhere else in the country. The farm buildings at Daneway could be made to answer the purpose of workshops; and the house would be most useful if you could allow us to place some of our finished pieces of furniture in the rooms, and this would not in any way prevent the house and surroundings being used as a pleasant place for visitors and sightseers. And further, could you consider, if we gave up our lease to Pinbury, building us three cottages on the land at the back of Park Corner Farm.[2]

These proposals were finally agreed upon by both parties a year later, in 1902, at about the same time that Ernest Gimson and Ernest Barnsley decided to enter into a formal partnership for the design and manufacture of furniture. Sidney Barnsley informed Philip Webb of this new development in a letter dated July 1902:

Fig. 65. Store cabinet veneered in English walnut with gesso gilt panels modelled by Gimson and an ebony stand. Designed by Gimson and made in about 1902.

Fig. 66. Peter van der Waals.

My brother and Gimson have already started workshops at Daneway having four or five cabinet makers and boys so far, with the hope of chairmakers and modellers in the near future. I am remaining an outsider from this movement and still going on making furniture by myself and handing over to them any orders I cannot undertake, and orders seem to come in too quickly now as we are getting known.[3]

It was the partnership between Gimson and Ernest Barnsley which led to the employment of Peter van der Waals as foreman/cabinet-maker of the new enterprise. Waals was a Dutchman, born in The Hague in 1870, who had worked extensively as a cabinet-maker in central Europe before coming to London in about 1899, possibly in connection with some ecclesiastical work. There is a possibility that Gimson may have already known of him through contacts in London before he answered their advertisement. Waals took up employment with Ernest Barnsley and Gimson in the Cotswolds in about 1901. His appointment was closely followed by those of the cabinet-makers, Percy Burchett and Ernest Smith, also from London, forming, together with Harry Davoll from the Cirencester workshop, the nucleus of highly skilled craftsmen who were to work at Daneway. The outbuildings of Daneway House were converted into spacious workshops for Ernest Barnsley, Gimson and the craftsmen, whilst the main rooms in the house itself, which had been previously renovated by Ernest Barnsley, provided a sympathetic setting for the furniture produced in the workshops. Sidney Barnsley remained separate from this development and continued designing and making furniture on his own. In his workshop, a converted outbuilding adjacent to his new cottage at Sapperton, he tackled those commissions which he could reasonably execute, working on his own, and passed the remainder over to his friend and his brother at Daneway.

These new developments at Sapperton were paralleled by the move of C. R. Ashbee's Guild of Handicraft to Chipping Campden, some twenty miles distant, in 1902. When the lease of his premises in the East End of London expired, Ashbee decided, for idealistic rather than practical reasons, to move his enterprise to the country, possibly influenced by Gimson's and the Barnsleys' removal some nine years earlier. The decision however was a democratic one; a vote being taken amongst all the Guild members, a course upon which one cannot imagine Gimson and the Barnsleys embarking under similar circumstances. Despite the fact that Ashbee moved so near to Sapperton and that all four men had so much in common, in terms of their work, there seems to have been very little contact between the two groups of craftsmen. More significant for the development of the new partnership between Gimson and Ernest Barnsley were the contacts with their friends and former colleagues in London. In 1902, for example, they were commissioned by the architect, A. Randall Wells, to provide furniture and metalwork for the Church of Edward the Confessor at Kempley, Gloucestershire. This was one of the major projects undertaken by the two men during the short period of their partnership, and is discussed in greater detail in a later chapter.

Amongst the collection of working drawings by Ernest Gimson in Cheltenham Museum are five, all dated 1902, signed 'B. & G.' These designs relate to the partnership between Ernest Barnsley and Gimson and, although all the drawings appear to have been executed by Gimson, one must assume that Ernest Barnsley made a significant contribution to their conception. These drawings illustrate quite clearly the influence of the initial work by Ernest and Sidney Barnsley at Pinbury, in the field of furniture design. A drawing of two folding tea tables shows Gimson and Ernest Barnsley trying to tackle a design problem to which Sidney Barnsley had already offered at least two solutions. It is difficult to judge the practical merits of Gimson's and Ernest Barnsley's design, which includes only a single support for each flap, from the drawing, although this is the only surviving record of this piece. Another 'B. & G.' design, a washstand in English oak, shows the influence of Sidney Barnsley's bow-fronted dresser in the simple, rectangular outline, the treatment of the cupboards, and the use of gouged decoration. This design is also reminiscent, in its proportions, of the oak dresser designed by Gimson and made by Kenton and Co. in 1891. This latter piece of furniture was acquired by Ernest Barnsley and was used in his home throughout his lifetime, The use of chamfered decoration on the washstand, and on other designs from this period, reflects Ernest Barnsley's enthusiasm for this traditional technique. Its use by the two men is seen at its most effective in the drawing of an oak half-tester bed. The 'country' feel of this bedstead is emphasised by the 'waggon-back' design of the footboard with the upturned ends of the top rail left protruding, as they would have been on a cart. A similar 'waggon-back' bed

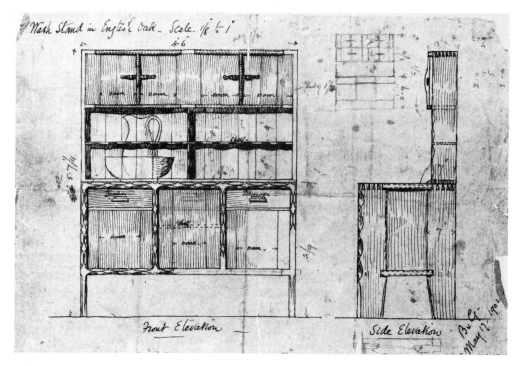

Fig. 67. Design for an oak washstand. Drawing in ink on tracing paper to a scale of $\frac{1}{8}''$ to $1''$, signed and dated 'B. & G., May 17 1902'.

Fig. 68. Design for a half–tester bedstead in English oak, signed and dated 'B. & G., May 17 1902'.

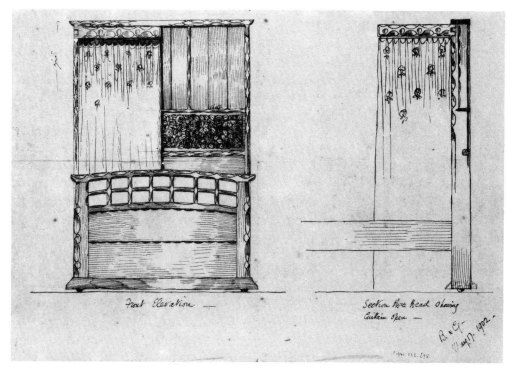

Fig. 69. Waggon-back bed in English oak, designed and made by Sidney Barnsley in about 1903 and seen in this contemporary photograph in its intended setting, the bedroom of Stoneywell Cottage, Leicestershire.

was made in oak by Sidney Barnsley for Mr and Mrs Sydney Gimson at Stoney-well Cottage, near Markfield, Leicestershire, at about the same time.

Although Gimson and Ernest Barnsley rapidly developed their furniture-designing activities and their workshop at Daneway, Sidney Barnsley continued to retain the greatest interest in this field. At the seventh Arts and Crafts Exhibition, held at the New Gallery in London between January and March 1903, he was one of the Society's committee members responsible for displaying the exhibits. He showed roughly the same amount of work, all executed by his own hand, as did Ernest Barnsley and Gimson together. Sidney Barnsley's exhibits included a sideboard in oak, with a chamfered plate rack, which has its drawer runners expressed externally as ribs on the side of the carcass. This constructional feature, which was adopted by all three men, made its first appearance in Sidney Barnsley's designs during this period. A dresser [Fig. 70], of a similar design, was made in Gimson's Daneway workshops in about 1910, and was acquired by the silversmith, Harold Stabler. The use of chamfering, which was so popular with Gimson and the Barnsleys, had originated with the craft of the wheelwright, as a means of reducing the overall weight of his product without weakening the structure, and was subsequently developed as an integral part of the design of most traditional carts and farm waggons. The technique was adopted by the three men because it was a traditional skill and, although the weight problem was not a significant one, in most pieces of furniture, chamfering remained a useful technique, requiring skill and thought in its execution, to soften sharp corners and edges and to anticipate wear. In terms of furniture design, its main

Fig. 70. Oak dresser designed by Gimson for the silversmith, Harold Stabler, and made in the Daneway workshops in about 1910.

qualities were to emphasise and add variety to an outline. Its effective use as a decorative technique is best illustrated by the oak chest of drawers designed by Ernest Barnsley and made by H. Pugsley in 1902 [Fig. 71]. Many of the right angles on the front of this piece of furniture are softened by the use of bold chamfers, cut so that all the planes catch the light to a different degree. This work was usually executed using a draw knife alone, without any recourse to the spoke-shave or to sandpaper. This chest of drawers was originally priced at £12 and was a product of the partnership between Ernest Barnsley and Gimson. A more delicate use of chamfering can be seen on the feet of furniture designed by both Gimson and Sidney Barnsley. The two- or three-step feet frequently used by both men have their angles softened and rounded by delicate chamfering, whilst the stretcher rails joining these feet were similarly chamfered with a series of gentle curves.

The contributions of all three men to the 1903 Arts and Crafts Exhibition

Fig. 71. Oak chest of drawers designed by Ernest Barnsley during the period of his partnership with Gimson, c. 1903.

illustrate the impact of Peter Waals's experience on the development of their skills and range as furniture-makers. Even Sidney Barnsley appears to have profited from the proximity of skilled and sympathetic cabinet-makers, with the result that he began to use panelling and other more sophisticated constructional features in his designs. The oak writing cabinet made by Sidney Barnsley, in 1902, for his wife, and exhibited the following year, has very simple square panels, in burr oak without any moulding, on the fall-front and sides. However, another example of his work, also exhibited at this exhibition, a small cabinet in English walnut, illustrates a more sophisticated use of double-fielded panelling. The enthusiasm of both Sidney Barnsley and Gimson for this technique was such that they were soon using multi-fielded panels to a great extent, both on oak and on other woods with more decorative figures. Under Waals's influence, the octagonal fielded panel, seen for example on the sideboard illustrated on page 120, became a recurrent feature of both men's work, whilst Gimson was particularly fond of the half-ovolo moulding worked on to the edge of fielded panels. This

Fig. 72. Oak writing desk with square panels of burr oak designed and made by Sidney Barnsley and exhibited by the Arts and Crafts Exhibition Society in 1903.

laborious detail was carried out using a very delicate, hollow plane which would not mark the surface below each fielding.

From the review of the 1903 Arts and Crafts Exhibition in *The Studio* magazine, it appears that Gimson and the Barnsleys were not considered amongst the foremost furniture designers in their field by their contemporaries. The lack of publicity which their work received was partly due to their move to the Cotswolds, where they were working in comparative isolation from the London art world. *The Studio* magazine's greatest praise and fullest commentary was justly reserved for the contributions of Charles Voysey and Ambrose Heal, but Gimson and the Barnsleys deserved more attention than that lavished on some of their contemporaries. Sidney Barnsley was understandably the best-known of the trio, as a result of his serious commitment to furniture design since about 1896. He was mentioned in the magazine's first notice of the 1903 exhibition in the same breath as Charles Spooner, who ran a furniture workshop in London, as sharing a common concern 'for simplicity and lightness in furniture'.[4] Despite this comparison, both Gimson and Sidney Barnsley were to have a far greater impact as furniture designers during their careers, so that in 1916, for example, Spooner contributed three pieces of bedroom furniture, made in his workshop to Gimson's design, to the Arts and Crafts Exhibition at the Royal Academy.

In contrast to the low-key discussion of the furniture designed by the three men in *The Studio* magazine, their contribution to the 1903 Arts and Crafts Exhibition greatly impressed visitors from the continent. Seven years earlier, the Prussian Board of Trade had sent Hermann Muthesius, a German architect, to London to report on the development of British design, in an attempt to emulate British achievements, but Britain was still considered to be the most advanced country in Europe in terms of design. *Der Moderne Stil*, a German art periodical published by Julius Hoffmann in Stuttgart, devoted almost two full pages of one issue to illustrations of the work of Gimson and the Barnsleys from the 1903 exhibition. The example of Gimson's work chosen for illustration was an oak sideboard executed by Peter Waals and priced at £45. A working drawing of a very similar piece [Fig. 73] illustrates the very effective use made of the clean lines and simple four-square designs developed by Sidney Barnsley at Pinbury and subsequently used by all three men.

The partnership between Ernest Barnsley and Gimson which had initiated the development of the workshops at Daneway was short-lived. The reasons for its dissolution appear to have been personal rather than in connection with their work, but, whatever their nature, they had a major impact on relations between the two men, which were more or less non-existent after about 1905. Edward Barnsley has said that there was never a written agreement between the two men, but Ernest Barnsley was the senior partner with responsibility for dealing with clients and engaging workmen. However, 'Gimson had a certain tenacity of purpose denied to Ernest Barnsley . . . when it came to the crunch or any sort of crisis, Gimson wouldn't compromise in any sort of way'.[5] After the collapse of the partnership, Ernest Barnsley relinquished any serious interest in furniture design, and devoted the remainder of his career to his architectural work.

Under Gimson's direction, the workshops at Daneway went from strength to strength. Both Gimson and Sidney Barnsley found themselves with more work than they, each working in his different way, could handle. The fact that some

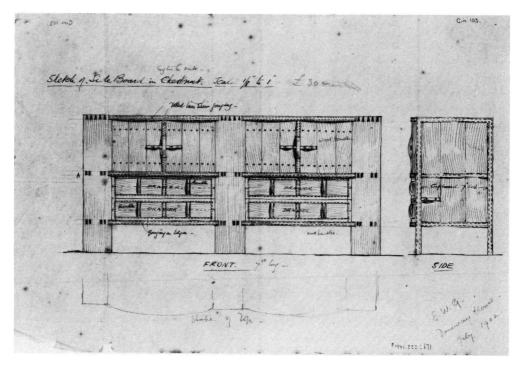

Fig. 73. Design for a sideboard to be made in English oak or chestnut by Ernest Gimson.

eight hundred of Gimson's working drawings of furniture, as well as about one hundred of Sidney Barnsley's, have survived to the present day is an indication of their application to their work. It is unfortunate that no similar documentation relating to Ernest Barnsley has survived. Peter Waals's role as foreman of the Daneway workshops became progressively more important in the development of Gimson's work. According to Sir George Trevelyan, who worked with Waals after Gimson's death:

> Gimson would be the first to acknowledge the immense debt he owed to him [Peter Waals] as colleague. Though Gimson was, of course, the inspiration and genius, he used Waals from the outset in close co-operation. The association of these two men was an essential factor in the evolving of the Cotswold tradition.[6]

The team of craftsmen, working directly under Gimson's and Waals's supervision, soon became expert at interpreting the former's ideas whilst maintaining the excellence of craftsmanship demanded by the latter. Gimson worked very closely with his craftsmen, discussing technical and design problems as they arose in the workshops, and, if necessary, providing modifications to his original plans. However, criticism of Gimson's work, from either his craftsmen or his friends and associates, was rare. Edward Barnsley recalls Oliver Powell pronouncing an adverse judgement on a design by Gimson, in the presence of his uncle,

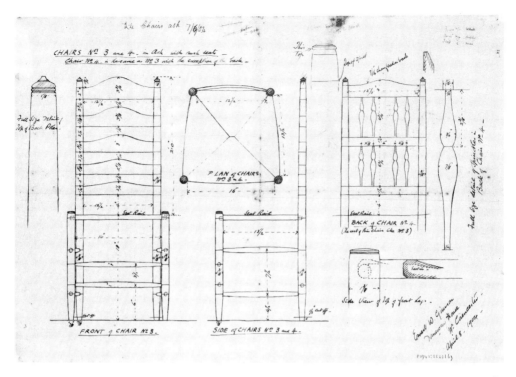

Fig. 74. Gimson's design for chairs nos. 3 and 4 in ash, dated 8 April 1904. Both chairs are of a basic ladderback design, but the second incorporates bobbin-turned supports in its back.

Alfred Powell, only to be reprimanded for criticising 'the master'. Apart from his continuing enthusiasm for the design and manufacture of decorative plaster-work, Gimson executed only a very small number of his own designs after 1900. However, in his case, because of his close sympathy with and understanding of the crafts involved, this was not a disadvantage. His success as a designer has been perceptively analysed by George Trevelyan:

> It is a puzzle to some that, apart from his exquisite plaster work and his spindle-back chairs, Ernest Gimson was not a working craftsman. He was an architect designer – but with what a difference! Too often when architects design furniture, their lack of true feeling for material and construction is revealed to the craftsman's eye. There may be unnecessary ingenuity in solving problems, or solutions that the craftsman himself dislikes. Not so with Gimson. His genius was such that he could put himself completely into the understanding and experience of a craft, so that as far as makes no matter, he *was* the craftsman in that skill. He thought as a craftsman, knowing exactly what he could ask of the men, and he had their complete confidence through the inevitable 'rightness' of each design.[7]

Because Gimson held the respect and confidence of his craftsmen, his authority over them was never questioned, and he was thus able to extend their skill beyond their own conception of their capabilities.

Fig. 75. Edward Gardiner, photographed in his Rugby workshop.

Fig. 76. Alfred Bucknell.

Gimson was also a good judge of character, as well as being extremely fortunate in his craftsmen. He developed chair-making and metal-working enterprises at Daneway, by employing young men who were relatively untried, and training them to reach the same standards of workmanship as his more experienced craftsmen. Gimson developed the chair-making side of his furniture work shortly after 1903. The popularity of the light 'Sussex' chair, promoted by Morris and Co. from the 1870s onwards, proved that there was a tremendous demand for this type of simple, moveable furniture, and the same success was repeated by Gimson at Daneway. Requiring more chairs than he himself could turn on the pole lathe, he first sent his designs to High Wycombe, the main centre for chair-making in the country. However, the inferior quality of the wood used, and the poor workmanship left him dissatisfied with the finished objects, and he decided to see if a more satisfactory product could not be made locally, using the waterwheel at the Daneway sawmill to drive a lathe. Edward Gardiner, the son of the sawmill owner, was initially given the job of turning small items such as stretcher rails, but, when Gimson realised the young man's natural talent in this direction, he offered him the opportunity of full-time work as a chair-maker. Edward Gardiner wrote of his introduction to the craft in a letter to Edward Barnsley, written in 1956, two years before his death:

I knew nothing about woodturning so I bought a book on the subject, but I really got the right ideas and some knowledge about it from that wise old

112

craftsman, carpenter, blacksmith and what not, William Bucknell of Tunley. . . . He not only showed me what he could, but took me with him on a visit to see men turning at a Mill at Chalford and to Woodchester to the wood turning department of Workman Bros. There I saw how the tools were used, the force the men put behind their tools and the amazing rapidity and accuracy by eye alone, of their production. This was a revelation to me and later on I employed a Chalford wood turner at Daneway and learned a lot more.[8]

Edward Gardiner also had to master the art of rush seating and bead turning, through a process of trial and error:

After making a few chairs in plain turning, Mr Gimson brought down his first design in bead turning for chairs, soon followed by a design for a beaded settee. I was much disquieted by this as being only a beginner Mr Gimson was treating me like an experienced craftsman and I was not at all sure I could rise to it.

I had by this time got to know the men at Daneway House, and appreciate the quality of the work they were doing and I did not intend that my work should be in any way inferior to theirs in quality and accuracy, therefore, I took great pains to make a perfect job of each chair.[9]

The chair-making venture proved so successful that Edward Gardiner soon took on several assistants and apprentices. He remained at Daneway until 1913, when he moved to Warwickshire, intending to continue his craft there. His plans were forestalled by the outbreak of war, and it was not till 1920, when Sidney Barnsley asked him to make sixty chairs, to Gimson's design, for the Bedales Memorial Library, that he took up his craft once more. He soon found that the demand for such chairs was plentiful, and he continued in business until his death. Happily, his work is continued today by Neville Neal, based at Rugby, who makes a wide range of turned chairs, many to Gimson's original designs.

Another offshoot of the Daneway workshops was the metalworking concern. Gimson had an early interest in metalwork design, demonstrated by drawings of seventeenth-century firedogs, executed during a visit, with W. R. Lethaby, to Haddon Hall in Derbyshire, in 1889. It was inevitable that his high standards should lead him to design the metal fittings for his furniture, rather than to rely on commercially available items, and it was to fill this need that metalworking was begun at Daneway. Gimson's friend, Alfred Powell, who lived for a short while in the village of Oakridge, saw the work of Alfred Bucknell, the son of the village blacksmith at nearby Tunley, and suggested to Gimson that the young man showed promise. Gimson set Alfred Bucknell up with his own smithy, in the wheelwright's yard at Sapperton, in about 1903, and the two men, neither of them trained in the intricacies of fine metalwork, worked closely together to produce wonderful interpretations of Gimson's designs in iron, brass, polished steel and silver. Eventually there were four men working in the smithy: Bucknell

Above left Fig. 77. A pair of firedogs in pierced and chased wrought iron designed by Gimson and made in the Daneway smithy.
Above right Fig. 78. Pencil drawing of a seventeenth-century brass firedog at Haddon Hall, executed by Gimson in 1889.
Left Fig. 79. Two pairs of strap hinges and a bolt in wrought iron designed by Ernest Gimson and made in the Daneway smithy.
Below left Fig. 80. Door handle made by Alfred Bucknell to Gimson's design.
Below Fig. 81. Detail of a walnut wardrobe, designed and made by Sidney Barnsley in 1903, showing the stamped brass handles.

himself, Steve Mustoe, Fred Gardiner and Fred Messenger, whose place was later taken by Whiting, producing a wide variety of work, including handles, locks and other items for furniture, fireplace fittings, candlesticks and sconces, ecclesiastical metalwork, and architectural fitments such as window casements, latches and gates, all to Gimson's designs, and bearing his distinctive touch which gave vigour and individuality to the most mundane item. The candle sconces and firedogs made to Gimson's design, some of which are illustrated in these pages, show perhaps most successfully his treatment of naturalistic patterns. In most instances, Sidney Barnsley used the metal fitments made by Bucknell and his colleagues, to Gimson's designs, on his own furniture. He did however design at least one type of metal handle, which, he made himself on his own lathe. This delicate drop handle, made of either brass or gun metal, is found on a number of pieces of furniture made by Sidney Barnsley between about 1902 and 1905. Alternatively, he occasionally used commercially-produced fitments, such as brass ring handles, which he would stamp with a variety of simple designs, using metal dies.

The range of media encompassed by Gimson's activities was very wide. As well as designing plasterwork, furniture and metalwork, he also ventured into the field of two-dimensional pattern design. The book plate [Fig. 86] is a rare example of Gimson's work in this medium and he also produced a number of designs for leather book bindings. More common are his designs for needlework and embroidery, including several samplers. He relied almost entirely on nature as his source of inspiration for his embroidery designs, and their rhythmic flowing patterns and subtle colour schemes create what are amongst the most satisfying of his undertakings. The most effective and unusual designs are those executed in white silk thread on white linen [Fig. 84]. They were carried out by a number of individuals, including his wife, his sister, Margaret, his sisters-in-law, Phyllis and Nellie Lovibond, and Evelyn Bankart, the wife of G. P. Bankart who worked with Gimson on a number of plasterwork projects.

A correspondent to the magazine *Country Life* in 1908 criticised Gimson's furniture for having 'too close a kinship to the packing case'.[10] Despite this comment, Gimson and Sidney Barnsley developed a wide repertoire of decorative motifs early on in their careers, which they used on the whole range of their furniture designs. Many of the motifs were developed out of the techniques of construction used by both men. Such features as exposed dovetails were first developed by Sidney Barnsley at Pinbury, and were retained and refined in both men's work throughout their careers. Cogged dovetails were sometimes cut to different sizes so that a pattern of larger and smaller rhomboids would run down the sides of a piece of furniture. The idea of honesty of construction, developed by Sidney Barnsley at Pinbury, reversed the process of evolution in furniture design which, up until the mid nineteenth century, had been concerned with the progressive concealment of constructional features through the cabinet-maker's skill. The new obsession with honesty of construction, in the second half of the nineteenth century, through such features as exposed joints, was

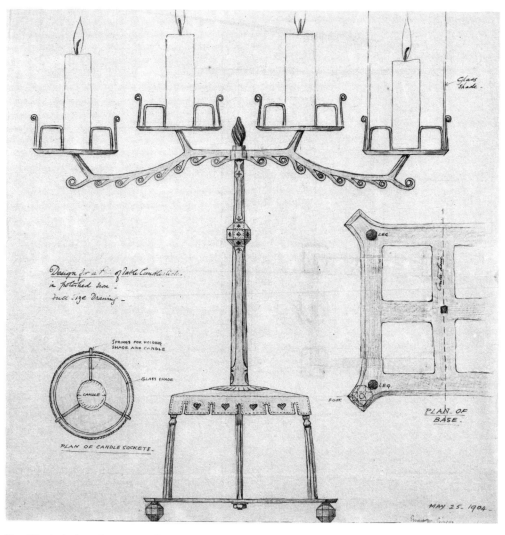

Fig. 82. A design for a pair of table candlesticks in polished iron, signed and dated 'Ernest W. Gimson, Designer, May 25 1904'. Full-size drawing in ink and crayon on tracing paper.

introduced in the work of Philip Webb and Ford Madox Brown, and had additional qualities which appealed to Gimson and the Barnsleys. The furniture made to conform to these principles was also endowed with some of the strength and frankness characteristic of the best seventeenth-century furniture, which they admired. In addition, all the details of construction had to be accurate, and the product of good workmanship, as they were visible to the naked eye. This exposed constructional work was retained in all the furniture designed by Gimson and Sidney Barnsley, even in the execution of more elaborate pieces made from exotic and beautifully grained woods. Although details such as exposed dovetails and double-dovetail joints were not used quite as frequently in their later work, they never lost their constructional significance, unlike those used by some of their contemporaries, which served a purely decorative purpose in a form of inverted snobbery.

Fig. 83. Design for an embroidery executed in coloured crayons by Ernest Gimson.

Fig. 84. Detail of a white linen washstand runner embroidered in white silk by Margaret Gimson to her brother's design, c. 1890.

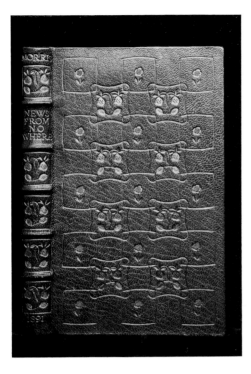

Fig. 85. A copy of *News from Nowhere* by William Morris, with leather binding designed by Ernest Gimson.

Fig. 86. A bookplate designed by Gimson for his brother, Sydney A. Gimson.

By about 1905, three main aspects of furniture design had emerged in the work of Gimson and Sidney Barnsley. Much of their oak furniture was influenced by vernacular woodworking traditions in its design and construction, although, in most cases, these traditions had never before been applied to furniture. Features such as hayrake and wishbone stretchers were derived from traditional designs, developed over many centuries by wheelwrights and other woodworkers to serve a practical purpose. In much the same spirit, these features were adopted by Gimson and Sidney Barnsley from the farm waggons, carts and farming implements, which were still in general use in the Cotswolds, to construct utilitarian and well-made furniture which also maintained a strong link with English vernacular traditions. The tables designed by the two men were particularly successful. Sidney Barnsley made a number of oak tables for Rodmarton Manor in this style, including the one illustrated here [Fig 88], which measures over two metres in length. The table top is made up of three planks of wood joined by wedged double dovetails which go right through its depth and serve a decorative as well as a functional purpose. The sturdy hexagonal legs are boldly buttoned to the horizontal surface, and the under-framing is completed by a vigorous combination of hayrake and wishbone stretchers, lightly chamfered to achieve their taut shape and maximum efficiency. Features of this vernacular style were often incorporated into more sophisticated designs. The chamfered shaping of the triangular supports of the mirror [Fig. 143] indicates the vernacular origins of the design, despite the delicate workmanship. Similarly, the walnut sideboard [Fig. 89] has a boldly-chamfered brown ebony underframing, and a plate rack whose inspiration had been clearly derived from the headboard of a farm waggon.

Fig. 87. Heel rake used for raking hay into winnows and for the final clearing of fields, from Tirley, Gloucestershire.

Fig. 88. Detail of a table designed and made by Sidney Barnsley for Rodmarton Manor, showing the use of hayrake and wishbone stretchers in its construction.

Fig. 89. Walnut sideboard with ebony underframing and plate rack, and chequered holly and ebony laid stringing, designed by Gimson and exhibited at the Arts and Crafts Exhibition, 1916.

The unusual oak chest with exposed ribbing [Fig. 134] was designed and made by Sidney Barnsley in 1905. Its design was derived from the raves and elbows which form the structure of the body of a farm waggon.

Inevitably, the most common decoration found on the simple 'cottage' furniture, designed by Gimson and Sidney Barnsley, was carried out using the techniques traditionally used by craftsmen to express their enjoyment and skill in their handling of the wood and their tools. Gouging was one such technique, and occasionally the difference in its use by the two men can provide a useful clue as to the designer of unprovenanced furniture. When used by Sidney Barnsley, the making of a line of gouged decoration on a piece of furniture was a relatively simple process, which he called 'tickling' the wood, and which could be done very quickly in two movements, when working with the grain on a pleasant wood. Using a small gouge, a sharp, downwards incision was made into the wood followed by a gentle upwards stroke, the sides of which would spread outwards. Gimson's use of gouging tended to be more precise, each incision having parallel sides, and therefore requiring more time and effort from the craftsman in its execution. The reason for this difference lay in the different lengths of time which each man could justifiably devote to the decoration of his furniture designs. Sidney Barnsley, because he was working entirely on his own, could not afford to undertake the precise style of gouging carried out by Gimson's craftsmen in the Daneway workshop. At the same time, however, gouging and chip-carving, usually in the form of a repeated square or diamond, were the simplest types of decoration used at Sapperton to add interest and to emphasise an outline or a plane.

Not all the oak furniture made by Gimson and Sidney Barnsley was in the vernacular, 'cottage' style. Instead its originality lay in the pruning of the design down to its basic essentials. It was the spirit of William Morris's dictum that all furniture should be made of planks and beams taken to its logical conclusion. At the same time, they were laying some of the foundations for the functionalism of the Modern Movement, in the twentieth century, although they called it 'workmanship, propriety or fitness for purpose'. The same approach to design can be seen in some of the work of other nineteenth- and early twentieth-century innovators such as Godwin, Mackmurdo, Voysey and Mackintosh and a parallel development can be seen in the work of several American designers, including the traditional furniture of the Shaker sect. The functional element in the work of the Cotswold School, based on plain surfaces and clean lines, was developed initially by Sidney Barnsley at Pinbury in the 1890s, at which time the simplicity of his designs was quite startling. The simplicity apparent in the design of such basic items as the oak settee [Fig. 64] and the walnut and chestnut sideboards [Figs. 89 and 145], designed by Gimson, provided a major challenge to most Victorian and Edwardian design, and, although the inspiration was often derived from traditional sources through their admiration for historical work and vernacular traditions, it was also used purely for its practical advantages. However, there was nothing consciously quaint in their approach as their nostalgia for the past and for rural pursuits was combined with an honest and straightforward attitude to design.

Throughout their careers, Gimson and Sidney Barnsley continued, with obvious enjoyment, to make what William Morris called 'state furniture', intended 'quite as much for Beauty's sake as for use'.[11] Their designs in this field were based on the careful and sympathetic study of the best old examples of furniture in museums and country houses. An obvious influence came from the seventeenth- and early eighteenth-century furniture makers of England and Holland, whose effective use of marquetry and inlaid decoration was particularly admired. Perhaps the most important contemporary influence was that of George Jack, who designed most of the furniture for Morris and Co. in the 1890s. George Jack's escritoire and stand [Fig. 90], made by Morris and Co. in 1892, and now in the collections of the Victoria and Albert Museum, was covered with flowing naturalistic patterns executed in marquetry of sycamore and other woods. The influence of such examples of contemporary furniture, as well as older pieces, was absorbed by Gimson and Sidney Barnsley, and, combined with their love of nature and respect for handwork, emerged in their furniture designs as something fresh and individual.

Gimson's participation in the mainstream of the Arts and Crafts Movement,

Above Fig. 90. Escritoire and stand with elaborate inlaid decoration designed by George Jack for Morris and Co. in 1892.
Right Fig. 92. The couch by Alfred Stevens referred to in the text, dating from the middle of the nineteenth century.

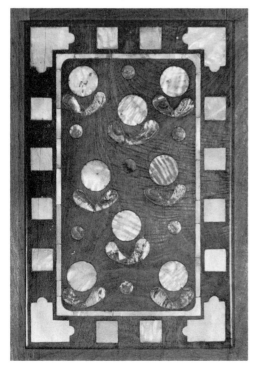

Fig. 91. Detail of mother-of-pearl inlay in the panel of a walnut wardrobe designed and made by Sidney Barnsley in 1903, and now in the collections of the Crafts Study Centre, Bath.

and in the design of 'state' furniture, can be seen at its strongest in his contributions to the 1916 Arts and Crafts Exhibition, where he was involved in the design of two room settings. Both he and Sidney Barnsley contributed furniture to the room laid out by Louise Powell, which featured twelve panels painted in egg tempera, surmounted by a plaster frieze designed and modelled by Gimson. He also designed a bedroom setting with May Morris which included furniture designed by the former and painted in vermilion by the latter. The centre piece of this room setting was a bedstead made at Daneway, decorated by May Morris, Ethel Everett, Alfred Powell and A. E. Swinney, and furnished with embroidered hangings. This piece was singled out for comment by the *Daily Chronicle* in its review of the exhibition:

> Am I exigent in saying that I find much of the modern furniture too self-conscious. Mr Ambrose Heal seems to me to hit the happy compromise in the war between decoration and structure; but Mr Gimson should be condemned to spend an hour a day for a week before a certain couch by Alfred Stevens[12] in the Bethnal Green Museum. And it rather spoils my afternoon to see a bed, however lavishly decorated, costing £170.[13]

A recurrent recipient of their elaborate workmanship was the cabinet, equipped with numerous pigeon holes, drawers and cupboards, often with a fall-front, on a stand. This type of furniture was derived from Spanish and Portuguese examples from the sixteenth and seventeenth centuries known as the 'vargueno'. Gimson and Sidney Barnsley would have been familiar with examples of this

Fig. 93. Mid-sixteenth-century vargueno.   Fig. 94. Macassar ebony cabinet on a stand.

type of furniture, in South Kensington Museum, which they used as the inspiration for their own designs. The cabinet [Fig. 95] with chequered walnut veneer is a fine example of Gimson's adaptation of the traditional 'vargueno' cabinet. The rectangular shape of the cabinet itself, dating from about 1903, is softened by the subtle faceting of the sides. The monotony of the chequered squares of veneers is enlivened by the herringbone inlay, outlining the basic silhouette of the cabinet, and by the central roundels of inlaid decoration. The cabinet sits on a very simple rectangular stand, whose only decoration derives from the brass ring handles and the half-ovolo moulding down the outer corners of each of the four legs. Gimson's ebony cabinet inlaid with mother–of–pearl [Fig. 94], made in the Daneway workshops in about 1907, illustrates another variation of the 'vargueno' design.

Various forms of inlaying were used by Gimson and Sidney Barnsley. At its most elaborate, this form of decoration consisted of panels of either naturalistic or abstract designs carried out in a variety of materials, including wood, bone, ivory, mother–of–pearl, coral or silver. It was Gimson, in particular, who refined this type of decoration, and applied it very successfully to furniture and ecclesiastical fittings, such as the candlesticks designed by him for the Debenham family, [Fig. 96]. The technique of inlaying was most commonly used by the two men on furniture, in the form of dark and light stringing, usually in ebony and holly or some other light-coloured fruitwood. Sheets of alternate holly and ebony veneer of equal thickness were glued together. The block thus formed was

Fig. 95. Walnut cabinet with a drop-front, faceted sides and inlaid herringbone stringing. The stand is very plain apart from ovolo mouldings down the sides of the legs. Designed by Ernest Gimson in about 1907.

Fig 96. Altar cross and candlesticks in black ebony and ivory, the cross additionally inlaid with red coral set in silver. Designed by Gimson in 1917 for St Peter's Church, Vere Street, London, and dedicated to the memory of Keith Debenham.

clamped together between two sheets of brown paper while it dried. When it was properly dry, slices, made up of alternate holly and ebony stripes, were cut off, using a small circular saw. The paper at either end of each slice was removed and lines of the required thickness were cut in the opposite direction. These lines, consisting of small pieces of alternate holly and ebony, were inlaid into a groove cut into the furniture. This decorative technique was used on much seventeenth-century furniture, particularly English and Dutch chests. Gimson originally used it in a similar fashion to these early craftsmen, flush with the surface, and up to half an inch wide, in his designs for Kenton and Co. In the Cotswolds, however, both he and Sidney Barnsley often left the inlaid stringing slightly proud from the surface, thus increasing its visual impact, whilst reducing its width. The technique was also used by a number of their contemporaries in the 1890s, including George Jack and Lewis F. Day, but its consistent use by Gimson and the Barnsleys has made it one of the hallmarks of their work.

The sheer quantity and variety of work carried out by Gimson and the Barnsleys in the field of furniture design provide an impressive testimonial to their achievements, which this more or less chronological account has attempted to survey. However, before the organisation of their workshops and their relationships with their clients can be discussed in greater detail, it is necessary to look at the architectural work which was tackled alongside their involvement with handicrafts, and which, in many cases, played an integral part in the development of their theories of design, and of their attitudes to standards of workmanship.

126

Chapter 8
Architectural work

Gimson and the Barnsleys continued to work as architects throughout their careers. As students of the profession, in London, they had absorbed the general precepts of Arts and Crafts theory, in relation to architecture, from pioneers in the field such as Philip Webb, John Sedding and Norman Shaw, and they continued to rely on these guidelines in all their building work. As far as they were concerned, the most important ideas to emerge from the Arts and Crafts Movement related to the need for simplicity, for the function to be honestly expressed, and for the establishment of a national style through the revived use of traditional constructional methods and local materials. The importance of 'manners' in architecture, of designing buildings which enhanced rather than dominated their surroundings, was a concept which recurred regularly in Arts and Crafts writings on the subject during this period, and one which was very relevant to all three men's work. Both Ernest and Sidney Barnsley fulfilled this criterion successfully, and their architectural work shows a profound sympathy for the natural surroundings, for vernacular traditions, and for the building materials and techniques adopted. Gimson's architectural work, particularly when one considers the scope of his designs, as well as his completed buildings, demonstrates all the qualities demanded by Arts and Crafts theory, enlivened by the impact of his original and individual approach, which links him with some of the most interesting and influential architects of the period such as W. R. Lethaby and Edward Prior.

It must be stated, however, that the amount of architectural work carried out by all three men was limited, firstly, by their preoccupation with handicrafts, particularly furniture-making; secondly, by their painstaking approach to the execution of their architectural projects; and thirdly, by the relatively few commissions received by them in this field. Most of their work, in common with that of the majority of Arts and Crafts architects, was concerned with small-scale domestic building, almost invariably in a rural setting. In addition, Gimson and the Barnsleys maintained their connection with the Society for the Protection of Ancient Buildings, and Gimson and Ernest Barnsley, in particular, undertook advisory and restoration work under its aegis throughout their careers.

The great proportion of Ernest and Sidney Barnsley's architectural work was carried out in the Cotswolds. Ernest Barnsley's career was dominated by Rodmarton Manor, the country house near Cirencester on which he began

Fig. 97. A contemporary photograph, formerly in the possession of Ernest Gimson, showing the construction of a cottage by traditional building methods.

work in 1909, after the collapse of the furniture-making partnership with Gimson, and which was not completed until after his death in 1929. He was only able to execute such a grandiose project as a result of the experience gained through his early work in the Cotswolds. He invariably worked very much at his own pace, and, following Philip Webb's example, he would take a keen interest in the design and execution of every minor detail in the construction of his buildings. According to Norman Jewson:

> He always had as much work as he wanted to do in his leisurely way, making all his own drawings and spending a great deal of time supervising the work, often staying with his clients, who enjoyed his company.[1]

On their removal to Pinbury Park, in 1894, it was Ernest Barnsley who was given the responsibility for alterations and renovations at that house, and at Daneway House, by their landlord, Lord Bathurst. His restoration work in both buildings was undertaken with a great deal of sensitivity to, and respect for, their original character. In a letter to Lord Bathurst, dated 1901, detailing the work already undertaken at Daneway, Ernest Barnsley wrote:

> Then in the autumn Mr Anderson [Lord Bathurst's estate manager] sent me instructions for the principal rooms to be painted white, the windows now plastered up to be reopened, and the range in the Dining Room to be

128

Fig. 98. Beechanger, the cottage at Sapperton built by Sidney Barnsley in about 1902.

removed. I went to see him and explained that this work would be thrown away unless the floors and the ceilings were made secure, and he agreed with me that this should be done. I had the floor boards removed from the walls in the rooms with the decorated plaster ceilings and then discovered (what is probably the case through the house) that the floor joists had rotted away where they were built into the walls, and this is the cause of the damaged ceilings. I had light scaffolding erected inside the rooms from floor to floor and the ceilings carefully packed, and the rotten ends of the joists were then removed and new pieces bolted onto the joists and made firm in the masonry; after this had been completed some months I had the scaffolding removed and I am glad to say the floors have not sunk at all and no injury has been caused to the ceiling.[2]

In anticipation of the return of the Bathurst family to Pinbury Park, Ernest Barnsley was commissioned, in 1902, to rebuild the early nineteenth-century wing at the rear of the house. The ground floor of the extension, conceived as one large room, was decorated with a plasterwork ceiling, designed and executed by Ernest Gimson, which admirably complements the oak-panelled walls and chimneypiece, also carried out to his design.

On the removal of Gimson and the Barnsleys to Sapperton, in 1902, each man built himself a cottage in that village. On the sloping site which fell to Ernest

Barnsley's share was a small, narrow, Cotswold stone cottage which, instead of demolishing, he used as the basis for a more imposing building, by the addition of a sizeable new wing at either end. The incorporation of existing vernacular structures into new buildings was a significant feature of Arts and Crafts architecture, indicative of the romantic enthusiasm for this aspect of the country's heritage, and was typical of Ernest Barnsley's concern for the preservation of the traditional environment. In this case, the restrictions imposed by the retention of the cottage, and the steepness of the site, gave rise to an imaginative solution in the final design of the building. Much of the character of Upper Dorval House, as Ernest Barnsley's home was named, derives from the impressive, tower-like three-storey structure at one end which makes an effective use of the steep gradient and owes much of its inspiration to the High Building added to Daneway House in the seventeenth century. This contrasts with the low-slung original cottage, whose interior was knocked into one room, and the kitchen wing. Ernest Barnsley made full use of Cotswold traditions in the materials, techniques of construction, design and proportions of his house, whilst at the same time creating a building which reflected the individuality of its designer and original owner. All the materials used in the building of Upper Dorval House came from the locality; the walls were of local stone, quarried from Sapperton Common, a lavish use was made of dressed stone from Minchinhampton for the window lintels, and stone tiles were used for the roofing. Ernest Barnsley gave this estimate of his building costs in an article in *Country Life* in 1909:

Mason – labour on house	580	0	0
,, ,, ,, stable, etc	98	7	10
,, ,, ,, hauling	32	0	0
Carpenter – labour on house	350	0	0
,, ,, ,, stable, etc	50	0	0
Tiler & plasterer – labour on house	199	0	0
,, ,, ,, ,, stable	45	0	0
Plumbing on house	91	0	0
Plaster floors	45	6	3
Dressed stone	110	0	0
Timber	80	0	0
Cement	20	0	0

£1700 14   1[3]

These figures indicate that Upper Dorval House can in no way be described as a cottage, according to Lawrence Weaver's definition in *The Country Life Book of Cottages*, published in 1913, which strictly excludes any building whose cost exceeded £600. In both the conception and the design of his house, Ernest Barnsley was clearly influenced by his work at Daneway and Pinbury Park; he commissioned Ernest Gimson to decorate the structural cross beams in the long hall on the ground floor with running plaster friezes, modelled in low relief, in a similar manner to the sixteenth-century plasterwork at Daneway House.

Fig. 99. A pair of cottages at Combe End Farm, near Cirencester, designed by Sidney Barnsley in about 1915.

Ernest Barnsley was also responsible for the design of two other buildings in Sapperton: a pair of cottages bordering Sapperton Common, at the west end of the village, and the Village Hall, built with the assistance of Norman Jewson in 1912, both of which were designed and carried out in the spirit of the Cotswold style and traditions, so that today they are impossible to distinguish at a glance from the older buildings in the village. In 1907, he received a commission to carry out alterations on a Cotswold stone cottage, then known as York House, in the village of Broadway, Worcestershire, from the bookbinder, Katharine Adams. The success of Ernest Barnsley's efforts to preserve the original character of the typical Cotswold building, whilst providing the necessary alterations and amenities, is borne out by this comment from an article on 'The Passing of Cotswold Architecture':

> And almost opposite the Eadburgha Bindery is a proof that by simple and tasteful alterations a little whitewashed village shop can be adapted for the residence of a lady and the carrying on of a craft whose products are sought by connoisseurs in many lands.[4]

Sidney Barnsley captured the same harmony, in keeping with the existing buildings, in the design of his cottage at Sapperton. Built on a smaller scale than Upper Dorval House, with a strong horizontal element typical of Cotswold vernacular building, and using local stone for the walls and roofing, this cottage, named Beechanger, was only the second building to be designed and built by Sidney Barnsley. The plan of the cottage was simple, straightforward and functional, in keeping with the modest requirements of the architect and his family. The living room incorporated one unusual feature in its design. Rough-hewn oak shelves were suspended by leather straps from the ceiling cross-beams, providing a visually successful solution to the storage of books.

Subsequently, in 1915, Sidney Barnsley undertook building work at Painswick, for Frederick Gyde. The commission included a terrace of almshouses and the Public Baths, both designed in an unassuming but totally appropriate style, which is echoed by the plain but beautifully-proportioned lettering carved in stone over the doorways of the latter by the calligrapher, Eric Gill. The growing concern for well-designed lettering, particularly in connection with architectural work, was fostered by a number of individuals within the Arts and Crafts Movement. It was W. R. Lethaby who, two years after his appointment as principal of the Central School of Arts and Crafts in 1896, established the first lettering classes, and installed Edward Johnston as their teacher. Amongst Johnston's original and most successful pupils was Eric Gill, who subsequently worked with Gimson and the Barnsleys on a number of projects. The modest design and sympathy for Cotswold traditions characteristic of Sidney Barnsley's work at Painswick can also be seen in his design for a pair of cottages at Combe End Farm, near Cirencester, built at about the same time. The dominant feature is the bold pattern of the corner-stones, reminiscent, in both function and appearance, of the exposed dovetails used in his furniture designs.

Sidney Barnsley showed the same respect for historic buildings and vernacular traditions as his elder brother, in the execution of three commissions received for the alteration and extension of large Cotswold houses in the 1920s. His first commission of this nature was for the enlargement of Combend Manor, a seventeenth-century house in the village of Elkstone, Gloucestershire, in 1921, which was followed by similar work at Painswick Lodge and at Cotswold Farm, near Duntisbourne Abbots, between 1924 and 1926. The latter building, an impressive stone farmhouse which dates from the seventeenth century, was extensively enlarged by Sidney Barnsley, and also contains a plasterwork ceiling designed and modelled by Norman Jewson, as well as stained glass designed by William Morris and Edward Burne-Jones.

Work on Rodmarton Manor began in 1909, when the Hon. Claud Biddulph, a banker based in London, commissioned Ernest Barnsley to design a small residence for himself and his family, which he called his 'cottage in the country',[5] on his Rodmarton estate. There was no suitable large house in the parish, the original manor house having been demolished in the eighteenth century, and Ernest Barnsley was given a virgin site and a more or less free hand in the design of this building. He was most fortunate in that his employer's ideas coincided very closely with his own.

Fig. 100. Rodmarton Manor, near Cirencester, Gloucestershire, designed by Ernest Barnsley and built by traditional methods, using local materials and workmen, between 1909 and 1929.

Mr Biddulph's plan in building was to spend £5,000 a year for a number of years. It seems that once work was underway, Ernest Barnsley elaborated the possibilities of the venture so beguilingly that his client's enthusiasm kindled and Rodmarton became not only a large country house but a centre for crafts and the education of the tenantry.[6]

The inscription on the front of the house of the following lines from Oliver Goldsmith's poem 'The Deserted Village', illustrates admirably the ideals of both client and architect:

> Ill fares the land, to hastening ill a prey,
> Where wealth accumulates, and men decay;
> Princes and lords may flourish, or may fade,
> A breath can make them, as breath has made;
> But a bold peasantry, their country's pride,
> When once destroyed can never be supplied.

In his design for Rodmarton Manor, Ernest Barnsley was attempting to repeat, on a large, imposing scale, what he and his brother had already achieved in the construction of their own cottages at Sapperton; that is, to build, decorate and furnish a house using only local materials and labour, and thus to revive local traditions and skills. He worked closely with the estate's workmen at Rodmarton, who were under the direction of the foreman/carpenter, Alfred Wright. Fred Baldwin, the local blacksmith, was responsible for all the ironwork and the metal door- and window-fittings, whilst the gardens were laid out by another local man, William Scrubey. All the stone and slate was quarried nearby, brought on to the site by farmcart, and cut, shaped and laid by local masons. The oak used for the roof timbers and floors was felled and seasoned on the estate, and the local carpenters and joiners who worked on it also made much of the furniture for the house, using, in some cases, designs provided by Ernest and Sidney Barnsley, and working under their supervision.

Fig. 101. The Kitchen Court, Rodmarton Manor, the first wing of the house to be built, and the most modest in scale and conception.

Ernest Barnsley's conception of the design of Rodmarton Manor grew as the work progressed, and the modest country residence which Claud Biddulph had originally envisaged developed into what has been described as the 'last great house built in England'.[7] The earliest part of the house, the kitchen wing, on the eastern side, is built on a smaller scale, and to a more modest design, than the later additions. The main scheme consists of a three-storey building, with its north-facing, multi-gabled facade forming three sides of an octagon. The forecourt, encircling an imposing expanse of lawn, creates a powerful rhythm as it sweeps round the façade and the subordinate wings. The asymmetrical grouping of the gables, the hipped roofs and the eaves, and the variety in design of the chimneys are all closely based on vernacular Cotswold types. According to *The Builder*:

> From the length of its frontage and the multiplicity of its gables (character-istic as they are of the Gloucestershire type), it has the somewhat unfortunate skyline effect of an upturned and magnified saw, but apart from this, is marked by interesting grouping and details.[8]

The inclusion of two loggias, probably used as open-air bedrooms when the English climate permitted, on the first floor of the main block at Rodmarton, blurs the differentiation between indoors and outdoors. The south-facing side of the building, which provides the outlook for the main living rooms, commands

134

Above Fig. 102. Rodmarton Manor, the chapel wing to the west, from an early photograph taken before the gardens were laid out. Note the loggia on the first floor, with an almost Italianate balcony.

Right Fig. 103. The Chapel, Rodmarton Manor.

the most impressive views of the lush garden and, in the distance, the rolling countryside of the Berkshire Downs. The garden was designed as an integral part of the conception of Rodmarton Manor, with a fairly formal layout, which becomes wilder, and more in tune with nature, at a distance from the house. In adopting this device, Ernest Barnsley was putting into practice the theories of his former employer, the architect, J. D. Sedding, expounded in *Garden Craft Old and New*, published in 1891. The splendour of this vista is set off by the simplicity of the interiors, which are decorated with plain, white walls and brown oak doors and ceilings. In many cases, the ceiling beams provide the most striking features of the interiors, with the intermediate, as well as the cross-timbers, exposed. This feature of the interior design is most effectively exploited in the chapel, where the cool, Spartan surroundings are enriched by the cambered and chip-carved ceiling beams in mature brown oak. The powerful contrast between masses of dark and light creates an almost abstract pictorial effect, which constantly draws one back to this part of Rodmarton Manor. It fulfills, without doubt, Lethaby's definition of architecture as 'building touched with emotion'.[9]

The completion of Rodmarton Manor was held up by the outbreak of the First World War in 1914, and, although it was occupied full-time by the Biddulphs from 1917 onwards, work continued for a further twelve years. After Ernest Barnsley's death, in January 1926, the building work was supervised by Sidney Barnsley, and finally completed by Norman Jewson in 1929. The strong craft element which played such an important role in the building of Rodmarton Manor was fostered by the benevolent patronage of the Biddulphs. The local inhabitants were encouraged to visit the house for instruction in useful and traditional handicrafts. In 1920, for example, classes in woodworking were held, under the supervision of several of Peter Waals's cabinet-makers. The house and the ideas which lay behind its conception made a tremendous impression on C. R. Ashbee, whose visit to Rodmarton in October 1914 inspired the following entry in his journal:

> I've seen no modern work equal to it, nothing I know of Lutyens or Baker comes up to it. And when I ask why I find the answer in the system, the method rather than the man. It is a house built on the basis not of contract but of confidence and Barnsley has been allowed a free hand to put all his personal knowledge and technique into the work. The Eng. Arts and Crafts Movement at its best is here – so are the vanishing traditions of the Cotswolds.[10]

Rodmarton Manor remains largely unaltered today, and, furnished as it is with the work of two generations of Barnsleys, Peter Waals, and contemporary craftsmen working in the same tradition, provides an impressive monument to the fine design and craftsmanship of the Cotswold School.

Ernest Barnsley's only major commission, apart from Rodmarton Manor, was for work at Bledislowe Lodge, Coates, near Cirencester. In 1921, he rebuilt

Fig. 104. A pair of cottages near Markfield, Leicester, built for James Bilson in 1897. These were the first of four buildings designed by Gimson to fit into the rugged landscape of the Charnwood Forest.

Fig. 105. Stoneywell Cottage, Leicestershire, designed by Gimson as a summer retreat for his elder brother, Sydney, in 1898. The original thatch roof and part of the main chimney stack were replaced after a fire.

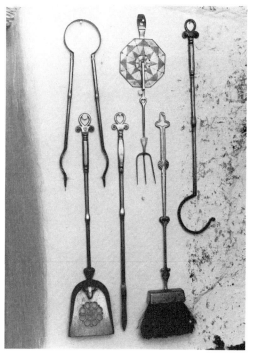

Fig. 106. Interior of the upper floor of Stoneywell Cottage.

Fig. 107. A set of fire-irons designed by Ernest Gimson for Stoneywell Cottage.

this late eighteenth-century house using stone from Ham House, an Adam-style mansion near Birmingham, which had been recently demolished. He also built a cottage, Rowbrook, on a remote part of Dartmoor, which only survives today in photographs. These show a very attractive, stone-built cottage, dominated by a powerful exposed chimney stack at one end, with a thatched roof. This is the only example of Ernest Barnsley's use of thatch; it was not a type of roofing indigenous to the Cotswolds and therefore not appropriate to the majority of his work.

All Gimson's architectural work after the completion of the White House, at Leicester, in 1896, was rural in its setting, although some of the finest examples of his subsequent buildings were carried out in the vicinity of his home town. During the course of his career, he built five cottages in Charnwood Forest, a very beautiful but remote and rugged area to the north-west of Leicester, with which Gimson had been familiar since early childhood. The first pair of cottages to be built were for James Bilson, and laid the foundations for the design of Stoneywell and Lea Cottages, built by Gimson between 1898 and 1899 as summer houses for his brothers, Sydney and Mentor Gimson. The ground plan for Stoneywell was dictated by the outcrops of hard rock on the site which were used wherever possible as the foundations, whilst local stone, including large rough boulders and old dry walls, was used as the basic building material. On the highest point of the natural foundations was built a large chimney, dominating the design, whilst the rest of the cottage continues downward from this point, following the natural contours of the slope in an open zigzag. It is these factors which give Stoneywell its 'organic' quality, and kinship with the natural landscape, which many Arts and Crafts architects struggled self-consciously to achieve. The originality of this cottage was acknowledged by the architectural commentator, Lawrence Weaver, who described it as 'frankly an unusual product of the building art'.[11] However, his fears that the exposed site and the Spartan interior would discourage all but the most hardy of inhabitants who shared Gimson's brand of puritanism and love of the simple life have, in the long run, been proved groundless, for Stoneywell Cottage is still inhabited and, with the alterations subsequently carried out by Gimson's nephew, Humphrey, now provides a comfortable home throughout the year.

Detmar Blow's contribution was particularly useful as far as the masons' work was concerned, for he had begun his architectural career by apprenticing himself to that trade in Newcastle-upon-Tyne. Under Blow's supervision, the colour, shape and placing of each stone were carefully chosen, before being laid in thick mortar joints, whilst the disused quarries near the site provided slates for the lintels over the doors and windows. The interior decoration was as sparse and powerful as the building itself. Detmar Blow found a massive shard of slate in a disused quarry, weighing approximately one and a half tons, which was used as the lintel over the kitchen fireplace. All the walls were whitewashed, contrasting with the brown oak woodwork, and the variations in levels, and sharp angles, created by the combination of the zigzag plan on the sloping site provide a constant source of visual interest. The constructional timbers and internal wood-work were provided by Richard Harrison, and the Sapperton blacksmith was responsible for all the metalwork. Despite this division of labour between Leicestershire and the Cotswolds, and the unusual character of the cottage, the final cost of Stoneywell, £920, was not excessive for its size. However, from the following note, appended to a working drawing by Gimson for the design of stables and outbuildings at Stoneywell, the cost of the cottage appears to have been more than its owner expected:

> Dear Syd., I should like your comments on this plan – I have been into the cost of the carpentry with Harrison *carefully* and exclusive of railway carriage and hauling from Bardon it comes to about £165 – in larch – in addition to this of course there is the mason's work in the foundations and chimney and the cost of the slating, glazing and small painting – and also the yard.
> If you are really inclined to have it done this year, it would be a great help to Harrison if it could be quickly decided as the trees could then be cut before the sap begins to rise. I should like this time to get estimates from Harrison and Chapman so that you don't have to rely on my 'probable cost' (as if you ever would again).[12]

Both Stoneywell and Lea Cottages were originally thatched although, in both cases, the thatch has subsequently been destroyed by fire. Stoneywell now has a slate roof but Lea Cottage has had its thatch replaced, presenting a very picturesque appearance in combination with its lime-washed walls. They were both furnished almost entirely with furniture and metalwork designed by Gimson and the Barnsleys. The fifth cottage designed by Gimson in the Charnwood Forest was Rockyfield, a rather modest exercise in a similar style, built in 1908 for his sister, Margaret, at a cost of £600.

The contemporary photographs showing the cottage which Gimson built for himself at Sapperton in 1902, about 100 yards down the road, away from the village, from that of Sidney Barnsley, illustrate admirably Gimson's skilful manipulation of different textures in his buildings. The combination of the rough-hewn stone walls surmounted by the luxuriously thick thatch roof executed by John Durham, a master-craftsman in this field, from Fifield, Oxford-shire, created a powerful contrast. The numerous dormer windows and the undulations of their hoods carry the eye from one end of the cottage to the other. The original thatch was destroyed by fire in 1941, and the roof was subsequently stone-tiled, which, although more in keeping with local practice, does not impart the same organic quality to the building, itself much altered since its construction. The interior of the cottage was modestly decorated with plain, white walls and oak beams and floors, and furnished with the products of his own and Sidney Barnsley's workshops, as well as pieces of simple seventeenth- and eighteenth-century furniture which were amongst his and his wife's well-loved treasures.

The only one of Gimson's thatched cottages whose original roof has not been destroyed by fire is Long Orchard, at Budleigh Salterton, Devon. This cottage was designed in 1912 for Basil Young, who had been employed for a brief period as one of Gimson's architectural assistants at Sapperton, and who acted as his own builder on this project. The walls of the cottage were of cob rather than stone. Gimson chose to use this technique, which was at that time a dying craft, in a conscious attempt to revive its use, and he left this description of the process used in the construction:

> The cob was made of stiff sand found on the site; this was mixed with water and a great quantity of long wheat straw trodden into it. The walls were built 3 feet thick, pared down to 2ft. 6ins., and were placed on a plinth standing 18ins. above the ground floor, and built of cobble stones found amongst the sand. The walls were given a coat of plaster and a coat of rough-cast, which was gently trowelled over to smooth the surface slightly.
> I believe eight men were engaged in the cobwork, some preparing the material, and others treading it into the top of the walls. It took them about three months to reach the wall plate, the cost was six shillings a cubic yard, exclusive of the plastering. No centering was used.
> The joists rested on plates and above them the walls were reduced to 2ft. 6ins. in thickness to leave the ends of the joists free. The beams also rested on wide plates and the ends were built round with stone, leaving

Fig. 108. Lea Cottage, Leicestershire, designed by Gimson in 1898 and built with lime washed granite walls and a straw-thatched roof. The clerk of works supervising the building of both this and Stoneywell Cottage was Detmar Blow.

space for ventilation. Tile or slate lintels were used over all the openings. The cost of the whole house was 6½d. a cubic foot.

Building with the cob is soon learnt – of the eight men only one of them had any previous experience, and I believe he had not built with it for 30 years. This is the only house I have built with cob.[13]

Gimson employed three architectural assistants whilst working at Sapperton. The first and most important of these was Norman Jewson, who was taken on as an 'improver' in 1907, and spent the rest of his career at Sapperton, working for both Gimson and Ernest Barnsley, as well as on his own account. Two other assistants, G. Basil Young and Walter Gissing, son of the novelist, George Gissing, were taken on for a short time in 1910. These assistants would often superintend building work on site for Gimson; for example, according to Jewson, in 1914 Walter Gissing was responsible for supervising the construction of the cottages designed by Gimson for May Morris at Kelmscott. Gimson's assistants were also often involved in projects initiated by the Society for the Protection of Ancient Buildings. William Weir, who had taken over responsibility for the Society's practical work from Philip Webb, worked throughout the country with his own team of trained builders and craftsmen, but often turned to Gimson for assistance, particularly where woodworking was involved. In 1911, Norman Jewson was sent to Norfolk to supervise the installation of interior fittings at Salle Church. The drawing for this project by Gimson which is in Cheltenham

Museum, shows how the original seatends, with carved poppy-heads or finials, were retained in the new seating. It was also the Society's policy that, where original stonework tracery was destroyed, it should not be 'restored' in stone in an imitation of the original style. Instead, wood was sometimes used so that the repair would be immediately obvious, and Gimson was called upon to assist the Society's team of craftsmen in many such cases. Perhaps his most successful scheme was in the repair of the tracery to a window at Whaplode Church, Lincolnshire, carried out in English oak, and creating a harmonious but original substitute for the destroyed stonework. Gimson was concerned with restoration work, in conjunction with the S. P. A. B., in numerous buildings throughout the country, including Ratcliffe on Soar Church, Nottinghamshire (1905), Staverton Church, near Daventry (1909), Ranworth Church, Norfolk (1910), Tredunnoc and Skenfrith Churches, Monmouthshire (1910), Llandletty Church, Bwlch, Brennock (1912), Ferry Hinksey Church, near Oxford (1913) and, according to Norman Jewson, a fourteenth-century priest's house at Mulchelney, Somerset.

Gimson's major architectural achievement was his work for Bedales School, Hampshire. His original contact with the school was made through Oswald Powell, Alfred Powell's brother, who taught at Bedales. Links between the school and the craftsmen at Sapperton were further strengthened when Sidney Barnsley sent his two children, Grace and Edward, there. Gimson's original commission from Bedales was for an assembly hall, which was built in 1910 by

Fig. 109. The Hall, Bedales School, Petersfield, Hampshire, 1910. In this design, Gimson successfully applied decorative features, such as hipped gables, dormer windows and asymmetrical bays, developed in his small-scale domestic architecture, to a much larger, brick-built, public building. The effect achieved is an imposing if rather severe one, with exciting contrasts of texture between expanses of roof tile and brick, and the variety of curves and angles within a basic rectangular framework.

Fig. 110. The Library, Bedales School, built to Gimson's design after his death by Geoffrey Lupton and Edward Barnsley under the supervision of Sidney Barnsley, 1920.

Fig. 111. The interior of the Hall at Bedales, built to Gimson's design by Geoffrey Lupton.

Fig. 112. Memorial Cross, Minchinhampton, Gloucestershire, designed by Sidney Barnsley in 1919.

Fig. 113. Design for a proposed cottage at Sonning, Berkshire, for William Holman Hunt, dated June 1900.

Geoffrey Lupton, who had attended the school before working as a pupil of Gimson at Daneway. The materials used in the construction of the hall were local, hand-made bricks, plain, hand-cut roof tiles and English oak, to create a simple but impressive barn-like structure. The internal use of massive oak buttresses, which rise to support the roof, is reminiscent of the technique used, in stone, by Edward Prior at Roker Church between 1904 and 1907. In 1919, Gimson completed his plans for an addition, in the form of a library, to the group of War Memorial buildings for Bedales School. This Library was not constructed until after his death, by Geoffrey Lupton with the assistance of Edward Barnsley, under the supervision of Sidney Barnsley. The ironwork was made locally by Stevie Mustoe who had previously worked in the smithy at Daneway.

The end of the First World War, in 1918, and the resulting spate of memorials erected throughout the country, provided several commissions for Gimson and Sidney Barnsley. As well as the War Memorial Buildings at Bedales, Gimson designed a Memorial Cross for the village of Fairford, erected in the churchyard, which was the last piece of work completed before his death in August 1919. Sidney Barnsley designed a number of memorials for villages in Gloucestershire, including stone crosses for Poulton and Minchinhampton. The latter, illustrated above, is a particularly fine example of this type of work, incorporating sober but attractive naturalistic patterns in its design.

Some of Gimson's most original and exciting architectural work is known

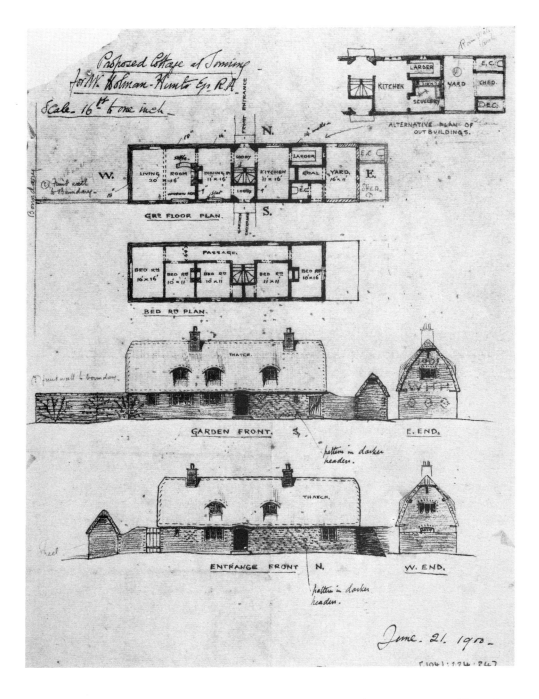

only through his working drawings. One cannot help feeling a sense of loss that some of his most interesting architectural projects were never built. A drawing dated June 1900 shows plans and elevations for a proposed cottage for the Pre-Raphaelite painter, William Holman Hunt at Sonning, Berkshire, which was never built. The simple, barn-like structure was intended to be constructed in red brick, with darker headers forming a pattern over the entire surface area. The strong, horizontal and low-pitched design of this cottage is emphasised by

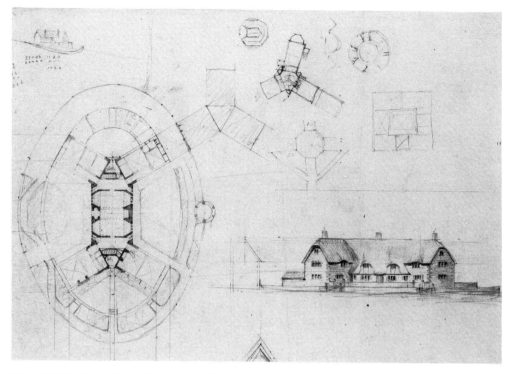

Fig. 114. Undated design for a 'butterfly' plan cottage by Ernest Gimson, probably about 1900.

the thatched roof, whilst the asymmetrical placing of the doors and windows contributes to its unusual character. Gimson's interest in the craft of thatching remained constant throughout his career, and, unlike Ernest and Sidney Barnsley, he tended to use thatch as a roofing material irrespective of any local traditions. In 1914, Gimson wrote to Mervyn Macartney, then editor of *The Architectural Review*, offering to write an article on thatching for the journal. Although the response from *The Architectural Review* was enthusiastic, the article never went into print, and, indeed, may never have been written, bearing in mind Gimson's reluctance to write about his work when he could be doing it.

Several of Gimson's architectural designs make an interesting use of the 'X' or butterfly plan, introduced most effectively as a feature of Arts and Crafts architecture by Edward Prior in the layout of The Barn, at Exmouth, Devon, built in 1897. The latter has been described as 'one of the two or three most original and influential houses of the Arts and Crafts Movement in the 1890s both in plan and in use of materials'.[14] Gimson was acquainted with Edward Prior from his student days in London, and subsequently worked for him in the furnishing of Roker Church, Sunderland, between 1904 and 1906. The 'X' plan was also used by Gimson's friend and colleague, Detmar Blow, in the design for a house at Happisburgh, Norfolk, built in about 1900. According to *The Architectural Review*:

146

This house is situated on the coast of Norfolk on high sandy ground close to the sea, in a small village of flint-built houses with reed-thatched roofs and a church with a very lofty tower. The house is built entirely of beach shingle and flints bonded with bricks; the roof covered with reeds grown on the estate; with the exception of some woods and glass, nothing was imported. It was built by the men of the district, assisted by a foreman and other leading men who work with the architect on buildings in various counties. The house was designed for a seaside residence, and planned to give shelters from wind in the gardens. On the ground floor are the usual sitting-rooms and offices, and cellars below. On the first floor and attic floor are eighteen bed and dressing rooms. The floors are of fire-resisting concrete. The cost, including the terraces, gardens, houses, coach-house and stabling for three horses, was £4,500.[15]

It is possible that one of the 'leading men' who worked with Detmar Blow on this project may have been Ernest Gimson, for there exists, amongst the latter's working drawings, a ground-floor plan identical to that of this house, which appears to be in his hand. Detmar Blow acknowledged the role played by Gimson in the conception of this design. According to Lawrence Weaver, writing in 1919:

Houses with wings set at angles are now not at all infrequent, but the crop of them has risen recently. Mr Prior was one of the first to carry out the idea of a sun-trap plan, in a house at Exmouth. That, however, had such wings on one side only, so that to Mr Blow must be given the credit of taking the lead in building one with a double pair of them. He does not himself lay claim to the idea but says that it 'Originated with my friend, Mr Ernest Gimson, who sent the little butterfly device on a postcard'.[16]

Gimson himself designed several houses which experiment with variations on the basic 'butterfly' plan, including one intended for the Norfolk village of Bacton. This house, which was never built, appears to have been rather more modest in its conception than the one at Happisburgh, although relying on the same local materials, and Gimson's drawings, illustrated here [Fig. 114], indicate his effective exploitation of the striking coastal site.

Gimson appears to have been acutely conscious of his failure to accomplish any major work in the field of architecture, and of his estrangement from the mainstream of the architectural profession in the early twentieth century. This attitude on Gimson's part provides an explanation for his entry in two major architectural competitions in about 1911 as his only course to establish his reputation as an architect. The first of these competitions was for the Port of London Authority Building on the Trinity Square site in the City of London. The winning entry was produced by Edwin Cooper, whose vigorous Edwardian Baroque design was built between 1912 and 1922. Gimson's entry for this competition [Fig. 115] was a free and simplified translation of the work of early eighteenth-century architects such as Wren, Hawksmoor and Vanburgh, the

Fig. 115. Gimson's design for the new head offices of the Port of London Authority.

style which had been generally adopted by the Arts and Crafts Movement as a suitable inspiration for large-scale public building. The first influential recourse to this source was provided by John Belcher, in his entry for the Victoria and Albert Museum competition in 1891. Although Belcher's design was unsuccessful, it made a profound impression on many of his contemporaries and, in particular, on his fellow-members in the Art Workers' Guild. The use of turrets and arches in Gimson's Port of London Authority design show clearly the influence of Belcher's work and of Norman Shaw's New Scotland Yard, as well as Gimson's own acute observations of proportions and details of design from seventeenth-century buildings throughout England. The geometric placement of masses in the tower structure of Gimson's design bears some similarity to the Midland Bank building in Manchester, designed by Edwin Lutyens in 1929. This is by no means the only comparison which can be drawn between the two men's work and it is interesting to conjecture whether they ever met; it is possible they may have done so in 1907, when Lutyens was building a group of almshouses in the Cotswold village of Upper Slaughter.

At almost the same time, Gimson also entered the international competition sponsored by the Australian Government for the new state capital at Canberra. The winning entry came from the American architect, Walter Burley Griffin, and the runners up were architects from Holland and France. Very few British architects entered this competition, as the conditions set for the judging of entries by the Australian Government did not meet with the approval of the R. I. B. A.

Fig. 116. Aerial view of Gimson's competition design for the new state capital of Canberra, executed for the designer by Alfred Powell.

According to the *Town Planning Review* of October 1912: 'probably not more than half-a-dozen competitors – and these men who do not represent the cream of the profession – submitted designs from this country'.[17] The fact that Gimson was amongst these half-a-dozen illustrates his eagerness to achieve some recognition in the architectural field. Gimson's design for the Canberra site was dominated by an artificial lake, created by a weir across the Molonglo River, which would provide recreational facilities for the new city, as well as enhancing the natural landscape. The 'X' plan reappeared in his design for the State Hall, around which many of the other public buildings were grouped. In addition to the city centre consisting of public and recreational buildings and shops, he also included an industrial area and a garden suburb on his plan, and his report included the following paragraph for the design of the streets and roads:

> To give a sheltered walk in the hot and wet weather a covered arcade is suggested 20 feet across and running nearly the whole length of the road on the lake side as shown in the two views. This arcade in the author's opinion while screening in some measure the near part of the lake from the ground floor windows of the houses opposite, would enhance rather than diminish, the interest of the wider views. The houses on this road would be set back 40 feet. It is assumed that they would have wide frontages and that their principal sitting rooms would be on the first floor. The first street parallel to the embankment road would be a residential street with the houses set back 16 or 20 feet. The second parallel street would be a

broad avenue with shops in the central part set back under arcades making the widths of paths and roadways 120 feet.[18]

In these and other ways, Gimson endeavoured, not altogether successfully, to reconcile his vision of the self-sufficient community in harmony with its surroundings with the needs and demands of a twentieth-century city. The importance which Gimson himself attached to his designs for Canberra is indicated by the fact that his sole entry to the eleventh Arts and Crafts Exhibition, in 1912, was three drawings related to this project.

In the last years of his life, Gimson worked as an architect in partnership with F. L. M. Griggs, better known today for his work as an engraver. They executed several commissions together, including extensive work at Stonyhurst College, Lancashire, and a house at Norsebury, near Winchester. Griggs's tribute to Gimson in the *Life and Work* memorial volume includes this paragraph, which is a fitting conclusion to this brief survey of the architectural work of Gimson and the Barnsleys:

> It will be understood that in building, as in his other crafts, his 'designs' were not drawn to look well on paper. The purpose of the building was kept before him, the site carefully noted, local labour and materials and their traditional usage studied, and then followed – not a mimicry of any bygone 'style', but something of today, so honest and natural, so familiar to the ground and welcome to the site, that it was, as it were, of local family and descent. It soon looked as if Nature herself had taken a hand in maturing it, and a good deal 'older' (as in truth it was) than the 'gothic' and 'Jacobean' houses of yesterday. I heard a visitor once ask him the age of his house, expecting to hear a history. 'Let me see', he replied, 'it must be nearly seventeen years old'. There was an excuse for the question, – modern houses do not look like that. Yet there was nothing old in that room except a clock and a few books and such like, nor anything that pretended to be old. Newly cut stone and oak, bright steel and glass, and white walls reflecting the sunshine – nothing was there but for use or comfort, and all without any sort of make-believe.[19]

Fig. 117. A front elevation of the same competition entry, executed in pencil and watercolour by Alfred Powell to Gimson's design, 1911.

Chapter 9
Woodworking

Gimson and the Barnsleys restricted themselves almost entirely to the use of locally-obtainable timber in the early stages of their careers at Pinbury. Oak was the staple wood used in the execution of their furniture designs, although examples in deal, elm and chestnut are also found during this period. Gimson relied on ash to make his turned chairs, though a few examples survive in yew or beech. Sidney Barnsley, the only one of the three men to be consistently involved in furniture-making at Pinbury, worked mainly in oak, for several reasons. Firstly, in much the same way that he used local materials and vernacular traditions in his architectural work, he used oak because it was available locally and was the traditional material used in furniture-making. Secondly, the fact that oak was readily available meant that it was cheaper than most other woods, an important consideration as Sidney Barnsley was developing woodworking skills by a process of trial and error. Thirdly, oak had a strong national and emotional appeal; it was the basic material used by the furniture-makers of the seventeenth and early eighteenth centuries, to whose work Sidney Barnsley was strongly attracted, and was thus very suited to his designs. Above all, oak has many pleasing and enduring qualities, which become apparent through sympathetic treatment by the designer and woodworker; it is long-lasting, hard, with an attractive though unassuming figure, and has a pleasant colour which matures well. However, it is worth bearing in mind that, by the end of the nineteenth century, oak was not used in the construction of most 'cottage' furniture, for the average villager could not afford items made from this traditional material and relied instead on furniture manufactured from poorer quality beech or deal.

When designing furniture for Kenton and Co., Gimson and Sidney Barnsley had enjoyed using imported woods, such as mahogany and ebony, often in combination with exotic veneers, yet they were still able to make effective use of oak when they first settled in the Cotswolds. The oak used by Gimson and the Barnsleys at Pinbury and, later, at Sapperton was acquired from a number of local sources, including the Sapperton carpenter and wheelwright, Richard Harrison, with whom they developed a close working relationship, enabling them to obtain the amount and quality of wood which they required. Harrison would fell the trees locally, and some of the necessary seasoning would be done on his premises. Most of the wood used by Gimson and the Barnsleys would have been air- rather than kiln-dried, a process which took a number of years to reach completion. The majority of oak logs used would have been quartered

Fig. 118. Oak cabinet on a stand with inlaid stringing of holly and ebony and metal drop handles designed by Sidney Barnsley for the architect and etcher, F. L. M. Griggs, 1910. *Right* Fig. 119. Dresser in oak made in the Daneway workshops to Gimson's plain but sophisticated design for F. L. M. Griggs, 1917, and *below left* detail of the wooden handles of the dresser doors.
Below right Fig. 120. Miniature cabinet of drawers in oak with multi-fielded panels and metal drop handles designed by Gimson in about 1906.

which, although wasteful, provided an attractive figure. One of the most successful pieces of oak furniture produced at Sapperton is the cabinet, designed and made by Sidney Barnsley in about 1910, and subsequently acquired by F. L. M. Griggs [Fig. 118]. The wide expanse of undecorated surface allows the natural beauty of the material free play, whilst the colour of the wood, originally a pale yellow, has mellowed to a rich light brown. F. L. M. Griggs also commissioned an oak dresser, from Gimson, for his house at Chipping Campden. This piece was designed with great subtlety, giving an overall impression of simplicity whilst avoiding all the pitfalls of heaviness and clumsiness inherent in this type of traditional 'cottage' furniture. This was achieved partly through the variations in the outline – the dresser has a slight bow-front whilst the upper part has a shallow break-front – partly through the quality of the wood and the workmanship, particularly noticeable in the mitred and cushioned shaping of the cupboard doors, and partly through the vitality of the gouged decoration. Another effective use of oak can be seen in the lattice-back settee, designed by Gimson and made for his house at Sapperton, whose bold chamfers and powerful design give this piece of furniture a very dramatic and rough-hewn impact.

Although, by the end of their careers, the scope of the work undertaken by Gimson and Sidney Barnsley in the field of furniture design was much wider than it had been at Pinbury, neither of them ever forsook the simple oak furniture which had been the mainstay of their early work. Gimson has been said to have preferred this type of furniture to the more elaborate pieces upon

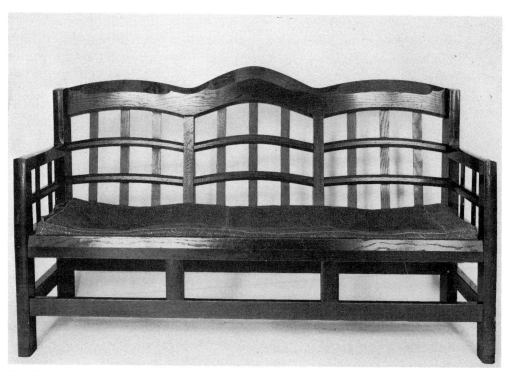

Fig. 121. Oak settee with a chamfered back rest, closely resembling a design by Gimson for a sedilia for Roker Church, Sunderland, in 1906.

which the economics of his situation encouraged him to concentrate. Sidney Barnsley's output in his later years was also dominated by more elaborate work using expensive woods, although he continued to make some plain oak furniture, similar in character to the chests and dressers which he had made at Pinbury. One of the last pieces which he produced at Sapperton was in this vein; an oak dresser with wooden handles, unornamented apart from some chip-carved decoration. This dresser was commissioned in 1922 by Ambrose Heal, a director of the London store of the same name, and a gifted furniture designer in his own right. It was Ambrose Heal who, as early as 1898, had produced a *Catalogue of Plain Oak Furniture*, launching the range of furniture which was to become a staple part of the output of Heal and Sons, and which established the store as one of the major suppliers of contemporary furniture designs in Britain. Ambrose Heal took great interest in Sidney Barnsley's design for the oak dresser, and the working drawings for this piece which have survived all include his annotations. The fact that a colleague of the stature of Ambrose Heal, who was at the forefront of contemporary design in the 1920s, should have given Sidney Barnsley this commission, indicates the esteem in which the latter was held by many of his more discerning contemporaries.

With the expansion of their furniture-making activities after 1900, Gimson and the Barnsleys began using a much wider range of woods. In particular, they became fond of using English walnut, because of its fine grain and figure, and its rich colour. Walnut as a material for furniture-making had fallen progressively

154

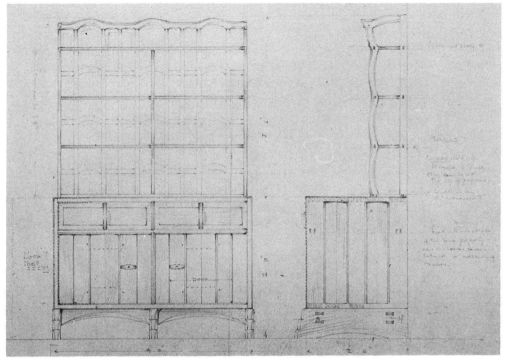

Fig. 122. Design for a dresser in English oak by Sidney Barnsley in 1922, with annotations by the client, Ambrose Heal.

into neglect since the second half of the eighteenth century, because of its susceptibility to woodworm as well as the growing availability of imported woods, and was unpopular amongst their contemporaries. However Gimson and the Barnsleys encouraged a revival of interest in walnut furniture through their constant and effective use of the material. This revival has continued to the present day, even though the cost of walnut has increased some thirty-fold since the early part of this century, restricting its use almost entirely to veneered work.

Although the work of Gimson and the Barnsleys is traditionally connected with the use of oak and other English timbers, they did not disapprove of the use of more exotic imported woods, nor did they ignore their possibilities in the field of furniture design. On the contrary, Gimson and Sidney Barnsley, in particular, took great pleasure in selecting types of wood for different purposes, and in combining different textures and colours in their designs. They regularly used Cuban and Honduras mahogany and macassar ebony, either alone or in combination with other woods. They also made occasional use of rosewood and satinwood, as well as the bold, striped figures provided by zebrawood and coromandel wood, often used in the solid as well as in veneers. These combinations were not always successful, as in the case of the furniture in satinwood veneer and ebony designed by Gimson, towards the end of his career, for a client in Yorkshire. The contrast between the dark ebony and the highly figured and coloured satinwood was not a sympathetic one, and, after Gimson's death, Peter Waals found it very difficult to dispose of these pieces, which had been rejected by the

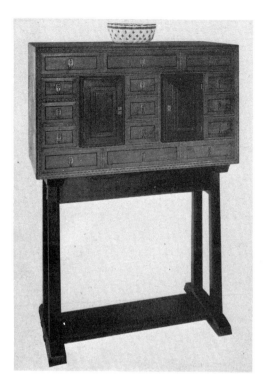

Fig. 123. Cabinet in cedar of Lebanon with macassar ebony cupboard doors on an ebonised oak stand, designed and made by Sidney Barnsley in about 1904. The drop handles were turned by Sidney Barnsley on his own lathe.

original client. A unique and striking piece of furniture is the cabinet of drawers in cedar of Lebanon, designed and made by Sidney Barnsley in about 1904, where the character of the wood makes a powerful appeal to all the senses through its texture, colour and fragrance. The impact of this cabinet is heightened by the contrasting use of macassar ebony for the two cupboard doors.

Veneered work was more frequently employed at Daneway after the employment of Peter Waals in 1902. The veneers used, usually on a groundwork of Honduras mahogany, were a far cry from the wafer-thin specimens used today, being up to a quarter of an inch thick. Oyster pieces, burrs and pollard woods were also used in veneered work. A writing cabinet in walnut, designed by Gimson and exhibited at the 1906 Arts and Crafts Exhibition, received this praise from *The Studio* magazine for its use of the decorative grain created by the pollard wood:

> This piece of furniture is an excellent example of the application of natural effects to decoration. It supplies a high conception of the laws upon which legitimate and beautiful decorative value may be obtained, and which frees the designer from any obligation to attempt more artificial methods of ornamentation.[1]

Another successful example of their veneered work is the fall-front writing desk, veneered in burr elm with ebony stringing, designed by Gimson in about 1911, and made by Peter Waals at Chalford in the early 1920s [Fig. 150].

156

The wood for such pieces of furniture would have been bought in London, from foreign wood and veneer merchants, such as Sam Westlake & Sons, of 51 Tabernacle Street, Finsbury Square, London, E. C. 2, from whom some accounts to Gimson have survived. Most of the actual selection and buying of timber was entrusted to Peter Waals, whose experience in conducting these transactions had the additional advantage of enabling Gimson to forego an unpleasant and unwelcome visit to London, and it seems possible that Sidney Barnsley might also have occasionally delegated this responsibility to Peter Waals. The timber was transported from London to the Cotswolds by rail, completing the final part of the journey from Cirencester to Daneway, or to Sidney Barnsley's workshop, by haulage using horse-drawn waggons, whilst many finished items of furniture underwent the same journey in reverse.

Gimson and Sidney Barnsley occasionally made use of staining in their furniture designs. This technique was widely used in the Victorian period to disguise poor quality wood, and to provide some of the colour and finish of fine timber and, in this context, it is difficult to understand why it was used at Sapperton. However, staining was used by William Morris and his friends in the 1860s and 1870s, and in connection with the growing interest in Japanese furniture, which developed as part of the Aesthetic Movement in the second half of the nineteenth century. The only consistent use of this technique at Sapperton was in the staining of the turned ash chairs, designed by Gimson and made by Edward Gardiner at the Daneway sawmill. Gimson also stained a few pieces of furniture, including the oak dresser used in his house at Sapperton, and now in the collections of Cheltenham Museum, which is believed to have been treated with a black walnut stain in order to display his collection of lustre pottery to advantage. Both he and Sidney Barnsley occasionally used black-stained oak, to make bases and stands for cabinets and cupboards, as a cheap and readily available substitute for macassar ebony. In some cases, as for example the cedar of Lebanon cabinet designed by Sidney Barnsley [Fig. 123], an inappropriate use was made of stained oak in combination with an expensive wood on a very fine piece.

All three men were opposed to the indiscriminate use of French polish on furniture, an innovation which had been adopted with great enthusiasm by the furniture trade and the general public since its introduction into Britain in the early decades of the nineteenth century, as, when carelessly or overlavishly applied, it prevented the development of a patina which gave the wood character and a rich, glossy appearance as it matured. Where the function of a piece of furniture, such as the oak kitchen table designed and made by Ernest Barnsley for his own household, demanded, the surface was scrubbed. Most of the oak furniture was left unpolished, although some pieces were dipped in lime which, in the short term, enhanced the beauty of the wood. White French polish was used on mahogany, and other fine pieces, which were then rubbed down with glass paper and waxed. This polishing was a long and laborious process, involving many hours of a craftsman's time. However neither Gimson nor Sidney Barnsley

Fig. 124. Miniature chest of drawers in burr yew with ebony feet and metal drop handles. Designed by Ernest Gimson and made in his Daneway workshops.

believed that it was necessary to polish the interior parts of furniture, such as drawer runners, to help them to run smoothly if they were accurately cut and fitted. As a consequence, the constant friction has rubbed the wood down in these areas on some examples of their furniture.

In 1902, the Daneway workshops were established by Gimson and Ernest Barnsley, employing four professional cabinet-makers: Peter Waals, the foreman, Harry Davoll, Percy Burchett and Ernest Smith. By 1914, the business had expanded considerably, providing work for Waals, nine woodworkers, ranging from skilled cabinet-makers to apprentices, four metal-workers and Edward Gardiner, who made chairs on the pole lathe at the Daneway sawmill, with one or two assistants. Many of the Daneway craftsmen lived nearby, at Hill House Farm, which Gimson had leased for that purpose as part of the concern which he consistently maintained in their general welfare. The wages earned by these skilled men appear to have varied from job to job, and were also related to the experience of each individual. In 1914, Waals's wage for cabinet-work was 1s 2d an hour, the average wage of the other cabinet-makers was 10d an hour, whilst an apprentice averaged 3d an hour. One of Gimson's job books, which relates to the period from 1913 to 1919, has survived. From this evidence, most of the craftsmen appear to have worked at least a fifty-hour week, although this must have varied according to the pressure of work. The average weekly wage for cabinet-makers and metal-workers was between twenty and thirty shillings, about five to ten shillings more than the average weekly wage of an agricultural labourer. Waals received about £2 10s a week as foreman, rising to about £5 by 1918. It is interesting to note that, although in many cases the great bulk of the cabinet-work for one piece of furniture was apportioned to a single craftsman, it was very rarely the work of one man alone, and often the workshop appears to have worked very closely together, as a team, with the most skilled cabinet-makers involved in two or three projects at one time. Gimson's three assistants during the course of his career, Norman Jewson, Walter Gissing and Basil Young, were concerned mainly with his architectural projects although Norman Jewson, the only long-term assistant, did design some furniture at Sapperton, and was heavily involved in the execution of Gimson's plasterwork designs. Sidney Barnsley twice attempted to employ an assistant to ease the pressure of work. These attempts were unsuccessful, although one of his assistants, Fred Foster, later worked for Waals at Chalford. Malcolm Powell, Alfred Powell's brother, spent a year working on his own designs in Sidney Barnsley's workshop before setting up as a furniture-maker on his own account in Reading.

Gimson and the Barnsleys began designing and making furniture with the intention of producing it cheaply enough to be within the means of most people. In fact it was impossible for them to provide the local community with its furniture requirements when, as has already been mentioned, most villagers could not afford oak furniture, and had to make do with cheaper woods. Gimson and the Barnsleys talked of making a chest of drawers which could be sold for £5, but this ideal was never achieved. The average pre-war price for such a piece of furniture from Daneway, or from Sidney Barnsley's workshop, was £12, and prices seem to have remained fairly stable throughout their working lives until about 1918. Gimson would have liked to have produced the simple oak furniture in a less 'finished' form, more suited to its character and also cheaper than the quality of workmanship which Waals as foreman demanded of the craftsmen at Daneway. According to Norman Jewson:

> For the plain oak furniture, intended for cottage use, he would have preferred a less exacting standard of finish, both so that it could be produced at a lower cost and also as being more natural for that kind of furniture. He would have liked a finish more akin to that of the village wheelwrights, who worked more by eye and less by measurement than highly trained cabinet-makers. However, unfortunately, there was much less demand for the plain oak so he was obliged more and more to rely on the more expensive type to keep his men employed. Had there been more demand for the simpler work he would probably have got over the difficulty by having a separate workshop and training men for this type of work only. It was a real disappointment that he could not produce this cottage-type furniture at a price that working class people could afford to pay, but with these highly trained men and the perfect finish required, too many hours were spent on each piece for this to be possible. He had always intended that the maximum price for a chest of drawers should be £5 when it was to the simplest possible design, but in this he never succeeded.[2]

The nearest Gimson ever came to achieving this ideal was in a drawing, dated

September 1909, showing an oak chest priced at £5 and a marble-topped washstand priced at £4 10s.

The five costings for pieces of furniture made in the Daneway workshops between 1914 and 1919, which have been calculated from Gimson's job book for inclusion here, indicate the low profit margins which were maintained. Only between ten and fifteen per cent of the selling price actually accrued to Gimson for the upkeep of the workshop, and for his personal account. It is obvious that neither Gimson nor the Barnsleys could have continued their work without the additional support of a private income. The costings included here, which cover a wide variety of work, give a useful insight into the organisation of the Daneway workshops. The earliest example is a costing for six museum cases made for Tattershall Castle in Lincolnshire, which can be related to a drawing dated January 1914. The work took approximately six months to complete and can be split up thus:

Waals 10 hours, unpaid			
Orton 8 hours @ $11\frac{1}{4}$d an hour		7	6
Gardiner $18\frac{1}{2}$ hours @ $10\frac{3}{4}$d an hour		16	6
Ward $609\frac{1}{2}$ hours @ $7\frac{1}{2}$d an hour	19	1	3
Hunt 251 hours @ $6\frac{1}{2}$d an hour	6	14	4
Hill 165 hours @ 3d an hour	2	1	1
	29	0	8
Proportionate sum for Waals	14	10	4
	43	11	0
wood	11	15	0
glass	6	0	0
locks	1	15	0
	63	1	0
10%	6	6	0
Selling price	69	7	0

The wide range of wages paid to the five craftsmen involved in this project obviously indicates their different experience and the varying importance of the tasks with which they were entrusted. Waals did not receive any wages for his ten hours of cabinet-work, but instead received a sum calculated at half the total earnings of the other men, in his capacity as foreman. In this case, Gimson took ten per cent for himself and for the workshop account.

The second costing is for four trestle tables, the original design for which is featured in one of Gimson's working drawings [Fig 126]. Work was commenced in April 1914 and the order took approximately five weeks to complete.

Fig. 125. Settee in dark oak with a shaped lattice-work back and a rush seat, designed by Gimson and made in his Daneway workshops. This piece originally retailed for £13 10s 0d.

Fig. 126. Design for trestle tables, with oak trestles and rails and cedar of Lebanon tops, signed 'Ernest W. Gimson, March 1914'. Drawing in pencil to a one-inch scale.

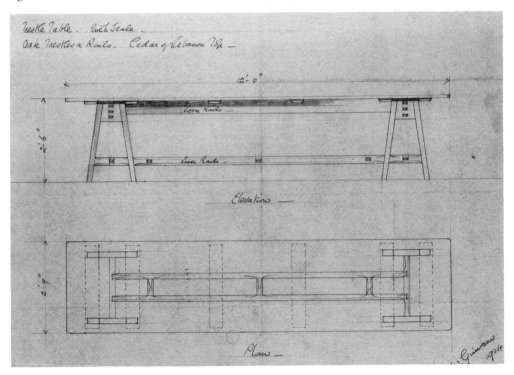

Burchett 210½ hours @ 1/- an hour........	10	10	6
Cobb 172½ hours @ 7½d an hour.........	5	7	5
Waals – proportionate sum	2	13	7
wood..............	5	10	0
hinges		15	0
	24	16	6
10%..............	2	9	6
Selling price	27	6	0

In this piece of work Percy Burchett undertook the major share of the cabinet-work, unsupervised, earning one shilling an hour. The other craftsman involved in this project, Cobb, was less skilled and therefore required Waals's supervision. Consequently a sum equivalent to half of Cobb's earnings was paid to Waals.

The walnut bureau made, for Harold Gimson, between June and August 1914, was a very fine piece of cabinet-work. Its cost can be calculated thus:

Smith 333 hours @ 8½d an hour	11	15	10½
Davoll 296 hours @ 8½d an hour.........	10	9	8
	22	5	6½
Waals..................................	11	2	9½
	33	8	4
wood..............	8	2	0
handles	4	10	0
locks	1	0	0
	47	0	4
10%..............	4	6	0
Selling price	51	6	4

The execution of this bureau was entrusted to two of the most experienced craftsmen at Daneway, Ernest Smith and Harry Davoll, each man working on the lower and upper part of the bureau respectively. Their wages appear low compared to those of Percy Burchett in the previous example, only eightpence halfpenny an hour compared to one shilling an hour, because they were working under Waals's supervision. As a consequence Waals took his full entitlement of half their total earnings for his work as foreman.

The fourth costing is for a walnut sideboard of a fairly simple design, similar to the one illustrated in Fig. 141, on which work was begun in July 1914 and continued for three months. All the cabinet-work was executed by Waals.

Fig. 127. Two ladderback chairs in ash stained black with rush seats designed by Gimson and made by Edward Gardiner.

Waals 224½ hours @ 1/2d	13	2	0
wood	3	10	0
	16	12	0
12½%	2	9	6
handles	3	0	0
	22	1	6
extras		3	6
	22	5	0

This piece was sold for £22. 10s.

The final costing is for the chancel screen at Crockham Hill Church, Surrey, which was completed by Sidney Barnsley after Gimson's death. The job was commenced in May 1919 and took approximately six months to complete. It illustrates the appreciable rise in wages which took place after the First World War, although there is evidence that in 1918 some apprentices were still paid as little as 2d an hour in the Daneway workshops. This last costing must be seen in the light of Gimson's long illness and eventual death, during which time much of the responsibility for the running of the workshops and the negotiations with clients was assumed by Peter Waals.

Waals 336½ hours @ 2/-	43	15	0
Smith 56 hours @ 2/-	5	10	0
Orton 625 hours @ 1/7d	49	10	0
Gardiner 812 hours @ 1/6	60	18	0
Hunt 500½ hours @ 1/3	31	5	0
Hill 567½ hours @ 9d	21	6	0
	212	4	0
rise in wages	18	8	0
	230	12	0
50%	115	6	0
	345	18	0
timber	68	15	0
	414	13	0
Waals	20	5	6
	434	18	6
15%	65	5	0
Cost of screen	500	3	6

The costings of the products of the metal-working shop were calculated in much the same way, with the four craftsmen involved, Bucknell, Whiting, Mustoe and Gardiner, earning between about sixpence and one shilling an hour.

The financial organisation was slightly different in the costings of the chairs made by Edward Gardiner at the Daneway sawmill, for Gimson had made him a partner in this concern. Edward Gardiner included this costing from his time book in a letter to Edward Barnsley:

Cost, time and materials for Ledbury armchair .	13s 6d
Mr Gimson 10%	1s 4d
Self 10%	1s 4d
Capital account...........................	1s 4d
in plain, unstained wood – sale price	17s 6d
Extras were: Staining and French Polishing	2s 0d
Packing	1s 0d
Delivery to Railway Station.....	6d
Total price of finished chair was	£1 1s 0d[3]

The practice of woodworking was of fundamental importance to Gimson's and Sidney Barnsley's work. The latter became more and more involved in the physical processes of woodworking, and believed that all the stages in the production of a piece of furniture, however routine, should be undertaken by the craftsman. His physical enjoyment of his craft, as well as something of the effort involved, is illustrated by this extract from a letter written by him to Philip Webb in May 1904:

> My workshop which I have to my 'lone self' is a great improvement upon the Pinbury one, much better lighted and being thatched is warmer and drier, and from the end window I have a most wonderful view across the valley to the hanging wood you would remember. I am still occupied principally in making good solid oak furniture with occasional pieces of a more delicate kind as a rest and change. I have just finished two tables of English oak, $12'0'' \times 3'6''$ each, the tops out of three inch and with only one joint in the width and they have given me a fair dressing down and by night time I have felt fair tired out.[4]

Sidney Barnsley also seems to have enjoyed the problem-solving aspect of the design and construction of furniture for its own sake. This can be illustrated by the fact that, from the evidence of his working drawings, Sidney Barnsley appears never to have designed a chair. Eleven armchairs in the library at Bedales, which are the only examples credited to him, were based closely on a design by Gimson, and were made in Lupton's Froxfield workshop by Walter Berry. The only explanation for this major gap in Sidney Barnsley's output is that he found the design and manufacture of chairs unsatisfying and time-consuming, and therefore refrained from making this very basic type of furniture, passing on any orders to the Daneway workshops.

Gimson, who, like Sidney Barnsley, was very much influenced by the teachings of Ruskin and Morris, also believed that the physical involvement in wood-working was essential to the happiness and well-being of his craftsmen. Although Gimson's comments, quoted by Alfred Powell, 'Let machinery be honest – and make its own machine buildings and its own machine furniture; let it make its chairs and tables of stamped aluminium if it likes: Why not?'[5] have been interpreted as his total rejection of machinery in furniture-making, his attitude to machinery and machine production was, in fact, much more realistic and tolerant. He accepted the necessity of machine production to fulfil the demands of twentieth-century society, but he was aware that he himself was not suited to designing for industry, basically because of his refusal to accept any sort of compromise as far as his work was concerned. It must be remembered that both Gimson and Sidney Barnsley did use a certain amount of the woodworking machinery which was then available, for craftsmen and small concerns, in their respective workshops. Edward Barnsley has written:

> A certain element of mythology has grown up about the machine and its use by craftsmen. It is seldom realised that Morris never spoke or wrote that

the machine must not be used. What he held can best be summed up in words following closely those which he used himself. He urged that machines should not be used if their use removed from the work of making, the pleasure of it. And this was the approach of the Barnsleys and Gimson. Especially the latter because he employed assistants, and wished their work to be an integral part of their lives and a satisfaction and pride to them. It is not often appreciated that, in the 1880s and into the twentieth century, machines of a pattern and scale suitable for use in the production of the craftsman's work had not been invented and therefore the whole question, in a sense, broke down. And though it has been written that Gimson 'abhorred the machine', this is not correct. And when the move was made to Pinbury and Sapperton, circular saw machines were installed in both the workshops. Sidney, knowing that he had to produce all his furniture without assistants, chose a large circular saw, a magnificent saw for its time, hand and foot powered, made by the Britannia Co. At Daneway there was a much smaller saw bench, and I believe that this choice was made intentionally, suitable only for such work as cutting out lines for inlay etc., but not for the heavier work which Gimson considered important that the craftsmen should themselves carry out, to be closely in touch with their materials at every stage.[6]

It is somewhat surprising that, despite their different methods of working, and the existence of separate workshops for over fifteen years, the furniture designs of Gimson and Sidney Barnsley were so similar. According to Harry Davoll, one of the first cabinet-makers to be employed by Gimson and Ernest Barnsley in 1901, 'Mr Sidney Barnsley . . . his designs were very similar in every respect, we could just tell the difference a little but, taking it on the whole, they were very much like one another'.[7] Neither methods of construction nor details of decoration provide any consistent evidence to enable one to differentiate between the two men's work. The only satisfactory method to accurately ascribe a piece of furniture to either Ernest Gimson or Sidney Barnsley is by the use of surviving documentary evidence, their working drawings, contemporary sources such as magazines, photographs and catalogues, and the provenance of individual items.

As far as both men's working drawings are concerned, approximately 800 of Gimson's furniture designs have survived, as opposed to only about 100 of Sidney Barnsley's. These cannot be taken as an accurate guide to the output of either man as, because of the way in which they worked, not every piece of furniture would have required a preparatory working drawing. From the alterations and annotations which have been made, some of Gimson's drawings appear to have had a working life of up to ten years. In addition, both men's designs have been re-used by other furniture-makers, and many must have been destroyed in the course of time. However, those drawings which have survived do provide a basis for estimating the proportion of work undertaken by both men, and they indicate that Gimson's output was much larger than that of Sidney Barnsley. The difference between the two men's output is understandable

Fig. 128. The dining room at Rodmarton Manor, Gloucestershire, showing the fitted oak dresser made by Alfred Wright in 1923 to Sidney Barnsley's design.

when one considers that Gimson employed a workforce of up to fifteen craftsmen to execute his designs, whereas Sidney Barnsley worked entirely on his own. The only known occasion when someone else carried out his designs was in the furnishing of Rodmarton Manor. The oak dresser built into the dining room at Rodmarton in 1923 was made by the estate's cabinet-maker, Alfred Wright, to Sidney Barnsley's design.

In addition to Gimson's furniture designs, many working drawings have survived of designs for metalwork, plasterwork, needlework and architectural projects. Although some of the drawings are preliminary sketches, the majority of these are drawn to scale, as are the final drafts. Edward Barnsley remembers Gimson working with a pencil in his right hand and a ruler in his left thus enabling himself to draw freely and to scale.[8] There is very little evidence of any full-scale drawing by Ernest Gimson, and none by Sidney Barnsley; they almost always worked to $\frac{1}{8}$ or $\frac{1}{12}$ scale and had no need to draw details such as the internal parts of chests of drawers. This is particularly true of Sidney Barnsley's drawings, which were executed entirely for his own benefit. As well as drawings of specific commissions, both men included drawings of possible designs for potential clients. Gimson's working drawings also included sheets of slightly differing designs for such basic items as chests of drawers, plate racks or beds, as illustrated on page 168, which provided customers with a range of alternatives in material, design and price. From this type of drawing one must conclude that Gimson and

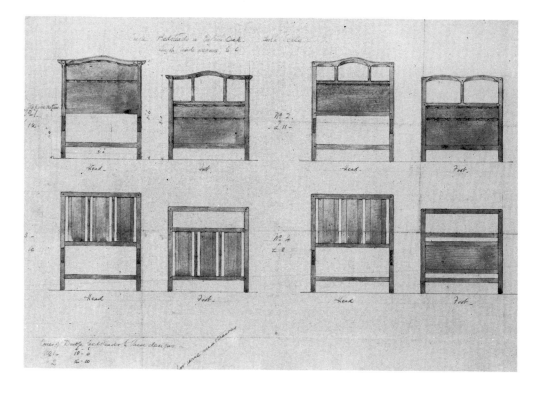

Sidney Barnsley did not work entirely on a one-off basis, and that certain designs could be repeated, or even reproduced, several times.

The manner in which Gimson and Sidney Barnsley worked was not always conducive to co-operation with the more traditional commercial concerns. The following rather bemused letter from a firm of wireworkers, J. Nichols & Sons Ltd., of Birmingham, to Ernest Gimson, dated March 1914, illustrates this point:

Dear Sir, We have your letter with reference to the mahogany frame mattress, and notice you tell us to make it. We will supply it without the holes being bored in the frames. It would not be possible for you to drill the holes after it is made up in the cross pieces in which the wire meshes are attached.

If you will tell us what position you want the holes boring we will bore accordingly. We do not know whether you mean none of the holes to be bored, but we cannot see how we are to make a mattress satisfactorily of a special size unless we have a chance of fitting it together and we cannot fit it together unless the holes are bored. . . . We shall be glad if you will give us the outside measurements of the mattress required both for length and width. We cannot trace that you have given us any sizes. We certainly had a sketch which was returned. If you will give us particulars we will at once give it our attention.[9]

Unfortunately, there is no record of Gimson's answer to this.

Fig. 129. A sheet of designs for single bedsteads in English oak by Ernest Gimson. Prices varied from £8 to £12 according to variations in design.

Fig. 130. Small cabinet on a stand in English walnut with the pattern of panelling and inlaid holly and ebony stringing repeated on the stringing. Designed and made by Sidney Barnsley in about 1914.

Despite his independent attitude, Sidney Barnsley was not afraid of working on a large scale and of devoting many hours to achieve the required decorative effect. It is said that when, in the course of fitting up a large piece of furniture, he reached the point where some physical assistance was essential, Sidney Barnsley would go round to Gimson's cottage to enlist the help of his gardener, Mr Eldridge. Edward Barnsley remembers that his father's first action, on receipt of an order, was often to take his rule to the stable, where the packing cases were kept, to see whether he had one of a suitable size. In this way, basic items such as chests of drawers, were produced to standard sizes unless definite specifications were provided by the client. Both Gimson and Sidney Barnsley made most of their furniture with detachable feet or bases which could be simply dowelled on when required, for ease of construction and packing. Both men found that there was more demand for their elaborate pieces than for the plain oak furniture, yet ornate pieces proved long undertakings. The walnut cabinet on a stand, made by Sidney Barnsley for C. H. St John Hornby in 1914, for example, required approximately one month of full-time work to complete. This cabinet [Fig. 130] has ten drawers and a central cupboard, the fronts of which have multiple fielded panels emphasised by the inlaid lines of dark and light stringing. It was intended to be free-standing within a room setting, as the pattern of the panelling and inlaid stringing on the front of the cabinet is repeated on the back. Such high quality of workmanship and attention to detail, in both Sidney Barnsley's and Gimson's workshops, provided an inspiration both for their contemporaries and for successive generations of craftsmen.

Chapter 10
Clients and colleagues

All the surviving documentary evidence, such as Sidney Barnsley's letters to Philip Webb, indicates that there was never any shortage of commissions in either his or Ernest Gimson's workshops. Furniture-making rapidly developed as the major concern of both men and, as their reputations as designers and woodworkers became more widely known, their architectural training and experience were progressively overlooked, both by those responsible for the allocation of architectural commissions and by many of their own clients. Gimson's architectural background was disregarded to such an extent that he found it necessary to write to Sydney Cockerell, on one particular occasion in 1916, in defence of his action in designing chairs for the Senate House, Cambridge, without having seen the building for which they were intended:

> As regards my seeing the building – I made as you know all arrangements for coming and Benson had to put me off, postponing my visit until this month when I should have been very glad to have come. In order to make the most of the intervening time I got measurements sent me of the dais and full size drawings of all the details and these, with the help of a very clear photograph, gave me all the information I wanted for making the designs. You know I am an architect and am used to designing to plans and sections before the actual buildings are in existence.[1]

The extent of Gimson's and Sidney Barnsley's reputations as furniture designers is illustrated by the numbers of visitors attracted to their workshops at Sapperton. When Ernest Barnsley was commissioned by Lord Bathurst to undertake repairs to Daneway House, the main reception rooms, with their sixteenth-century plasterwork ceilings, were restored, with the intention that access to them should be granted to interested visitors. When Gimson and Ernest Barnsley entered into partnership in 1901, they came to an agreement with Lord Bathurst that, as well as using the outbuildings at Daneway as workshops, they could also use the main rooms of the house, which were accessible to the public, as showrooms for their furniture. These simply decorated but attractive rooms provided admirable settings for the wide range of furniture produced in the Daneway workshops. The success of their scheme for the use of Daneway House is borne out by the numbers of visitors attracted to it, the majority of whom came on purpose to see the furniture and workshops, although the pleasant surroundings provided by the house and the countryside were an additional bonus.

Fig. 131. Daneway House, one of the main rooms in which the products of Gimson's Daneway workshops were exhibited. This photograph dates from about 1905.

Gimson's visitors' book, with entries appertaining to short periods in 1904 and 1907, has survived, and indicates a constant and large influx of visitors to the extent that, on some days, one wonders whether the routine of the workshops was not totally disrupted. The numbers are particularly impressive when one considers the lack of private transport facilities in the early twentieth century, particularly to a relatively remote part of the country such as the Cotswolds. On the three days between 29 and 31 January 1904, for example, over a hundred people signed Gimson's visitors' book, having come from as far afield as Aberdeen, Nottingham and Chicago, U.S.A. However, the great majority of visitors came from London, and included a professor from the Royal College of Art, a party from the School of Wood Carving and three representatives of the press: from the *Morning Post*, the *Westminster Gazette* and the *Manchester Guardian*. Many of the visitors were titled, and the majority of those from London had addresses in the 'best' parts of the West End. Although these would obviously have been the people with their own transport, or those who could afford to travel for pleasure, it is interesting to note how, relatively early on in his career, Gimson found his patrons from amongst the wealthiest sections of the community. In contrast relatively few local people appear to have visited the workshops and showrooms, according to the 1904 section of Gimson's visitors' book. The only local names which occur are those of Sidney Barnsley, who was obviously a regular visitor, and the Rev. H. D. Cropper, rector of Sapperton, whose cautious attitude to Gimson and the Barnsleys was described by Norman Jewson:

When Gimson and the Barnsleys came to Sapperton, the rector didn't quite know what to make of them. He couldn't understand anyone who hadn't got to do so, making furniture with his own hands, as Sidney Barnsley did, or any 'gentleman' having workshops for furniture making and smith's work like Gimson.[2]

However by 1907 Gimson's reputation in Gloucestershire appears to have spread, with visitors coming to Daneway from Cirencester, Stroud and Cheltenham as well as from the surrounding villages.

Amongst the familiar names in Gimson's visitors' book are those of A. Romney Green, the schoolmaster turned woodworker; Eric Gill, the calligrapher and stonecarver; Georgina Burne-Jones, daughter of the painter Edward Burne-Jones; George Jack, chief furniture designer with Morris and Co.; and Charles M. Gere, the Gloucestershire-based painter. There were also many visitors from schools of art throughout the country, in particular from the London County Council Central School of Arts and Crafts, whose students were probably encouraged to make the visit by the Principal, W. R. Lethaby, and a considerable number of foreign visitors, predominantly from the United States of America, Australia, Scandinavia and Germany.

It is reasonable to assume that many of those who made the relatively arduous journey to Sapperton to see Gimson's workshops and showrooms would also have visited those of Sidney Barnsley, although no similar documentation has survived. However the appearance in Gimson's visitors' book of some of Sidney Barnsley's most important clients confirms that many visitors took the opportunity to view both men's work. On 14 March 1904, for example, the name of Mrs Austan Eckhard of Broome House, Didsbury, Manchester appears in Gimson's visitors' book. Mrs Eckhard was already an important client of Sidney Barnsley, having commissioned a suite of bedroom furniture in 1903 as a present for her daughter, on the occasion of her marriage to Sidney Waterlow, a peripheral member of the Bloomsbury Group. The wardrobe, chest of drawers and mirror which formed the major part of this commission are now in the collections of the Crafts Study Centre in Bath. It seems likely that Mrs Eckhard's visit to Sapperton in 1904 took in the workshops of both craftsmen, perhaps in connection with further commissions.

Neither man ever issued a catalogue of his designs. Although the output of Gimson's Daneway workshops in particular was large enough to warrant such a publication, he was very conscious of the risk of his designs being copied by competitors. Instead of a catalogue, he therefore sent out photographs of specific designs, with prices, to prospective clients, with instructions that they should be returned to him.

Fig. 132. Chest of drawers and mirror inlaid with mother-of-pearl, designed and made by Sidney Barnsley. Part of a bedroom suite in walnut commissioned by Mrs Eckard of Manchester in 1903.

Fig. 133. Revolving bookcase in English walnut with holly and ebony inlaid stringing, designed and made by Sidney Barnsley for St John Hornby, in about 1909.

Fig. 134. Oak coffer, ribbed and braced externally, designed and made by Sidney Barnsley and painted in oils by Alfred Powell, c. 1905.

Many of Gimson's and Sidney Barnsley's regular clients are featured in the visitors' book, including several members of the Hornby family. C. H. St John Hornby, the founder of the Ashendene Press, and a partner of W. H. Smith and Son, provided Sidney Barnsley with his first professional sale by his purchase, from the 1896 Arts and Crafts Exhibition, of an oak gate-legged table [Fig. 51], designed and made by Sidney Barnsley. He and other members of the Hornby family continued to act as patrons of Sidney Barnsley and, to a lesser extent, of the other craftsmen working in the Cotswolds, both by buying work from exhibitions and by commissioning pieces directly from their workshops. Much of the furniture for the library of Shelley House, the Hornby family home on the Chelsea Embankment, was commissioned from Sidney Barnsley, including a revolving bookcase in walnut [Fig. 133], now in the collections of the Victoria and Albert Museum. This piece shows a particularly sensitive response on the part of the designer to a constructional problem; it was necessary to provide a pedestal foot which would remain stable whilst supporting a heavy weight and allowing the upper part of the bookcase to revolve smoothly. The system of pillar supports on a cross-shaped base, devised by Sidney Barnsley, fulfilled all these conditions successfully whilst remaining relatively unobtrusive.

C. H. St John Hornby also bought several cabinets designed and made by Sidney Barnsley from successive Arts and Crafts Exhibitions, and, where necessary, commissioned stands for them from their maker. Two of these cabinets were of a similar delicate design, using exotic materials, such as coromandel wood, in combination with painted decoration by Louise Powell. Both Louise Powell and her husband, Alfred, who are perhaps best-known today for their work as artist-potters in collaboration with the firm of Wedgwood, were long-standing friends of Gimson and the Barnsleys. They undertook the decoration of at least three major pieces of furniture designed by Sidney Barnsley, the two cabinets already mentioned, and an oak coffer dating from about 1905, [Fig. 134], enriching the wood with flowing naturalistic patterns executed in a limited range of oil colours. A more elaborate example of this type of collaboration is the cabinet in ebony, made by Peter Waals in about 1925, with painted decoration by Louise Powell. This cabinet [Fig. 154] was also acquired by the Hornby family, and it is interesting to note that, in the 1930s, Diana Hornby, St John Hornby's daughter, worked with Louise Powell on several projects, including the design and decoration of a suite of bedroom furniture.

Gimson also made several pieces of furniture for the Hornby family, including an octagonal shaving mirror on a simple but effective stand which is adjustable for height [Fig. 136]. This design was subsequently used in a slightly modified form by Peter Waals, and the version made for W. A. Evans of Inglewood, Leicester, is now in the collections of Leicester Museum. Other clients of Gimson whose names were featured in his visitors' book include the Countess Bathurst, Lady Manners and Joseph King. The latter's home, Sandhouse, at Witley, Surrey, was built by the architect and friend of Gimson, F. W. Troup, in about 1902, and furnished with many examples of Gimson's work.

Another valuable source of commissions for Gimson and the Barnsleys was provided by their friends and contacts in the architectural profession. Fellow-architects who had worked with the three men in the offices of Sedding and Shaw, such as William Lethaby, Robert Weir Schultz and Alfred Powell remained life-long friends and associates. Sidney Barnsley's contribution to the seventh Arts and Crafts Exhibition, in 1903, included an ebony mirror frame and box inlaid with mother of pearl which, according to the catalogue, were made by Sidney Barnsley and exhibited by R. W. Schultz, indicating that these two pieces had been previously acquired by the latter. Subsequently Sidney Barnsley designed furniture for Schultz's home at Hartley Wintney, Hampshire. Gimson also collaborated with Schultz on a number of the latter's architectural projects. In the 1890s, Schultz's work in Greece, with Sidney Barnsley, had brought him into contact with the Marquess of Bute and, in 1903, he was appointed official architect to the Marquess, with responsibility for the design of the interiors and gardens of the Old Place of Mochrum, Wigtownshire, rebuilt by Richard Park after 1873. Although much of the furniture was made to Schultz's designs in a heavy 'Celtic' style at the Bute workshops in Cardiff, the building also contains some pieces of more typically Arts and Crafts furniture, including two oak dining tables by Sidney Barnsley, (perhaps the ones in whose construction he was involved when he wrote the letter to Philip Webb, in 1904, quoted on page 165) and chairs and chests of drawers made in Gimson's Daneway workshops to his design. Gimson's workshops also produced fireplace furniture in wrought iron, metalwork fitments and wooden fixtures such as doors and

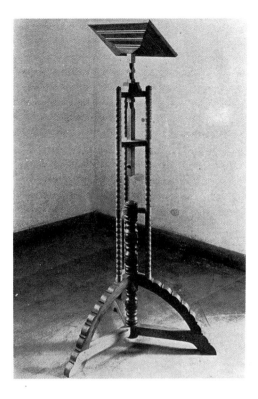

Far left Fig. 135. Detail of a cabinet in coromandel wood by Sidney Barnsley with painted decoration by Louise Powell, c. 1910.

Left Fig. 136. An octagonal walnut shaving mirror on an adjustable stand designed by Ernest Gimson in about 1910.

Right Fig. 137. A lectern designed by Gimson in collaboration with Robert Weir Schultz in 1914, and made in the Daneway workshops with other ecclesiastical furniture for the Cathedral at Khartoum, of which the latter was the architect.

handles for Mochrum, to both his own and Schultz's designs, implying the existence of a close understanding and respect between the two men. Gimson also supplied metalwork to two other country houses in Scotland through Schultz's recommendation: Knockenhair, Dunbar, in 1908, and the House of Faulkland, Fife, in 1910.

Gimson and Schultz also co-operated extensively on a number of ecclesiastical projects, including a church at Woolmer Green, Hertfordshire, built by the latter between 1899 and 1900, for which Gimson designed wood and metalwork fittings in 1908. In 1909, Schultz was entrusted with the design of Khartoum Cathedral, in the Sudan, and commissioned much of the church furniture for the Gordon Memorial Chapel from Gimson's Daneway workshops. The collaboration achieved in the process of designing the lectern for this Chapel is illustrated by the following letter, sent by Schultz, from Gray's Inn Square, London, to Gimson on 18 June 1914:

> Dear Gimson, I forgot whether I wrote to thank you for sending on the full-size drawing for the lectern.
>   Generally it seems all right and I should think would be quite light and also would not topple over easily. The only one point that I should like to refer to is the turning of the central pillar which looks rather 'Jacobean-y'. If this is not done already perhaps you would alter it a little bit to make it a little bit more like the enclosed which is an old example in the Cairo Museum

Fig. 138. The choir stalls in ebony inlaid with ivory, St Andrew's Chapel, Westminster Cathedral, London. The furnishings for this chapel were also designed by Gimson and Schultz, in about 1914.

Left Fig. 139. Lectern in oak inlaid with mother-of-pearl and ebony and holly stringing, designed by Ernest Barnsley for Kempley Church, Gloucestershire, and made in the Daneway workshops in 1903.
Right Fig. 140. Lectern in ebony inlaid with ivory, mother-of-pearl and silver, with candlesticks of polished wrought iron designed by Gimson for Roker Church, Sunderland, in 1906, and made in the Daneway workshops by Peter Waals.

and which I ought to have given you from the first. The cutting of the spurs on the supports to the legs on this old example is also I think a little better than the one you have drawn.[3]

At approximately the same time, Schultz was also involved in the design of St Andrew's Chapel, in the Roman Catholic Westminster Cathedral, in London, built by the architect, J. L. Bentley, between 1895 and 1902. Schultz received this commission through his connection with the Marquess of Bute, a prominent member of the Roman Catholic community in Britain. The choir stalls and pews for St Andrew's Chapel were made in the Daneway workshops, using brown ebony inlaid with ivory. The design of the stalls, judging from both men's working drawings for this project, was the result of close collaboration, the initial idea probably coming from Schultz with, of course, his prior familiarity and sympathy with Gimson's approach to woodwork, and being subsequently developed and refined by Gimson. The richness and contrast provided by the materials, and the variety of inlaid motifs, combine to make these stalls amongst the most successful pieces of ecclesiastical furniture executed at Daneway, and an effective complement to the predominantly Byzantine style of Bentley's Cathedral.

Gimson and the Barnsleys also worked on a variety of schemes under the direction of F. W. Troup, W. Curtis Green and the architectural partnership of Blow and Billerey. Gimson designed a large quantity of panelling and furniture for Wimbourne House, built by this partnership in Arlington St, London. Much of the work undertaken by Gimson and the Barnsleys in conjunction with other architects was of an ecclesiastical nature, which could be considered to be at variance with their lack of enthusiasm for the established church, a result both of their upbringings and their inclinations. However, they were all practical enough not to allow this attitude to interfere with their work, and, in many instances, the combination of simplicity of design with richness of materials proved very effective in an ecclesiastical setting.

All three men were long-standing friends of William Lethaby, and he remained an important source of encouragement throughout their careers, introducing many useful contacts and influential patrons to their work. Gimson executed several plasterwork ceilings in houses built by Lethaby, including Avon Tyrell, in Hampshire, in 1892. In 1903, during the period of their partnership, Gimson and Ernest Barnsley designed furniture and fittings for the Church of St Edward the Confessor at Kempley, Gloucestershire. The architect for this project was A. Randall Wells, a close associate of Lethaby and his clerk of works on several previous architectural projects, including the church at the nearby village of Brockhampton, completed in 1902. It seems likely that when Randall Wells was commissioned to design a church with a strong local and Arts and Crafts element, at Kempley, Lethaby recommended that he use the woodworking skills of Gimson and Ernest Barnsley who had the additional advantage of being local craftsmen. The lectern in the church at Kempley [Fig. 139] was made of oak, inlaid with mother-of-pearl and holly and ebony stringing, and is particularly interesting as one of the few pieces of decorative, rather than utilitarian domestic, furniture designed by Ernest Barnsley. The lectern illustrates his rather heavy, sculptural approach to furniture design, and provides an interesting comparison with the lectern designed by Gimson for Roker Church in Sunderland in 1906. The chamfered rib-shaped braces between the octagonal pillar and the cross-framed base in Ernest Barnsley's design illustrate an early version of the wishbone stretchers, which became a feature of the underframing of furniture, such as tables, designed by all three men. Another particularly attractive feature of this design is the variety of abstract patterns achieved by the inlay of mother-of-pearl in the oak. Gimson also worked with Randall Wells on a subsequent project, designing plasterwork and metalwork for Besford Court, Worcestershire in 1912.

Perhaps the most effective co-operation between Gimson and an architect, in an ecclesiastical setting, was in the furnishing of Roker Church, near Sunderland. This church was built between 1904 and 1907 by Edward Prior, a former student of Norman Shaw, and an early acquaintance of Gimson from that period. Roker Church is an impressive monument to the Arts and Crafts Movement and has been described as 'the best English Church of the early 20th century'.[4] Its tower, which was intentionally designed to be visible from far out at sea, is a massive, craggy structure of rough-tooled stone, and the same impressive effect was achieved in the interior by the powerful stone buttresses which curve upwards, meeting in a point to form the transverse arches of the roof. The internal panelling and fitments were designed by Gimson, in a similarly austere style, in oak, but the total impact of the interior is both heightened and enriched by what might be called the jewels of the design: the tapestry designed by Edward Burne-Jones and made by Morris and Co. in 1906, and the furniture and metalwork designed by Gimson and made in the Daneway workshops. These included a lectern in ebony inlaid with naturalistic motifs in ivory and silver [Fig. 140] and a set of crosses and candlesticks in polished wrought iron, pierced and chased with floral patterns. Amongst the other artists and craftsmen involved in the decoration of this church were Eric Gill, who carved the foundation stone, A. Randall Wells, who designed the font, and Henry A. Payne who designed some stained glass windows.

Sidney Cockerell, Curator of the Fitzwilliam Museum, Cambridge, was a long-standing friend of Gimson, whose acquaintance he had made at the meetings of the Society for the Protection of Ancient Buildings. Through his recommendation, Gimson received a number of commissions for work at Cambridge University, including furniture for Magdalene College Library, and for the Senate House, for which some working drawings have survived. The correspondence relating to this commission, a letter from Gimson to Cockerell, dated 16 August 1916, indicates that this particular commission was fraught with problems. Gimson, who was beset with difficulties caused by trying to keep his workshops in operation throughout the 1914 to 1918 war, refused to pander to the ideas of the authorities at Cambridge, and his reaction to their demand for 'period' chairs throws some light on his approach to furniture design. He wrote:

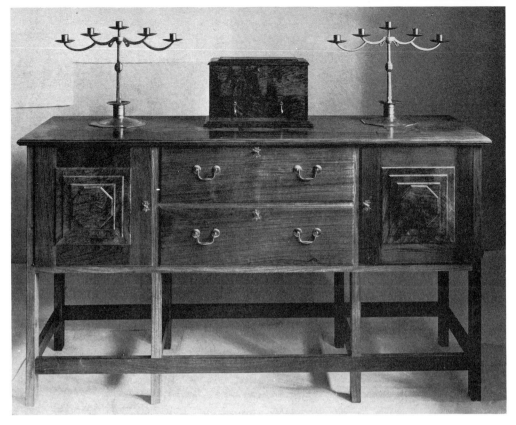

Fig. 141. A sideboard and a glove or handkerchief box, both in English walnut, and a pair of branched candelabra in wrought iron. All designed by Ernest Gimson and exhibited at Debenham and Freebody's London store in 1907.

The thing is that as fast as I submit designs, Benson and Dr James reject them as unsuitable because they don't follow in detail the style of 'the period', a curious reason for intelligent men and doubly so when both of them are members of the S. P. A. B. that exists to oppose that point of view. If they want *period* chairs, the best thing would be to buy old ones – at any rate they should understand that it's impossible for anyone to design them – a copy might be made of some old specimen or a hotch-potch of many and *called* a design – and we both know the folly of it. The only sensible course is to get a good bit of modern work that isn't unsympathetic to the expression of the building. This is the course the S. P. A. B. advocate and the one that Morris and Webb and Lethaby and any of us that have faced the problem of new work in old buildings have always followed. Benson and James only *assume* that my designs are unsuitable to the building because they fail to find in them any of those early 18th century tricks of design that they are looking for . . . As to making the chairs – Benson asked me to make one and Leach the other five. This of course would be a very unsatisfactory business and could not be successful. However I would have agreed to it to please Benson if he felt unable to wait till I could have made the six in my own shop. Things have been very difficult for me this year. Nearly all my men have gone and it has been with great difficulty that the tribunals have been persuaded to leave me the few that remain. Then the bulk of the work I had in hand was likely to fall through owing to the recent Munitions Office

order respecting building work. Thus it was not until last week that I could tell in the least what work I could do or even whether my shops could exist at all.[5]

Gimson also had a fruitful partnership with May Morris, the daughter of William Morris and a designer of jewellery, embroidery and fabrics in her own right. She and Gimson shared a stand at the Arts and Crafts Exhibition held at Burlington House in 1906, and again at the Royal Academy in 1916. In 1915, Gimson built a pair of cottages for May Morris at Kelmscott, and also designed the hall for that village, although this was not built until 1933. Both Gimson and Sidney Barnsley continued to exhibit fairly regularly with the Arts and Crafts Exhibition Society in London; examples of their designs were sold during the course of the exhibitions, and prospective clients were introduced to their work. Gimson was certainly more active than Sidney Barnsley in the field of exhibitions after about 1905, partly because of the larger output of his workshops, and partly because of his greater involvement in the commercial and art worlds. In 1907, he was given the opportunity to mount an exhibition of his work in the London store of Debenham and Freebody's, newly rebuilt on a palatial scale, by one of its directors, Ernest Debenham, who was an admirer of his work. The exhibition was very extensive, consisting of eighty items including forty-five pieces of furniture, turned chairs made by Edward Gardiner at the Daneway sawmill, and metalwork, and an illustrated catalogue was produced. This must have been the largest exhibition of Gimson's work to be held during his lifetime. The exhibition was reviewed thus in *The Builder* in December 1907:

Left Fig. 142. A small cabinet with a geometric marquetry design in holly, ebony and walnut and silver fittings designed by Gimson and included in his exhibition at Debenham and Freebody's in 1907.

Right Fig. 143. A toilet mirror with two drawers in walnut; a variation by Gimson on a traditional eighteenth-century design which was made by Harry Davoll at the Daneway workshops in about 1907.

On the first and second floor landings of Messrs Debenham and Freebody's sumptuous new premises in Wigmore Street there is at present on view an admirable collection designed and made under the direction of Mr Ernest W. Gimson, which is worth a visit from those who like to see furniture not only unexceptionable in taste but thoroughly well made. Mr Gimson's effects are got with little ornamental work, by means of simple lines, careful detail, thoroughly sound workmanship and a judicious use of the natural colour and grain of different woods. Among the most notable specimens are a chest of drawers in English walnut, inlaid in the front with a rather conventional floral ornament in walnut and cherry; this is not a mere thin veneer but is carried out in solid thick pieces. This is almost the only bit of elaborate ornament. . . . A small cabinet entirely covered with a chevron marquetry pattern in three alternating woods – ebony, holly and walnut – is most effective in appearance in spite of the simplicity of the pattern scheme, and is a model of careful execution of this kind of work depending on the accurate cutting and fitting of innumerable small pieces.[6]

This last piece of furniture is interesting because it illustrates the use of an overall geometric marquetry technique which Gimson had previously employed in the design of a cabinet for Kenton and Co. in 1891. The first decade of the twentieth century appears to have been a particularly fruitful one for Ernest Gimson as he was also well-represented in the Arts and Crafts Exhibition in 1910. He exhibited furniture, metalwork and embroidery designed by himself, and was the largest single exhibitor of furniture at the New Gallery that year.

Fig. 144. Oak table designed by Ambrose Heal.

It is interesting to note that Gimson subscribed to a press cutting agency during the period between about 1907 and 1916, partly because it indicates that despite his removal from the London art world, he retained a natural concern in its reaction to his work, and to the development of his career, and partly because of the mixed and often amusing reactions to his work in the press. The *Pall Mall Gazette*, in its review of the 1910 Arts and Crafts Exhibition, wrote:

> Mr Gimson's chest of drawers in plain English oak has a healthy severity which is not all solidity, for on approach the highly original handles show a dainty decoration of their own, and the fitting of component parts of the piece as a whole is as true as a die.[7]

The *Nottingham Guardian*, reviewing the 1916 Arts and Crafts Exhibition took a completely opposing view:

> There is not one piece of furniture, for instance, that achieves that blend of matter-of-courseness and decoration achieved by most furniture prior to the 19th century. Mr Gimson and Mr Ambrose Heal show furniture excellent in technique, often fine in detail, and of carefully chosen wood. Yet set one of Mr Gimson's cabinets besides an eighteenth century piece, and, now in the inappropriate form of the metal fittings, now in a want of unity between body and legs, the unsure touch of the modern craftsman would be apparent.[8]

The work of Gimson, and indeed that of many of his contemporaries, was constantly receiving unfavourable comparisons with the skills and designs of eighteenth-century cabinet-makers. A typical example of this attitude was evinced by *The Builder* in this review of the 1916 Exhibition:

> To some extent Mr Gimson has been forced to study the old work, and particularly in construction his methods surpass the work of the famous master craftsmen; but his theory of design is lamentable. The fault inheres in the narrowness of outlook, in a blind attempt to build up a new system of design for movables based on the requirements of the peasant, and in a vain attempt to stretch rude simplicity into terms of rich and pompous complexity. Such methods might, and probably do, snare the uninitiated, but the educated man rebels at the idea of being treated as a glorified peasant, hence his desperate appeals to the antique dealer or the charlatan of reproduction. . . . Perhaps Mr Gimson will in time overcome his passion for excessive inlaying and when peace is declared will pay a visit to Paris and there study the exquisite designs of the ebonists of the century before last?[9]

This was not the only occasion on which the inconsistency of his arguments was not perceived by the reviewer, whilst the possibility of Gimson's profiting from a study of the exuberant rococo designs of the French ebonists is most doubtful. However Gimson was not short of support from the press, as is illustrated by the following two extracts, the first from the *Manchester Guardian*, the second from *The Spectator*, which are both taken from reviews of the 1916 Arts and Crafts Exhibition held at the Royal Academy:

> The furniture shows a steady refining and respect for tradition that is very far away from the eccentricities of the [Arts and Crafts] movement. The workmanship, too, is of a remarkably high level. One comes away with the feeling that Mr Gimson is the presiding genius here. There is a set of fire irons which in design, appropriateness of decoration, and workmanship, is worthy of South Kensington, although I hope it will be put to better use in some sensible man's home.[10]

> His [Gimson's] works have those desirable qualities which it is hard to put into words. His work does not recall the style of any other designer, but it is difficult to say where the originality lies. It is beautifully designed, eminently practicable, entirely without affectation, and shows the happiest choice of material. . . . The workmanship, too, is of the finest kind. It is a delight to pull out the drawers of the table cabinet executed by Mr Burcheet [sic], so perfectly do they work.[11]

Despite these favourable comments, Gimson and the Barnsleys probably received more recognition as furniture designers on the continent than in Britain, during their own lifetimes. Their contributions to successive Arts and Crafts Exhibitions were frequently illustrated in continental periodicals, such as *Der*

Moderne Stil, and a considerable number of foreign visitors to the London exhibitions ventured out to their workshops at Sapperton. Gimson's work, in particular, was seen several times on the continent. He exhibited in Belgium, at the International Exposition of Arts and Crafts, at Ghent, in 1913, where his contributions were commented on thus in *The Times*:

> To the general public Mr Gimson's name is probably little known; but it should not remain so after this proof of his power over many kinds of wood, his love and knowledge of their surfaces and colour qualities. His furniture is strongly individual, yet never bizarre or 'artistic'; it is all choice, yet all thoroughly serviceable. When he makes a simple garden seat, it is unlike any other garden seat, and more comfortable than any other garden seat; his most elaborate little cabinet, inlaid on the outside, partly faced with white wood inside, as various and as dainty a piece as we have seen, has nothing in it otiose or impracticable; it is a positive temptation to collect love letters. . . . perhaps Mr Gimson's furniture may rob some of the rest of its interest.[12]

In the following year, Gimson also contributed some of his furniture designs to the exhibition of British Arts and Crafts held in Paris.

It was the influence of the British Arts and Crafts Movement, including individuals such as Gimson and the Barnsleys, which inspired the foundation of the Deutscher Werkbund in Germany in 1907. This association consisted of representatives from diverse fields, including artists, craftsmen, manufacturers and tradesmen, who adopted principles of design which were concerned mainly with the refinement of an object down to its essentials. This concern relates closely to that of the designer-craftsmen working in the Cotswolds but, in Germany, these principles were applied to all aspects of industrial as well as craft production. The influence of the Arts and Crafts Movement on these European developments was recognised even by contemporaries. According to *The Times*:

> Our industrial art, even for the Philistine, has a commercial value, as the Germans discovered some time ago. They studied it, imitated it and organised their industrial art by all the means in their power, with the result that they made a great commercial success of it, both in Germany and abroad. Meanwhile our shops remained for the most part at the mercy of the commercial traveller. They catered for his taste, which was no one's taste; the ideas of our artists were exploited, and profited by, in Germany.[13]

The Deutscher Werkbund was a particularly successful enterprise, and its ideas were adopted in many other countries as well as by the German art schools. The impact of the work of Gimson and the Barnsleys on this particular enterprise, as well as on the general developments in the field of continental design, were discussed by H. H. Peach, founder of the Dryad Works in Leicester, in 1924:

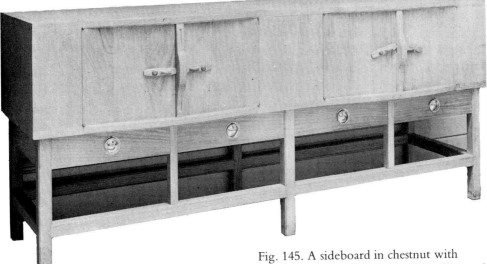

Fig. 145. A sideboard in chestnut with polished steel handles designed by Gimson in about 1905. The simple, four-square design is relieved only by the half-ovolo moulding on the underframing.

A German, who came over from Munich before the war, related how he asked in vain from the leading furniture manufacturers in London for a man called 'Gimson' of Sapiton (Sapperton) and was finally told to look up Surbiton! Gimson's work was better known abroad than here, in fact it could be seen in the continental museums before the war.[14]

Gimson's work was not only known in Europe; he also received orders from further afield. Examples of his work are known to have gone to Australia, Canada and South Africa. One of his European clients, Anton Possenbacher, an interior decorator and furniture-maker from Berlin wrote the following letter to Gimson in March 1914:

Dear Sir, I ordered you on the 26 February 4 highback armchairs and sent you a little sketch too, but I did never get any answer, nor an invoice from you. As I am needing the chairs at once, please will you send them off without any delay. . . . If you did not get the order, please send them now by express. 18/- each 4 high-back armchairs.[15]

With the imminent declaration of war, it must sadly be assumed that Mr Possenbacher never received his chairs.

In retrospect, Gimson and the Barnsleys stand out above most of their contemporaries in the field of furniture design. Comparisons were often made between Gimson and Ambrose Heal, one of the few individuals of comparable stature to emerge during this period. Despite certain similarities in their approach to furniture design, the course of each man's career was very different, a fact which can be partly explained by the differences between their backgrounds. Unlike Gimson and the Barnsleys, Ambrose Heal's family had a long connection with the design, manufacture and sale of furniture, the firm of Heal and Son having been established in 1810 for the manufacture of bedding and upholstery. Ambrose was born in 1872, and was one of the very few furniture designers within the Arts and Crafts Movement who did not begin his career by training as an architect. His lack of any architectural training was not significant as such, but it did mean that he did not participate in the general discussion and personal introspection, influenced by the work of John Ruskin and William Morris, which took place at the formative stage of most of his contemporaries' careers. Instead, after completing his schooling at Marlborough College, Ambrose Heal served an apprenticeship with a Warwickshire cabinet-maker between 1890 and 1893. He then joined the well-established family business, directing its attention towards the manufacture as well as the retail of furniture. From 1896 onwards, he was responsible for the design of a large proportion of the furniture sold in the store, as well as contributing unique pieces to exhibitions. Although his designs, in common with those of Gimson and the Barnsleys, were occasionally described as ugly and clumsy because of their simplicity and lack of ornamentation, Ambrose Heal was very successful as a furniture designer from early on in his career. Heal and Son were one of the few British firms to show at the Paris Exhibition of 1900, and their stand was a great success, bringing the talents of Ambrose Heal firmly into the public eye, both in Britain and on the continent. It was therefore inevitable that he, rather than Gimson or his colleagues, should participate in the controversial efforts to forge closer links between art and industry which dominated the art world for two decades, from about 1915 onwards.

Ambrose Heal was one of the founder-members of the Design and Industries Association which was set up in 1915, following precedents established by the Deutscher Werkbund, who had held a successful exhibition of their achievements at Cologne in 1914. The aims of the D. I. A. were fairly modest in character, and were concerned with the improvement of standards of design in industry. In his essay entitled *Art and Workmanship*, Lethaby, who was something of a father-figure to the D. I. A., wrote:

> The master-workman, further, must have control from first to last to shape and finish as he will. If I were asked for one simple test by which we might hope to know a work of art when we saw one, I should suggest something like this: 'Every work of art shows that it was made by a human being for a human being.'[16]

The importance of his basic humanism, and of his belief in the major role played by the handicrafts, in the development of Lethaby's theories of design is recognised by Gillian Naylor, who writes:

Lethaby's commonplace, however, like Webb's, reflected the highest rather than the lowest common denominator. It represented common sense and practicability and assumed the existence of a kind of folk-knowledge or instinct concerning the way things should be built and made. Such knowledge, however, was in danger of extinction, and it was threatened, not primarily by industrialisation but by the pursuit of the phoney and pretentious, by what Lethaby called 'sham artistic twaddle'.[17]

Although these sentiments were very similar to those of Gimson, Lethaby was unable to persuade him to join the D. I. A., despite a series of correspondence between the two men in 1916. Whilst he accepted, however reluctantly, the necessity for machine production to cater for the economic demands of twentieth-century society, Gimson was not prepared to compromise his own way of working to accommodate large-scale reproduction of his designs. He wrote to Lethaby, explaining the reason for his refusal to join the D. I. A.:

> What should be the point of view of those of us *who are interested in the crafts*? and I should like to find out just where the difference between us comes in – why you think I might do some good by designing bookcases for machines while I don't. I suppose all designers with workshops of their own have in unprosperous times been faced with the problem of machinery. It has faced me often – sometimes seemed to be a question of machinery or no shop at all and I have wavered about it but always ended by knowing that of the two alternatives I would rather have no shops at all. And I wish you thought this right – *from the craftsman's point of view*. If one's interest in the work were only that of design and utility it would be different but it is the men themselves too and their ways of work and through that to most other things in life as you know.[18]

Gimson's principles were such that he was unable to subordinate his own beliefs and his own work to a corporate venture, in the hope of producing long-term benefits for humanity – at least, not unless he could wholeheartedly support the aims and methods adopted by such a venture. He believed that the only way to influence people's attitudes was to pursue his own work to the best of his capabilities. Through his own efforts he certainly made a success of his workshops, on his own terms, as he testified in a letter to Sydney Cockerell, dated 20 September 1918:

> Until my shops had to close this summer for the time of the war they were very full of work, and the work could easily have been doubled or trebled if there had been the necessary workshop and cottage accommodation for the extra workers . . . As the old difficulties as regards prices and the competition of machine production have long ago disappeared and as the demand is constantly increasing there seems to be no object left in the way of success if once the problem of housing is solved.[19]

Chapter 11
Developments and divergences

Gimson and the Barnsleys made a success of their enterprises in the Cotswolds through their own efforts. Their reputation amongst their contemporaries was based solely on the evidence of their physical output. They left very little written documentation relating to their work, and, after leaving London, had only irregular contact with organised groups in the field of arts and crafts. Instead, they preferred to concentrate all their energies on the pursuit of their own ideals through their practical work, whilst maintaining a number of personal and professional contacts with individuals working in related spheres. As craftsmen and designers, Gimson and Sidney Barnsley, in particular, were impressively prolific. Gimson's contribution was such that Sir Nikolaus Pevsner has described him as 'the greatest of the English artist-craftsmen'. Despite the fact that they never sought public acclaim, the example set by the three men, both through their work as designers and through their respect for quality of materials and workmanship, was influential on many of their contemporaries and, to a greater extent, on successive generations of designers and craftsmen.

There was a continuous cross-current of contact and influence in the field of furniture design between individuals such as Charles Spooner, A. J. Penty and J. H. Sellers and the Cotswold Group. Certainly these craftsmen shared a respect for English traditions in design, and an appreciation of the decorative qualities inherent in the raw materials of their trade. The furniture, which was made in Spooner's London workshop to Gimson's design and exhibited at the Royal Academy in 1916, is one example of the contact which existed between them. However, probably the closest to Gimson and the Barnsleys, amongst their contemporaries, was Arthur Romney Green. Their influence on his work can be seen both stylistically and more clearly, in his approach to craftsmanship. Romney Green was certainly aware of their work in the Cotswolds from an early date, as he visited Gimson's workshops at Sapperton in 1904. He may also have come into contact with Gimson through his brother, W. Curtis Green, who commissioned woodwork from Gimson for a number of his architectural projects including two houses, one near Cambridge (1907), and the other in Hampstead. It was at about the same time that Romney Green gave up an academic career as a mathematician at Cambridge to concentrate on the design of furniture and woodworking. He established a workshop at Strand-on-the-Green in Chiswick, London, where he designed and made furniture which combined the use of geometric principles, in the underlying structure, with the simple, craftsmanlike approach pioneered by the Cotswold Group. Unlike Gimson, Romney Green wrote quite widely on the subject of woodworking and he appears, from these sources, to have expressed in writing many of the principles fundamental to the work of Gimson and the Barnsleys. He wrote:

> No kind of work is good, or likely to survive, merely because it is home-made, or merely because it is hand-made; good work of any kind, at all events in the absence of a sound tradition, can only result from constant slight emendations of his design by a designer who executes some at least of his own designs himself, and directly supervises the execution of all: and it is only after 25 years experience of this kind that I feel justified in any sort of self-advertisement, other than exhibiting or publishing illustrations of my work when invited to do so.
>
> Draw Tables, for example, I have been making for 25 years: and though they are now commonly produced by the trade, for 15 years I believe that mine was the only workshop in England to produce this, the earliest and best, and the most difficult to make of all types of expanding table. But though I have never seen draw tables, either old or new, better, or even as good as the best of my own, I am still so far from standardising my designs that I still expect to produce the best I have yet made for the next customer who wants it.*
>
> *Draw tables by the late Messrs Sidney Barnsley and Ernest Gimson would doubtless have been better than mine, but I am not aware that they ever made them.[1]

Romney Green's assistant from about 1921 to 1929, during which time he moved his workshop from Strand-on-the-Green to Christchurch, Dorset, was Eric Sharpe, who subsequently carried on and developed the woodworking tradition of Gimson, the Barnsleys and Romney Green in his own workshop at Winchester. Robin Nance and Stanley Davies followed in his footsteps, working with Romney Green before setting up on their own accounts at St Ives and Windermere respectively.

Edward Barnsley recalls that another furniture designer to visit both Gimson's and Sidney Barnsley's workshops in the early years of this century was the Swedish craftsman and teacher, Carl Malmsten. He was born in 1888, in Stockholm, where he trained as a cabinet-maker and subsequently established his own workshop and school for designers and craftsmen. Malmsten designed for a variety of media, including textiles and tapestry, but his primary concern was for furniture and woodwork. His designs in this field included a number of elaborate marquetry pieces, as well as simple yet carefully-detailed and well-finished domestic furniture, such as his table in acid-stained pinewood dating from 1945. The simple but effective design and the details of construction of this table are closely reminiscent of the work of Gimson and the Barnsleys. Like them, Malmsten believed passionately in allowing his designs to develop

Fig. 146. Oak chair with chip-carved decoration and a pigskin seat designed by A. Romney Green and possibly made by his assistant, Stanley Davies.

Fig. 147. Walnut sidetable with chamfered legs and stretchers designed and made by Eric Sharpe in about 1936.

out of local traditions, rather than participating in the general pursuit of modernity. According to one writer on contemporary Scandinavian design, 'He was one of those who worked most actively for the programme of the "more beautiful everyday things" movement before 1920, and was one of the bitterest opponents of the Stockholm Exhibition of 1930, i.e. of internationally-inspired functionalism'.[2] Malmsten was also an advocate of handwork which he considered to be the vital ingredient in any efforts to improve standards of design and manufacture. The same appreciation of craftsmanship, and of the characteristics of different woods, can be seen in the work of a number of contemporary Scandinavian designers, including the Norwegians, Alf Sture and Arne Halvorsen.

The influence of Gimson and the Barnsleys was also continued and extended by their immediate successors. Ernest Gimson died on 12 August 1919, at the age of fifty-five, after a long and painful struggle against cancer which cut short many of his plans and undertakings. It was a tribute to the affection in which he was held that, after his untimely death, many of his friends rallied round to complete as much as possible of his work. Frederick Griggs was probably the closest to Gimson and his wife in the months before Gimson's death, and subsequently provided Emily Gimson with his guidance and support. The couple were childless, and, after her husband's death, she continued to inhabit the house at Sapperton which Gimson had built in 1902, and remained an important figure in the village until her own death in 1940. The Daneway workshops remained in operation long enough to complete the work in hand, with Peter Waals in charge of the day-to-day running, and Sidney Barnsley taking overall responsibility, particularly for the business management. He found himself having to cope with several tricky problems, including one caused by a client who refused to pay for a considerable amount of furniture, claiming that the standard of work was not good enough. Armed with a letter from Gimson's elder brother, Sydney, Sidney Barnsley had to visit this recalcitrant client on the island of Jersey, in company with his brother, William, before this problem could be solved. Sidney Barnsley also took over the direction of Gimson's major architectural project, the building of the Memorial Library at Bedales School, Hampshire.

In 1920, the Daneway workshops were closed down, and Peter Waals set up his own furniture-making workshop just outside the village of Chalford, in the Golden Valley, near Stroud. He took over Haliday Mill, an old silk mill, one of many left derelict when the textile industry in Gloucestershire declined. At Chalford, Waals was able to make effective use of the railway, relieving some of the transport problems which had beset the Daneway workshops. Waals also took some of Gimson's stocks of wood and tools with him to Chalford, and the continuation between the two workshops was strengthened by the employment of many of the former Daneway craftsmen. Waals's relationship with his craftsmen at this crucial stage in his career is described thus by Sir George Trevelyan who was taken on as a pupil between 1929 and 1931, after graduating from Cambridge University:

Waals was much respected by his men as one who could lead them in their craft. Gimson had a delightful touch with the men and was able to contact them and show his appreciation in ways which were perhaps more difficult for Waals as a foreigner taking over the direction of the firm. Yet my powerful recollection of that workshop is the cohesion of the team, held by the greatness of their tradition and its standards. Never was that let down by any hint of skimping work or 'making do' with anything less than the best, even in the quality of the unseen back panels in cupboards. Each piece from the Waals workshop stands as an example of English craftsmanship at its best, and a lesson for an age when in so many directions standards of workmanship are allowed to slither. Each man of the group knew himself to be engaged in something far greater than himself, which he may not let down by any carelessness. The nature of the work, individual yet responsible to a group standard, built into them a human quality which made these men a veritable rural aristocracy.[3]

The contemporary photograph of the Chalford workshop [Fig. 148], illustrates something of the dedication and involvement which characterised this enterprise where ambition was subordinated to the common good.

The workshop at Chalford was quite small, measuring only 70 feet by 20 feet, and was equipped with a certain amount of woodworking machinery, including a band saw, circular saws, a planer, thicknesser and mortiser. There were rather more powered tools available for the use of the craftsmen at Chalford than there had been in the Daneway workshops, as Waals, being an eminently practical man, considered that the economic contribution they made to his newly-established business did not significantly compromise either the quality of the work or the involvement of his craftsmen. The truth of this belief is borne out by the lively description of the Chalford workshop written by Sir George Trevelyan:

After leaving Cambridge, undecided as to career, I suddenly realised a passionate longing to get down to it and make things with hands. 'What about crafts', a friend had said, and at those three words all became clear. Very soon I discovered that Peter Waals at Chalford was the fountain head to approach, and in the Cotswold spring, I started. That spring for me never faded. There was such endless joy in losing oneself in the making of fine things in a workshop where a dozen superlative craftsmen were doing the same. I would walk from Burleigh over the hill in the dewy morning, take cheese and beer in a pub beside the canal, and only chafe that the workshops closed at 5.30 and one could not work into the night. For a young man of 23 it was a wholly satisfying experience. I would pore over Waals' designs in his drawing office during the dinner hour. Each man was carrying out his own job, be it sideboard, wardrobe, table or set of chairs, and all could therefore watch each other's progress. My bench, looking up the canal, was next to that of Ernest Smith, the foreman, who had joined Gimson as an apprentice. Percy Burchett, also one of Gimson's original team, was my

Fig. 148. Peter Waals's workshop at Chalford in the early 1920s.

instructor, a tiny man, neat, gentle and polite, but absolutely firm in his demand for perfection in workmanship. Amongst others of the old heroes, Harry Davoll was very much at the top of his form, and to his great age went on making beautiful things in his home workshop. My friend and contemporary, Owen Scrubey, still working at Chalford on machine production, has continued making occasional pieces for me in the old tradition. . . . They were a wonderful group of men and the whole atmosphere of the workshop was permeated *by the standard of quality* as an unquestioned assumption.[4]

Also amongst the craftsmen at Chalford were Harry and Fred Gardiner, Tom Hunt and Fred Foster. Peter Waals and his wife moved into Chestnut House, adjacent to the workshop, and formerly the mill owner's home. Similarly close at hand was Alfred Bucknell, the foremost craftsman in the smithy at Daneway, who had set up on his own account at nearby Water Lane, and who continued to produce the metal fittings, to Gimson's designs, for the furniture made at Chalford.

Although Peter Waals relied heavily on his experience as Gimson's foreman in the development of his own workshop, and although he used to deprecate his own talents as a designer, he did make a significant contribution to the design of the furniture made at Chalford. It was inevitable that Gimson's legacy would be strongly felt, partly because of Waals's and his craftsmen's respect and admiration for his work, and partly because Waals inherited many of his clients. Waals's own

Fig. 149. A long-case clock in English oak made in Peter Waals's Chalford workshop to Norman Jewson's design. The clock was made in 1931 for Arthur Mitchell of The Glenfall, Charlton Kings, with a movement by W. E. Evans of Birmingham and a striking mechanism by Whittington and Westminster.

Fig. 150. Fall-front bureau veneered in burr elm with ebony stringing, made in Peter Waals's workshop in about 1921 after a design by Gimson dating some ten years earlier.

contribution to design is difficult to assess, as the great majority of his working drawings were destroyed by fire in 1938. He certainly seems to have lacked confidence in his own skill as a designer, and he often turned to Norman Jewson for assistance in this field. However, the furniture made at Chalford was only in a few instances a direct reproduction of Gimson's designs. In general, Waals followed the basic precepts of design laid down and developed by Gimson and the Barnsleys, with the addition of his own characteristic touches, including a slightly heavier, more sculptural approach to furniture design which can perhaps be ascribed to his Dutch origin. This element, which is closest in feeling to the work of Ernest Barnsley, can be seen in his treatment of the feet of the walnut sideboard [Fig. 151], which was a typical feature of many of his designs. This piece also illustrates the elaborate use of fielded panelling made by Waals at Chalford. His long experience as a cabinet-maker and furniture designer can be clearly appreciated in such pieces as the gentleman's wardrobe in oak [Fig. 152], one of a number of wardrobes made at Chalford in the late twenties and early thirties in a series of experiments with the light-reflective qualities of sunken and cushioned panelling.

Many of Gimson's former clients continued to come to the Chalford workshop with commissions for furniture. The tradition of aristocratic patronage was maintained; in April 1920, for example, Peter Waals delivered an ebony drawer-cabinet to the Earl of Plymouth's London home. He also made furniture for Rodmarton Manor, including two cabinets with painted decoration by Louise Powell. Amongst other Cotswold notables who patronised his workshops were the brothers, William Rothenstein and Albert Rutherston, whose own reputations as painters extended beyond the immediate locality. As well as commissioning furniture, William Rothenstein also painted a group portrait of five of the craftsmen connected with Chalford, which depicts them in a very straight-forward manner in the simple setting of their workshop [Fig. 157]. However, it was the interest of three clients, in particular, which ensured the survival of the Chalford workshop into the mid thirties. One of these clients, Arthur Mitchell, was the owner of The Glenfall, Charlton Kings, near Cheltenham, the house for which Sidney Barnsley designed and executed a quantity of interior panelling. Arthur Mitchell furnished this house with many examples of Waals's work and, in addition, was a close and sympathetic friend of the craftsman. Many orders for furniture also came from W. A. Evans who lived at Inglewood, the house in Leicester built by Gimson in 1892. Much of the furniture made at Chalford for the Evans family has since been acquired by the Leicestershire Museums Service. The third major client was W. A. Cadbury, a member of the Quaker family who founded the chocolate factory and village at Bournville, Warwickshire. He furnished his house at King's Norton, near Birmingham, with many examples of Waals's work. Public commissions came from a number of sources, including the University of Leicester and Eton College, whilst the firm of W. H. Smith and Son, which had a longstanding connection with the Cotswold craftsmen through the Hornby family, bought a quantity of furniture for their head office at Strand House, Portugal Street, London. Frank Pick,

Fig. 151. Walnut sideboard with moulded decoration and multi-fielded panels designed by Peter Waals and made in his Chalford workshop in 1934. Although the use of two concentric octagonal panels with a $22\frac{1}{2}°$ difference in their axes is an interesting development from this decorative device typical of Waal's work, in practice it is a slightly irritating distraction from the beauty of the figured walnut.

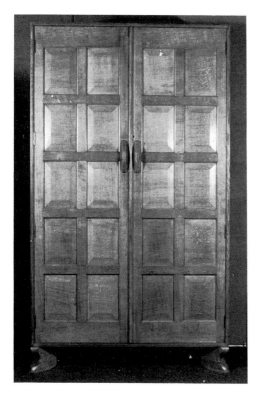

Fig. 152. Oak wardrobe with sunken, cushioned panelling designed by Peter Waals in 1931 as one of a series on which he was experimenting with the light effects produced by variations in panelling.

chairman of the London Passenger Transport Board, bought furniture from Waals in the twenties, and may also have been responsible for a commission from the Institute of Industrial Art in 1922. In 1923, Waals was commissioned by the architect, Edwin Lutyens, to design and make a set of bedroom furniture for the Queen's Dolls' House. This was probably the most unusual order to be executed at Chalford, and was followed by several other smaller orders for royal dolls' house furniture. Queen Mary's, and other royal dolls' houses can be seen at Windsor Castle. The growing interest in craftsman-made furniture in the twenties is illustrated by the existence of a retail outlet in London, 'The Cotswold Gallery', in Frith Street, W. 1. Between 1921 and 1927, Waals supplied the gallery's owner, Mrs Finberg, who was the wife of the celebrated art historian and Turner expert, A. J. Finberg, with furniture which was presumably intended for re-sale.

Like Gimson, Waals worked closely with a number of architects, many of whom had long-standing connections with the former. He continued to work with Ernest and Sidney Barnsley until their deaths in 1926. During that year, for example, Waals was contracted to undertake joinery work at Lodge Farm, Painswick for Sidney Barnsley's client, L. B. Murray. He also, between 1925 and 1929, made furniture for three houses built by Norman Jewson, including Hidcote House, near Campden, Gloucestershire, whilst in the early twenties Robert Schultz Weir commissioned the execution of interior woodwork and metalwork for Netherton Hall, near Honiton, Devon. Peter Waals provided wood for Norman Jewson, in exchange for building repairs, as well as for the carver and puppet maker, W. G. Simmonds, who lived and worked in the Cotswold village of Far Oakridge. The close links which Gimson and the Barnsleys had built up with the Society for the Protection of Ancient Buildings were maintained by Waals who, in 1925, received orders for a screen for Oddington Old Church, Gloucestershire, and for desks and doors for the Old Chapel, Hawarden Castle in the county of Flint.

However, possibly the most interesting and unexpected example of Waals's co-operation with another architect and designer was his work carried out, between 1921 and 1923, for C. F. A. Voysey. Charles Voysey is recognised today as one of the major figures in the field of twentieth-century design for his work as an architect, furniture designer and pattern designer. His interest in furniture design dates from about 1895, and his approach was based on similar principles to those of Gimson and the Barnsleys, with emphasis on the need for simplicity, for quality and for fitness for purpose. His designs are characterised by their sense of proportion and strong vertical element, showing the influence of his close friend, A. H. Mackmurdo. He worked almost entirely in oak, which was usually left unpolished, and often enhanced by the use of brass strap hinges and other fittings. He never worked as a furniture-maker himself, nor set up his own workshop. Instead, his designs were executed by a number of craftsman firms, including the London-based concern of F. C. Nielsen, and that of Arthur Simpson in Kendal. Although Voysey never established particularly close

Fig. 153. A carved ceremonial table in oak with cross-framing and hayrake stretchers designed by Peter Waals for Leicester University College, c. 1929.
Fig. 154. A cabinet in ebony designed and made by Peter Waals and elaborately painted in oils by Louise Powell, c. 1925.

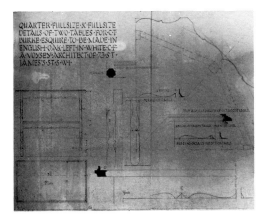

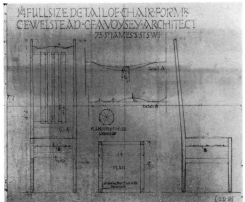

Fig. 155. A design for two oak tables by Voysey, probably made by Peter Waals.

Fig. 156. A design for a chair, one of several pieces made for Voysey at the Chalford workshop.

relationships with any of these firms, and although his connection with Waals was short, the co-operation between the two men is of interest. Peter Waals made furniture at Chalford for three of Voysey's clients, both to his own and to the latter's designs. Much of the work was for C. T. Burke, for whom Voysey had designed a house at Penn, Buckinghamshire, in 1907. Amongst the pieces which were made for this client were a clock case and two tables, for which Voysey's designs have survived [Fig 155]. Although there is no reference to Waals on Voysey's drawings, the connection is clearly made in Waals's ledger. According to this ledger, Voysey also ordered three more tables and a box, for C. T. Burke, to be made to Waals's design. The other clients included C. E. Welstead, who commissioned four small chairs, an armchair and a clock case from Voysey in 1921. All six items were made at Chalford. From Voysey's design for the chairs [Fig. 156], it appears that this order would not have differed greatly from the majority of the work undertaken at Chalford in the Gimson/Barnsley tradition, although it is fairly typical of the former's work. Waals's craftsmen would be well-equipped to execute details such as the precisely-chamfered rails and the octagonal-shaped legs which were recurrent features of Voysey's designs. Finally, in 1923, a number of pieces of dining room furniture were made at Chalford for Voysey which were intended for Mrs T. Eastwood, but were sent instead to Vodin, the house at Pyrford, Surrey, built for Mr F. Walters in 1902. Although Voysey would have been familiar with both Gimson's and Waals's work through the Arts and Crafts Exhibition Society, and through their mutual friend, Edward Prior, it is an indication of the respect which Waals's work as a craftsman and cabinet-maker could command that Voysey should co-operate with a workshop which had developed such a distinctive style of its own.

The workshop at Chalford continued in existence until Waals's death in 1937 His wife subsequently made a brave attempt to keep the workshop in operation, but her efforts were put to an end by the fire in 1938 which also destroyed Waals's working drawings. Although the workshop was disbanded, many of the craftsmen who had been involved in the enterprise and, in some cases, with

Fig. 157. 'Cotswold Craftsmen, Far Oakridge', a painting in oils by Sir William Rothenstein, c. 1920. From left to right: Harry Davoll, Harry Gardiner, Fred Gardiner, Alfred Bucknell and Tom Hunt.

Gimson's Daneway workshops, continued their involvement with their craft on an individual basis. Harry Davoll, Fred Foster, Ernest Smith, Fred Gardiner and Owen Scrubey were amongst those who set up their own workshops, making fine quality furniture in the tradition in which they had worked for so many years. Sir George Trevelyan wrote of the courage and dedication of one of these craftsmen thus:

> Ernest Smith established a tiny workshop in his garden and for some ten years executed pieces to my design until he suddenly went blind. Calling on him I found to my surprise, a new little garden gate to his terraced Chalford house, with the fielded panels and champered edges typical of the tradition. In gallant defiance of fate Ernest had made this gate, blind, as the closing act of his great career of craftsmanship. He died at 90, still reminiscing of the days when they sawed the great logs by hand in a pit-saw at Sapperton, for a trivial wage, but with joy and delight in great and manly workmanship which is characteristic of the Cotswold Tradition.[5]

Similarly, Alfred Bucknell's smithy at Water Lane prospered. He continued to make fine quality metalwork, as well as more mundane items, and the tradition was ably carried on by his son, Norman, until his recent retirement.

Ernest and Sidney Barnsley outlived Ernest Gimson by seven years. Ernest Barnsley died on 6 January 1926, leaving his major work, the building of Rodmarton Manor, unfinished. The final stages of the work on this great house were supervised first by Sidney Barnsley and then by Norman Jewson, who had previously acted as Ernest Barnsley's assistant on the early stages of this project. Ernest Barnsley's friend and fellow-architect, Francis Troup, wrote of him thus after his death:

> His thorough knowledge of the making of furniture readily extended itself to woodwork and carpentry. The building of his own house in Sapperton, in which he took the part of master of works rather than architect, opened to him all the 'mysteries' of the mason's and the slater's and the plasterer's traditional ways of work. He truly became a master of all the building crafts as they were practised from time immemorial in the district of the Cotswolds. . . . Though Barnsley's bent and first desire was for quality both in materials and of workmanship, yet through it all ran a keen knowledge of value and care for money expenditure. It seemed as if his business aptitude had been inherited from the family of well known builders in Birmingham to which he belonged.[6]

Sidney Barnsley only survived his elder brother for a few months, dying suddenly at Sapperton on 25 September 1926. William Lethaby wrote the following tribute in a letter to his widow, Lucy:

> We have valued Sidney very much; Robert Weir, when he came in here one morning to tell me, showed how much. . . . It was only those who saw him in his home-life who could really know all his fullness, and understand why he has gone so rich in honour, so dearly loved and so quiet a help to all things beautiful. Something like that should be written on his tomb. In his quietness and withdrawal – whilst having his gifts – there was true greatness. He was a big Englishman. It is a very conscious world, and his keeping out of things so much and going his quiet way was part of his bigness. Our hope is that we may have more of the kind but there can never be just that again.[7]

Sidney Barnsley's son, Edward, took responsibility for the completion of his furniture commissions, whilst Humphrey Gimson, Ernest Gimson's nephew, completed the only architectural work in hand, the addition of a small chapel to the church at Wotton-under-Edge, in Gloucestershire. The two Barnsley brothers were buried at Sapperton, where they had lived and worked for so many happy years, in company with their friend and colleague, Ernest Gimson. The graves of the three designer-craftsmen were marked by granite slabs, carved with simple grace as a fitting memorial to their life and work in the Cotswolds.

Fig. 158. Pieces from a Wedgwood pottery service with underglaze painted decoration by Grace Barnsley, c. 1926.

Fig. 159. Jug with painted decoration by Grace Barnsley and F. L. M. Griggs.

Both of Sidney Barnsley's children carved out careers for themselves as designers, and made a considerable contribution to their chosen craft. Grace Barnsley, the eldest, attended Birmingham School of Art in 1914 after which she trained as a decorator of pottery with her father's friends, Alfred and Louise Powell. In about 1904, the Powells had set up a studio for the painting of ceramics at Millwall which had subsequently been transferred to premises in Red Lion Square, London. They concentrated almost entirely on lustre and underglaze painting, and were instrumental in reviving the employment of freelance artists as decorators by the Staffordshire firm of Wedgwood. In this context, it is interesting to note that Louise Powell was the grand-daughter of Emile Lessore, the renowned decorator of Wedgwood pottery in the mid nineteenth century. After training with the Powells, Grace Barnsley returned to the Cotswolds to pursue her chosen career. Although her work is not widely known today, it is remarkable for its great delicacy, both of colour and pattern, and its keen sense of rhythm. Her work was influenced both by the example of the Powells and by her love and close observation of plants and flowers. In the mid twenties and thirties, she also worked as a decorator for Wedgwood, and some of her most distinctive and successful designs embellish the fine earthenware services produced by the factory [Fig. 158]. She occasionally produced decorative schemes for ceramics in co-operation with F. L. M. Griggs, as well as with her husband, Oscar Davies, who invented the 'duopour', a dispenser for both milk and coffee, produced by Wedgwood. In 1938, Grace and Oscar Davies set up the Roeinga Pottery at Rainham, Kent, where they worked for a short time making and decorating pottery.

Grace Barnsley's younger brother, Edward, carried on from his father, Sidney Barnsley, in much the same way that Peter Waals continued Gimson's work at Chalford. Edward Barnsley's earliest recollections include the strong creative atmosphere of the joint Pinbury workshop, and his father's workshop at Sapperton, where, from the age of six, he was making small items in wood. After a short period of schooling at Cirencester Grammar School, he and his sister were sent to Bedales, the progressive boarding school in Hampshire where the curriculum placed an emphasis on the importance of handwork and physical skills. In 1919, at the age of nineteen, Edward Barnsley began making furniture seriously in his father's workshop, and, at the end of that year, he went to Geoffrey Lupton's workshop at Froxfield, Hampshire, to work as an apprentice. He also spent a year at the Central School of Arts and Crafts, between 1922 and 1923, working under the guidance of the furniture-maker, Charles Spooner. Edward Barnsley's pedigree must have been rather overwhelming for his teachers as well as his fellow-students, for Spooner once said to him, 'You know, Barnsley, you know more about this than I do – I can't teach you anything'.[8] In 1923, he returned to Froxfield, eventually taking over control of Lupton's workshop where he has lived and worked ever since.

Edward Barnsley's work as a furniture designer was initially very much influenced by the tradition into which he was born. He worked very closely with his father during the last years of the latter's life, executing a number of his commissions, and completing any outstanding work after his death. However, by the mid forties, he was beginning to question certain features of the Cotswold tradition, and to develop his own distinctive style. His work has continued the strong bias towards handwork, fine workmanship and good quality materials, but has culled its inspiration from a wide range of sources to create an individual mixture of simplicity and refinement. In retrospect, Edward Barnsley describes his development thus:

> What I like to think I've done is in some measure to improve on two backgrounds or traditions. One is the Gimson/Barnsley with which I started, on to which I like to think I've added something new; the other is the eighteenth century from which I derive most of my plans and thoughts.[9]

The widespread use in Edward Barnsley's furniture designs of curved outlines, slender uprights and slim inlaid sycamore lines, instead of the typical dark and light inlaid stringing, is indicative of the development of his style. One of the most attractive examples of his work, a long, bow-fronted sidetable in rosewood [Fig. 162], illustrates these features admirably.

Unlike his father, Edward Barnsley has always worked with assistants and apprentices, employing on average six men at any one time. Over the years he has built up a close working relationship with his foreman, Herbert Upton, which has contributed a great deal to the success of the workshop. Although the craft element is still fundamental to their work, factors of economics and supply

Fig. 160. Edward Barnsley.

Fig. 161. A dressing table in English walnut with ebony stringing and handles and a hinged top revealing an adjustable mirror. Designed by Sidney Barnsley in collaboration with his son and made in Edward Barnsley's Froxfield workshop in about 1926. Despite the simple design of the mirror, the multi-fielded panels on the sides and, in particular, on the top of this piece of furniture seem rather cumbersome and impractical.

Fig. 162. Rosewood sidetable with a shallow bow-front designed by Edward Barnsley and made in his workshop by Oskar Dawson under the supervision of Herbert Upton.

have inevitably led to changes in the methods of furniture-making used at Froxfield. Edward Barnsley, like his father before him, recognises the importance of using good quality timber. However, as English timbers are no longer in plentiful supply, a large proportion of imported woods such as Australian black bean, and Indian rosewood and padouk are now used. Most of this timber is kiln- rather than air-dried, although Edward Barnsley's open sheds contain some pieces which have been in store for nearly fifty years, waiting to be used in the construction of an appropriate piece of furniture. Similarly, he now uses a certain amount of laminates, such as blockboard and plywood, either in the construction of the back panels of furniture, or in conjunction with veneers. Despite these developments, the same care and consideration is given in Edward Barnsley's workshop to the selection of the appropriate type and piece of wood for each item of furniture as was ever given by his father or Ernest Gimson. Machinery is also used, sparingly, to remove some of the time-consuming effort from the basic chores involved in furniture-making, such as the sawing and planing of large pieces of wood. In this way, the craftsman has suitable powered tools as his servant and can use his time constructively in the execution of tasks where his skill is most important.

As well as employing assistants in his workshop, Edward Barnsley has taken on a succession of pupil-trainees during his career. Many contemporary furniture

Fig. 163. Edward Barnsley's workshop.

designers have undertaken part of their training in Edward Barnsley's workshop and are now working independently throughout the country. It is not possible to mention all the craftsmen involved, but the list includes Robert Townshend, now working at Saxmundham, Suffolk, and Oliver Morel who works at Moreton-in-the-Marsh, sharing premises with his former pupil, Hugh Birkett. Kenneth Marshall returned to his native Gloucestershire and set up a workshop at Coleford after training with Edward Barnsley. Another one-time pupil, Alex McCurdy, is best known today for his beautifully-made string instruments, whilst two of the most recent trainees, Sandy Mackilligan and Alan Peters, are amongst the most promising craftsmen and designers in Britain.

In addition to this impressive array of former pupils, Edward Barnsley, and Peter Waals before him, were responsible for instilling a profound respect for handwork and craftsmanship in a succession of students at Loughborough Training College. In 1935, Peter Waals was invited to take up the newly-created post of Design Adviser at the college, on the recommendation of Frank Pick, then chairman of the Design and Industries Association. The creation of this post was one of several attempts made during this period to improve craft teaching in colleges, and to promote a respect and understanding of good design amongst students. Under Waals's supervision, the students at Loughborough designed and made the furniture for Hazelrigg Hall of Residence. In 1939, the post of Design Adviser was taken over by Edward Barnsley. He takes a very practical approach to the mystique of design, saying 'If you can't see the thing that is being asked for in your mind's eye fairly quickly, then maybe you won't produce the thing to its best advantage'.[10] He used to advise his students to start a drawing with the basic information, such as the floor and the centre lines, as points of reference and build from there. Through the personal contributions of Peter Waals and Edward Barnsley, the work of Gimson and the Barnsleys was continued and brought to life for a significant number of students in the thirties and forties despite the fact that they themselves had neither written about their attitudes to furniture-making, nor talked about them as part of any formal teaching.

Although Peter Waals and Edward Barnsley in particular ensured the survival of the Gimson/Barnsley tradition in the field of craft furniture, it was left to others to apply the advances made by the three men in the design of furniture to the problem of industrial production in Britain. Under the influence of Ambrose Heal, the firm of Heal and Son continued to produce furniture which combined functional design with high quality workmanship, and these qualities have remained a feature of much of their stock up to the present day. Amongst other commercial designers of the thirties and forties whose work showed the influence of Gimson and the Barnsleys were John Stark, who designed furniture for Peter Jones Ltd., and C. A. Richter, who worked for the Bath Cabinet-Makers Company.

However, the foremost figure in this field, whose name is inextricably linked with the Cotswold School, is Sir Gordon Russell. He was born in 1892, and moved to the Cotswolds in 1904 when his father took over the Lygon Arms, in the village of Broadway. Gordon Russell's main interests in his youth included calligraphy, stone carving and leatherwork as well as machines and mechanical drawing, and he also became involved in the family antique and restoration business, prior to the outbreak of war in 1914. On his return to Broadway, in 1919, he began designing and making furniture which was sold by Russell and Sons Ltd., the firm established by his father. In his autobiography, Gordon Russell wrote of this period:

> Our earliest efforts were made entirely by hand and were directly inspired by the work of Ernest Gimson, many aspects of which I had greatly admired. I feel very strongly that handwork of the best kind is essential in any civilisation: in fact I would go so far as to say that, in the long run, I do not believe that fine quality machine work can exist without it. Handwork enables the worker to get to grips with his material and collaborate with it in a way that is infinitely more difficult if he is operating a machine.[11]

Gordon Russell began designing furniture seriously in the 1920s, having taken the advice of Percy Wells, who was in charge of cabinet-making at the London County Council Shoreditch Technical Institute. Under Russell's supervision, Edgar Turner, already an employee of the family firm, was trained to execute his designs. The connection between these new developments at Broadway and

Fig. 164. Part of a bedroom suite in oak
designed by Gordon Russell in about 1930.

Fig. 165. The first cabinet designed by
R. D. Russell for Murphy Radio, 1929.

Gimson's workshops was further strengthened when Harry Gardiner, who had previously worked in the smithy at Daneway, was employed by Gordon Russell to run a small metalworking shop.

In the 1920s, Gordon Russell was one of a number of manufacturers to join the Design and Industries Association. The influence of the association and its members encouraged him to extend the scope of his business. He wrote:

> Early in the 1920s I realised that the most urgent job of all was to teach the machine manners. The civilisation that had been built up was based on the machine, without which goods that were considered essential could not be produced for the masses. The kind of goods produced and the effect on the people producing them seemed to me most important. As we had a number of enquiries for furniture for schools, public houses, hotels, hospitals, and municipal buildings I determined to see what could be done about it.[12]

Thus, towards the end of the decade, the firm of Russell and Sons began to concentrate its output on lower-priced furniture designed for serial production. The impetus behind this change of direction was increased partly by the influence of Gordon Russell's younger brother, Dick, newly returned to the Cotswolds after the completion of his architectural training, and partly by the disastrous effects of the world-wide slump on the traditional markets, particularly in America, for expensive craft and antique furniture. In the thirties and forties, Gordon and Dick Russell designed and supervised the manufacture of possibly the most influential examples of contemporary furniture. According to Gillian Naylor:

> Production during this period tended to be concentrated on the domestic market, and more machinery was introduced to increase the output, a factor which was reflected in the rationalisation of the ranges, and in the design of the furniture itself, which with its under-statement, careful detailing and precision of form and finish established a vocabulary that was to be used by British furniture designers throughout the 1950s.[13]

Some of the firm's most impressive pieces from this period are the wireless cabinets designed by Dick Russell for Murphy Radio [Fig. 165].

Gordon Russell's long term impact on the furniture trade was felt most keenly through his involvement with the Utility Schemes during the Second World War. His pioneering work with Russell and Sons Ltd. led to his appointment on the Advisory Committee on Utility Furniture in 1942. Wartime conditions and the shortage of raw materials forced the government to control the production of a wide variety of goods. Under the influence of Gordon Russell, and with the support of the President of the Board of Trade, Hugh Dalton, the concept that the design and quality as well as the supply of basic household items should be controlled was accepted by the Advisory Committee.

In 1943, the Utility Furniture design team, under the chairmanship of Gordon Russell, produced the first range of functional, carefully detailed and well-made Utility Furniture. Although neither the furniture trade nor the public as a whole were entirely converted to this approach to design, according to Edwin Clinch, one of the designers working on the team, 'Furniture never went back to what it was like before the war – thank God'.[14]

It was thus that the principles of design developed by Gimson and the Barnsleys at the end of the nineteenth century gradually became accepted by the great majority of the furniture-buying public. Although one cannot be sure of their own reactions to these developments had they survived to see them, the role which they played in enabling them to take place adds immeasurably to their stature and reputation today.

Fig. 166. Walnut fall-front cabinet designed by Edward Barnsley in 1976, reworking a theme which had been used by both his father and Ernest Gimson. This piece was included in the 'Masterpiece' Exhibition held in London by the British Crafts Centre as its contribution to Queen Elizabeth II's Silver Jubilee.

Notes

Introduction

1. *Ernest Gimson, His Life and Work*, published in a limited edition by the Shakespeare Head Press, with essays by three of Gimson's closest friends, the architects and fellow-members of the Arts and Crafts Movement, William Lethaby, Alfred Powell and Frederick Griggs.
2. John Farleigh (ed.), *Fifteen Craftsmen on their Crafts*, Sylvan Press (1945), page 106.
3. Arts and Crafts Exhibition Society, catalogue to the eleventh exhibition (1916), page 207.

Chapter 1

1. F. J. Gould, *History of the Leicester Secular Society*, Leicester Secular Society (1900).
2. F. J. Hanes had previously worked with the architect, W. Eden Nesfield, on Kimnel Park, Denbigh, one of the major buildings in the design of which the latter pioneered the use of the Queen Anne style.
3. *The Builder,* Vol. LXI (1891), page 460.
4. *The British Architect*, Vol. XXII (1884).
5. Sydney Gimson, *Random Recollections of the Leicester Secular Society*, Part I (1932), page 22. Leicestershire Records Office.
6. Ibid, page 23.
7. It was in much the same way that, some thirty-five years later, the firm began its co-operation with the young Arts and Crafts architect, J. L. Ball, who worked with W. R. Lethaby on the design of the Eagle Insurance Building, Colmore Row, Birmingham. J. L. Ball's connection with the Barnsley family was firmly cemented by his marriage, in about 1880, to Edith, one of the daughters of Thomas Barnsley.
8. Birmingham *Daily Post*, 21 June 1909.

Chapter 2

1. A. W. N. Pugin, *The True Principles of Pointed or Christian Architecture*, London (1841).
2. *Lectures on the Results of the Great Exhibition*, London (1853).
3. John Ruskin, *The Nature of Gothic*, reprinted by the Kelmscott Press (1892).
4. H. S. Goodhart-Rendel, *English Architecture since the Regency*, London (1953), page 191.
5. May Morris (ed.), *The Collected Works of William Morris*, Vol. XXII, London (1914), page 262.
6. *Ernest Gimson, His Life and Work*, Shakespeare Head Press (1924), page 3.
7. Gillian Naylor, *The Arts and Crafts Movement*, London (1971), page 109.
8. Unpublished letter from Ernest Gimson to W. R. Butler dated 22 June 1890, Leicestershire Museums Service.

Chapter 3

1. Unpublished letter from Ernest Gimson to W. R. Butler, dated 22 June 1890, Leicestershire Museums Service.
2. Unpublished letter from Ernest Gimson to Ernest Barnsley, dated 19 February 1888, Leicestershire Museums Service.
3. Unpublished letter from Ernest Gimson to Ernest Barnsley, dated 4 May 1889, Leicestershire Museums Service.

4. Unpublished and undated letter from Ernest Gimson to Ernest Barnsley, Leicestershire Museums Service.

5. Unpublished letter from Ernest Gimson to Ernest Barnsley, dated 7 June 1890, Leicestershire Museums Service.

6. Unpublished memorandum written by Robert Weir Schultz and Sidney Barnsley in 1910, British School at Athens.

7. Idem, Ernest Gimson to W. R. Butler, 22 June 1890.

8. *The Studio*, Vol. II (1894), page 15.

9. *The British Architect*, Vol. XXI (1889).

10. Unpublished letter from Ernest Gimson to Ernest Barnsley dated June 1889, Leicestershire Museums Service.

11. The Soane Medallion was an architectural honour awarded by competition by the Institute of British Architects in memory of Sir John Soane.

12. Idem, Ernest Gimson to W. R. Butler, 22 June 1890.

13. *The Architectural Review*, Vol. XIII (1903), page 188.

14. *Ernest Gimson*, an exhibition catalogue, Leicester Museums (1969), page 34.

15. May Morris (ed.), *The Collected Works of William Morris*, Vol. XVI, Longmans Green and Co., (1912), page 221.

16. *Ernest Gimson, His Life and Work*, Shakespeare Head Press (1924), page 5.

17. Idem, Ernest Gimson to W. R. Butler, 22 June 1890.

18. The National Association for the Advancement of Art and its Application to Industry was founded in 1887 with the aim of encouraging industry to accept artistic values. The main method employed by the Association to further its aims was to hold congresses in the major provincial towns, including Liverpool and Birmingham, which brought together a wide spectrum of speakers and delegates.

Chapter 4

1. *The Builder*, 19 December 1891, Vol. LXI, page 458.

2. Preface to *The Hobby Horse*, January 1886, quoted by Gillian Naylor, *The Arts and Crafts Movement*, London (1971), page 117.

3. Reginald Blomfield, *Memoirs of an Architect*, London (1932), page 75.

4. Detmar Jellings Blow had been an architectural student in London in the 1880s. He later worked as Gimson's assistant on various architectural projects including Stoneywell Cottage, Leicestershire.

5. Unpublished letter from Ernest Gimson to W. R. Butler dated 22 June 1890, Leicestershire Museums Service.

6. Unpublished letter from Ernest Gimson to Ernest Barnsley dated 1 October 1890, Leicestershire Museums Service.

7. Idem, Ernest Gimson to W. R. Butler, 22 June 1890.

8. Idem, Ernest Gimson to Ernest Barnsley, 1 October 1890.

9. Idem, Reginald Blomfield, page 75.

10. Ibid, page 62.

11. *The Builder*, 19 December 1891, Vol. LXI, page 459.

12. *Ernest Gimson, His Life and Work*, Shakespeare Head Press (1924), page 2.

13. H. J. L. J. Massé, *The Art Workers' Guild, 1884–1934*, Shakespeare Head Press (1935), page 90.

14. Idem, Reginald Blomfield, page 76.

15. Ibid, page 76.

16. Quoted by Paul Thompson, *The Work of William Morris*, London (1967), page 73.

17. *The Builder*, 19 December 1891, Vol. LXI, page 458.

18. Ibid, page 458.

19. *The Studio*, Vol. II, (1893), page 3.

20. Idem, Reginald Blomfield, page 76.

21. Ibid, page 76.
22. *The Studio*, Vol. XVIII, (1899), page 281.
23. *The Builder*, 19 December 1891, Vol. LXI, page 458.
24. Idem, Reginald Blomfield, page 77.
25. *Ernest Gimson, His Life and Work*, Shakespeare Head Press (1924), page 6.
26. John Farleigh (ed.), *Fifteen Craftsmen on their Crafts*, Sylvan Press (1945), page 102.

Chapter 5

1. Norman Jewson, *By Chance I Did Rove*, published privately (1973), page 13.
2. Ibid, page 33.
3. Unpublished letter from Sidney Barnsley to Philip Webb dated 30 June 1901, Mr A. Davies.
4. Idem, Norman Jewson, page 3.
5. *Ernest Gimson, His Life and Work*, Shakespeare Head Press (1924), page 17.
6. Unpublished letter from Philip Webb to Alfred Powell dated 19 July 1902, Cheltenham Art Gallery and Museum.
7. Idem, Norman Jewson, page 79.
8. Idem, *Ernest Gimson, His Life and Work*, page 15.
9. Ibid, page 17.
10. Idem, Sidney Barnsley to Philip Webb, 30 June 1901.
11. Idem, Norman Jewson, page 34.
12. Unpublished letter from Edward Barnsley to the author dated 30 June 1976.
13. Idem, Philip Webb to Alfred Powell, 19 July 1902.
14. Idem, Norman Jewson, page 27.
15. *Ernest Gimson*, an exhibition catalogue, Leicester Museums (1969), page 35.
16. Idem, Norman Jewson, page 14.
17. Idem, *Ernest Gimson, His Life and Work*, page 32.
18. Unpublished letter from Philip Webb to Sidney Barnsley dated 5 May 1900, Mr A. Davies.

Chapter 6

1. *Cabinet Maker and Art Furnisher*, Vol. XVII, November 1896, page 117.
2. Ibid, page 118.
3. Paul Thompson, *The Work of William Morris*, London (1967), page 77.
4. *Cabinet Maker and Art Furnisher*, Vol. XVII, November 1896, page 115.
5. May Morris (ed.), *Collected Works of William Morris*, Vol. XXII, Longman Green and Co. (1914), page 261.
6. *The Builder*, Vol. LXXVII, October 1899, page 335.
7. Quoted in an unpublished notebook of Ernest Gimson, Local Studies Division (Cheltenham), Gloucestershire County Libraries.
8. William Millar, *Plastering, Plain and Decorative*, edited and revised by G. P. Bankart, Batsford (1927), page 285.

Chapter 7

1. Unpublished letter from Sidney Barnsley to Philip Webb, dated 30 June 1901, Mr A. Davies.
2. Unpublished letter from Ernest Barnsley to Lord Bathurst, dated 12 March 1901, Mr E. Barnsley.
3. Unpublished letter from Sidney Barnsley to Philip Webb, dated 6 July 1902, Mr E. Barnsley.
4. *The Studio*, Vol. XXVIII (1903), page 36.
5. Unpublished transcript of taped conversation between Edward Barnsley and Godfrey Beaton, 1975, Godfrey Beaton page 21.
6. *Ernest Gimson*, an exhibition catalogue, Leicester Museums (1969), page 43.
7. Ibid, page 43.
8. Ibid, page 32.

9. Ibid, page 33.

10. Ibid, page 7.

11. John Farleigh (ed.), *Fifteen Craftsmen on their Crafts*, Sylvan Press (1945), page 102.

12. Alfred Stevens was a sculptor active in the mid nineteenth century whose work was based on the forms of the Italian Renaissance. He also co-operated closely with many manufacturers of decorative metalwork, ceramics and furniture.

13. *Daily Chronicle*, 31 October 1916.

Chapter 8

1. Norman Jewson, *By Chance I Did Rove*, published privately (1973), page 13.

2. Unpublished letter from Ernest Barnsley to Lord Bathurst, dated 12 March 1901, Edward Barnsley.

3. *Country Life*, 10 April 1909, page 526.

4. *The Builder*, Vol. XCVIII (1910), page 587.

5. Quoted by Clive Aslet in *Country Life*, 19 October 1978, page 1180.

7. *Ernest Gimson*, an exhibition catalogue, Leicester Museums (1969), page 40.

8. *The Builder*, Vol. CXIII 1917, page 3.

9. *Ernest Gimson, His Life and Work*, Shakespeare Head Press (1924), page 2.

10. Quoted by Clive Aslet in *Country Life*, 19 October 1978, page 1181.

11. Lawrence Weaver, *Small Country Houses of Today*, Vol. 2 (1919), page 16.

12. Ernest Gimson, unpublished working drawing 1941.224.13, Cheltenham Art Gallery and Museum.

13. Idem, *Ernest Gimson*, an exhibition catalogue, page 5.

14. Alistair Service (ed.), *Edwardian Architecture and its Origins*, Architectural Press (1975), page 146.

15. *The Architectural Review*, Vol. XV (1904), page 219

16. Lawrence Weaver, *Small Country Houses of Today*, Vol. 2 (1919), page 22.

17. *Town Planning Review*, Vol. III, no. 3, University of Liverpool (1912), page 165.

18. Ernest Gimson, unpublished report on competition designs for Canberra, 1941.224.37, Cheltenham Art Gallery and Museum.

19. Idem, *Ernest Gimson, His Life and Work*, page 29.

Chapter 9

1. *The Studio*, Vol. XXXVII (1906), page 59.

2. Norman Jewson, *By Chance I Did Rove*, published privately (1973), page 24.

3. *Ernest Gimson*, an exhibition catalogue, Leicester Museum (1969), page 34.

4. Letter from Sidney Barnsley to Philip Webb, dated 1 May 1904, Mr E. Barnsley.

5. *Ernest Gimson, His Life and Work*, Shakespeare Head Press (1924), page 14.

6. *Good Citizen's Furniture*, an exhibition catalogue, Cheltenham Art Gallery and Museum (1976).

7. Quoted by B. G. Burrough in 'Three Disciples of William Morris: Ernest Gimson, part 1', *The Connoisseur*, Vol. 171 (1969), page 231.

8. Taped conversation between Edward Barnsley and Godfrey Beaton, 1976.

9. Letter from J. Nichols and Son Ltd. to Ernest Gimson, dated 20 March 1914, Cheltenham Art Gallery and Museum.

Chapter 10

1. Unpublished letter from Ernest Gimson to Sidney Cockerell, dated 16 August 1916, Leicestershire Museums Service.

2. Norman Jewson, *By Chance I Did Rove*, published privately (1973), page 73.

3. Unpublished letter from R. W. Schultz to Ernest Gimson, dated 18 June 1914, Cheltenham Art Gallery and Museum.

4. Alistair Service (ed.), *Edwardian Architecture and its Origins*, Architectural Press (1975), page 147.

5. Idem, Ernest Gimson to Sydney Cockerell, 16 August 1916.

6. *The Builder*, Vol. XCIII, 21 December 1907.

7. *The Pall Mall Gazette*, 18 January 1910.

8. *Nottingham Guardian*, 27 October 1916.

9. *The Builder*, Vol. XCI, 20 October 1916.

10. *Manchester Guardian*, 11 October 1916.

11. *The Spectator*, 14 October 1916.

12. *The Times*, 20 August 1913.

13. *The Times*, 7 October 1916.

14. *Leicester Mail*, 2 April 1924.

15. Unpublished letter from Anton Possenbacher to Ernest Gimson, dated 26 March 1914, Cheltenham Art Gallery and Museum.

16. W. R. Lethaby, *Form in Civilization*, London (1922), page 211.

17. Gillian Naylor, *The Arts and Crafts Movement*, London (1971), page 181.

18. Ernest Gimson to W. R. Lethaby, 18 April 1916, quoted by B. G. Burrough in *The Connoisseur*, Vol. 172 (1969), page 10.

19. Unpublished letter from Ernest Gimson to Sydney Cockerell dated 20 September 1918, Leicestershire Museums Service.

Chapter 11

1. A. Romney Green, *Instead of a Catalogue*, New Handworkers' Gallery, (1928), page 13.

2. Eric Zahle, *Modern Scandinavian Design*, Methuen (1963), page 88.

3. *Ernest Gimson*, an exhibition catalogue, Leicester Museums (1969), page 44.

4. Ibid, page 43.

5. Ibid, page 45.

6. Unprovenanced newspaper cutting in the possession of Mr A. Davies.

7. Unpublished letter from W. R. Lethaby to Mrs Sidney Barnsley, dated 24 October 1926, Mr A. Davies.

8. Unpublished transcript of taped conversation between Edward Barnsley and Godfrey Beaton, 1975, Godfrey Beaton, page 21.

9. John Norwood, *Craftsmen at Work*, John Baker (1977), page 124.

10. Idem, taped conversation between Edward Barnsley and Godfrey Beaton, page 37.

11. Gordon Russell, *A Designer's Trade*, George Allen and Unwin (1968), page 140.

12. Ibid, page 140.

13. *Utility Furniture and Fashion*, *1941–51*, an exhibition catalogue, Inner London Education Authority (1974), page 25.

14. Ibid, page 13.

Acknowledgements

I would like to acknowledge the following
whose advice, encouragement and criticism have
spurred me on and who have been generous
with the fruits of their own researches when
they overlapped with mine: Edward Barnsley;
Godfrey Beaton; Alan Crawford; Remo
Granelli; Lionel Lambourne; the staff of
Leicestershire Museums, especially Annette
Carruthers; Oliver Morel; David Otterwill;
Barley Roscoe of the Crafts Study Centre, Bath;
Alan Saville; J. C. Sharp; Gavin Stamp; Sir
George Trevelyan; the staff of the Furniture and
Woodwork Department, Victoria and Albert
Museum, especially Simon Jervis and Clive
Wainwright.

My thanks go to all those whose homes I have
visited, particularly the present members of the
Gimson and Barnsley families, for their assistance
and unfailing kindness.

I would also like to thank my father who
typed much of the original manuscript.

Above all, I am grateful to David Addison,
Director of Cheltenham Art Gallery and
Museum, and his staff, whose interest and
encouragement was a constant source of support.

Mary Comino

For permission to reproduce the photographs in
this book, the author and publishers are grateful
to the following:

Abbey Studios, Cirencester, Fig. 148
Mr E. Barnsley, Figs. 1, 19, 20, 21, 30, 31, 40,
   45, 48, 49, 52, 98, 112, 138
   (photo Dennis Moss) Figs. 99, 123, 153
Miss E. Barnsley, Fig. 102
Bristol City Art Gallery, Fig. 95
Cheltenham City Art Gallery and Museum,
   Figs. 3, 9, 13, 14, 16, 24, 34, 35, 36, 37, 39, 46,
   50, 53, 54, 55, 58, 61, 62, 63, 64, 67, 68, 69, 71,
   73, 74, 78, 79, 81, 83, 85, 86, 89, 91, 96, 97,
   100, 103, 104, 108, 109, 110, 111, 113, 114,
   115, 125, 126, 127, 128, 129, 130, 131, 135,
   136, 139, 142, 143, 145, 152, 154, 161, 162
   (photo B. Donnan) Figs. 2, 15, 57, 59, 82, 122,
   146, 149, 150, 151
   (photo Dennis Moss) Figs. 44, 77, 140, 141
   (photo S. F. Scorey) Figs. 33, 47, 80, 157
Crafts Study Centre, Bath, Figs. 163, 160
Alan Crawford, Figs. 17, 18
Country Life (photo Alex Starkey), Figs. 88, 101
Mr A. Davies, Figs. 23, 38, 42, 43, 72, 158, 134, 159
Design Council (photo Dennis Moss), Figs. 56,
   70, 120
Furniture and Woodwork Dept., Victoria and
   Albert Museum, Figs. 26, 27, 28, 29, 32
Mr and Mrs D. Gimson, Figs. 106, 107
Gloucester City Museums, Fig. 87
Mr N. Grimwood, Fig. 166
Hereford City Museum, Fig. 22
Mrs B. Keith, Fig. 137
Leicester Museums and Art Gallery, Figs. 4, 25,
   41, 51, 60, 66, 76, 84, 94, 105, 116, 117, 121
National Monuments Record, Fig. 8
National Portrait Gallery, London, page 28
Private collection, Figs. 118, 119, 144
Royal Institute of British Architects, Figs. 5,
   155, 156
Gordon Russell Ltd., Fig. 165
Salford Museum and Art Gallery, Fig. 6
John Saunders, Fig. 75
Sotheby's Belgravia, Figs. 147, 164
Victoria and Albert Museum, Figs. 7, 11, 12, 65,
   90, 92, 93, 124, 133
Mrs J. Waterlow, Fig. 132

Bibliography

Catalogues

The Arts and Crafts Movement, 1890–1930, The Fine Art Society, London 1973.

Catalogue of an Exhibition of Victorian and Edwardian Decorative Arts, Victoria and Albert Museum, H.M.S.O. 1952.

Ernest Gimson, Leicester Museums and Art Gallery, 1969.

Ernest Gimson and the Cotswold Group of Craftsmen, Leicestershire Museums Publication no. 14, 1978.

An Exhibition of Cotswold Craftsmanship, Cheltenham Art Festivals, 1951.

Good Citizen's Furniture, Cheltenham Art Gallery and Museum, 1976.

A Tour of Broadway and Chipping Campden, Victorian Society, 1978.

Articles

Aslet, Clive, 'Rodmarton Manor, Glos. I and II', *Country Life*, 19 and 26 October 1978.

Baker, Stephen, 'Gimson's Cotswold Furniture and its London Origins', *Apollo*, Vol. CIX, January 1979.

Beaton, Godfrey, 'Thinking About Chairs', *Crafts*, No. 32, May/June 1978.

Burroughs, B.G, 'Three Disciples of William Morris: 1. Ernest Gimson', two articles in *The Connoisseur*, Vol. 171, August–September 1969

Comino, Mary, 'Good Citizen's Furniture', *Crafts*, No. 23, November/December 1976.

Crawford, Alan, 'Ashbee in the Cotswolds', *Crafts*, No. 5, November/December 1973.

Derrick, Freda, 'Sapperton Craftsmen', four articles in *The Illustrated Carpenter and Builder*, July–August 1945.

Derrick, Freda, 'After Gimson', four articles in *The Illustrated Carpenter and Builder*, October–November 1952.

Lambourne, Lionel, 'The Art and Craft of Ernest Gimson' *Country Life*, Vol. CXLVI, August 1969.

Books

Alexander, R., *The Furniture and Joinery of Peter Waals*, Alcuin Press, Chipping Campden, 1930.

Aslin, Elizabeth, *Nineteenth Century Furniture*, Faber and Faber, 1932.

Blomfield, Sir Reginald, *Memoirs of an Architect*, London, 1932.

Bradshaw, A. E., *Handmade Woodwork of the Twentieth Century*, John Murray, 1962.

Brill, Edith, *Cotswold Crafts*, Batsford, 1977.

Farleigh, John (ed.), *Fifteen Craftsmen on their Crafts*, Sylvan Press, London, 1945.

Gloag, John, *The English Tradition in Design*, A. and C. Black, 1959.

Gloag, John, *Victorian Taste*, David and Charles, 1962.

Jewson, Norman, *By Chance I Did Rove*, reprinted by the Roundwood Press, Warwickshire, 1973.

Joel, David, *Furniture Design Set Free*, (first published as *The Adventure of British Furniture*), J. M. Dent and Sons, 1969.

Lethaby, William; Powell, Alfred and Griggs, Frederick, *Ernest Gimson, His Life and Work*, Shakespeare Head Press, Stratford on Avon, 1924.

MacCarthy, Fiona, *All Things Bright and Beautiful*, Allen and Unwin, 1972.

Morris, May (ed.), *The Collected Works of William Morris*, 24 volumes, Longmans, Green and Co., 1910–15.

Naylor, Gillian, *The Arts and Crafts Movement*, Studio Vista, 1971.

Pevsner, Sir Nikolaus, *Pioneers of Modern Design*, London, 1936, reprinted by Penguin Books, 1960.

Rogers, J. C., *Modern English Furniture*, Country Life, London, 1930.

Russell, Sir Gordon, *Designer's Trade*, Allen and Unwin, 1968.

Service, Alistair, *Edwardian Architecture*, Thames and Hudson, 1977.

Service, Alistair (ed.), *Edwardian Architecture and its Origins*, Architectural Press, London, 1975.

Thompson, Paul, *The Work of William Morris*, London, 1967.

Watkinson, Ray, *William Morris as Designer*, Studio Vista, 1967.